The free movement of persons between Switzerland and the European Union

Cover illustration:

Ruskpp, *Svizzera e UE*, Photo archive 123RF©

The free movement of persons between Switzerland and the European Union

Vincenzo Salvatore (ed.)

IUSTITIAM COLIMUS
G. Giappichelli Editore

PL ACADEMIC RESEARCH

G. Giappichelli Editore - Torino

www.giappichelli.it

ISBN/EAN 978-88-921-0410-5

International Academic Publishers
Frankfurt am Main 2016

www.peterlang.com

ISBN 978-3-631-67567-0

Peter Lang Academic Research is an Imprint of Peter Lang GmbH.
Peter Lang - Frankfurt am Main • Bern • Bruxelles • New York • Oxford • Warszawa • Wien

Bibliographic Information published by the Deutsche Nationalbibliothek
The Deutsche Nationalbibliothek lists this publication in the Deutsche Nationalbibliografie; detailed bibliographic data in available in the internet at http://dnb.d-nb.de.

This volume has been published thanks to a financial contribution granted by the European Commission in the framework of the Jean Monnet module on the *The Free Movement of Workers in the European Union and in the Regio Insubrica* (reference n. 553370-EPP-1-2014-1-1T-EPPJMO-MODULE).

The contributions collected in this book have been submitted to peer review prior to publication.

Printed: Stampatre s.r.l. - Torino (Italy)

Contents

Acknowledgements

This volume collects the lectures delivered by some of the colleagues involved in the teaching activities of the Jean Monnet module on the "*The Free Movement of Workers in the European Union and in the Regio Insubrica*", held at the University of Insubria, Varese, Italy. The publication of this book has been made possible by funds granted by the European Union to the University of Insubria, Varese (Italy) in the framework of the Erasmus+ Programme (reference n. 553370-EPP-1-2014-1-1T-EPPJMO-MODULE).
Special thanks are given to Cecilia Sanna for coordinating the Jean Monnet module and to Alice Pisapia for her most valuable support in liaising with individual authors and supervising editorial revision of their contributions.

Articles by Cecilia Sanna, Giulio Peroni, Maria Grazia Buonanno, Chiara Giussani, Gaetano Ragucci and Maria Pierro were originally submitted in Italian and have been subsequently translated from Italian into English by Viola Nicodano, to whom I am extremely grateful for the timely and accurate work done.

Responsibility for imprecisions and errors remains with each individual author.

Introduction

Switzerland is, geographically, politically and culturally a very close neighbour to the European Union. All the Swiss borders are shared with EU (Austria, France, Germany and Italy) or with EEA (Liechtenstein) countries. This makes Switzerland the third most important EU trading partner (behind US and China), whilst the EU is Switzerland's main trading partner.

With regard to individuals, according to the latest statistics[1], over 1 million EU citizens live in Switzerland and some 430.000 Swiss citizens live in the EU.

On top of that, approximately 230.000 cross-border workers commute daily to Switzerland to go to work.

This phenomenon is particularly relevant in Canton Ticino, where nearly 1 in 4 workers (around 23%) is a frontier worker.

It is than crucial for Switzerland to strengthen its relationship both with the EU and with neighbour countries and this has been done over the years by bilateral treaties, although further negotiations with the EU have been recently suspended and put at stake further to the outcome of the Swiss popular initiative against mass immigration.

This book outlines and analyses the legal framework governing free movement of persons between Switzerland and the EU, looking at it from an Italian perspective.

The intention is to provide students and economic operators with an accessible tool of basic documents and information concerning the rules governing cross-frontier relationship between Switzerland and Italy.

Actually, the contributions collected in this volume relate to individual lectures delivered at the University of Insubria, Varese (Italy), within a teaching module funded by the European Union within the Erasmus+ program (Jean Monnet). They tackle different aspects of the free movement of persons, with a focus on the mobility of cross-border workers and its main legal implications. I am fully aware that, due to their individual origin, subjects addressed by different authors may present some repetitions and overlapping. Nonetheless, when it occurs, I am inclined to consider it as an added value rather than a pitfall as it may offer the reader a different analysis perspective.

---

1 Source: European Union External Action Service, www.eeas.europa.eu, accessed on 19 March 2016.

The first two chapters aim at offering some introductory remarks on the relationship between Switzerland and the EU, considering its origin and its evolution, and on the Swiss-EU 1999 bilateral agreement on the free movement of persons (FMP). Most of the information and data contained therein are retrieved from European Union's institutional websites and from the Directorate for European Affairs (DEA) of the Swiss Federal Department of Foreign Affairs (FDFA), which represent a unique updated and unpaired repository of information whose sources are hereby acknowledged.

The following chapters offer a thorough and more in-depth legal analysis on selected topics such as the outcome of the 9 February 2014 referendum on the popular initiative against mass immigration and its impact on the FMP agreement; the comparison between the Economic and Monetary Union and Switzerland in the light of the economic crisis; the relationship between Switzerland and the EU on antitrust; the judicial cooperation between Switzerland and the EU; the impact of the agreement on the taxation of savings between the EU and Switzerland and the multilateral convention on common Reporting Standard on the bank secrecy, the tax treatment of cross-border workers and the effects of the FMP agreement; and the administrative cooperation between Switzerland and the EU financial authorities.

It goes without saying that without the most valuable contributions of all the individual authors, this book could not have been written and for that reason I express my deepest and sincere gratitude to each and all of them.

Varese, 31 March 2016 Vincenzo Salvatore

Vincenzo Salvatore*

The relationship between Switzerland and the European Union: Historical Evolution and Current Legal Framework

Abstract: The author analyses the evolution of the legal framework governing the relationship between Switzerland and the European Union, being Switzerland a member of the European Free Trade Association but not adhering to the European Economic Area. Specific attention is devoted to the content of the Switzerland-EU bilateral agreements "packages" and to sectoral agreements between Switzerland and Italy.

1 Introductory remarks

Not being part of the European Union (EU), the relationship between the Swiss Confederation (hereinafter referred to as Switzerland), the EU and the latter's member States are governed by a series of multilateral and bilateral international agreements. Two basic principles have to be borne in mind when looking at the concerned relationships: since the European Economic Community (EEC) was established pursuant to the Treaty of Rome signed on 25 March 1957, the treaty making power with regard to commercial policy has been identified as an exclusive responsibility of the EEC[1]; on the other hand, when with regard to (other) policies falling within the shared responsibilities of the EU and its member States agreement have not (yet) been negotiated nor finalized between the EU and a third State (saying Switzerland as far as we are concerned), the EU member States retain the bilateral treaty making power to the extent that the content of the agreement at stake does not clash with EU law and until EU *jus superveniens* repeals the bilateral relationship.

The above implies as a consequence that EU member States are prevented from entering negotiations and agreements affecting trade or, more in general commercial policy, between themselves and Switzerland as all commercial agreements between the EU and third States, whether bilateral between the

---

* Professore Ordinario di Diritto Internazionale, Università degli Studi dell'Insubria, Varese (Italy).

1 M. Kaniel, *The Exclusive Treaty-Making Power of the European Community up to the period of the Single European Act*, Kluwer, The Hague, 1996.

EU and another State or multilateral in the framework of an international organization fall within the exclusive remit of the EU. Conversely, there are still several bilateral agreements in force between Switzerland and EU member States either because entered before establishment or accession of the concerned member State to the EU, or because subsequent multilateral agreements between Switzerland and the EU contain provisions stating that the concerned agreement does not affect existing conventions to which EU member States are or will be parties in relation to the subject matter.

Another element to consider when looking at the relationship between the EU and Switzerland or between the latter and the EU member States is that Switzerland if a federal State, meaning that the treaty making power in Switzerland lies with the federal government in Bern whilst Swiss cantons do not enjoy foreign powers. This has not prevented frontier cantons (like Ticino, Grisons or Valais) to enter preferential arrangements with local authorities (such as regions or provinces in Italy) to further promote and strengthen their trans-frontier relationship[2]. A valid model of this approach is represented by the work community *Regio Insubrica*[3], which fosters cooperation between local Swiss and Italian authorities in the Alps Lakes Region to facilitate exchange of information and joint programs and support trans-frontier movement of people for work or tourism purposes. Nonetheless it has to be noted that spontaneous organisations like the *Regio Insubrica* or other kind of memorandum of understandings or protocols of intents between Swiss cantons and local authorities of neighbouring countries (such as *Regione Lombardia* or *Tyrol*[4]) cannot generate nor be source of legal obligations according to general principles of public international law, as the treaty making power remains with the central government of the contracting parties.

---

2 For a more in-depth analysis of the regional transborder cooperation in Italy, see G. Saputelli, *The Regions and Their International Activities*, in S. Mangiameli (Ed.), *Italian Regionalism: Between Unitary Traditions and Federal Processes. Essays on Federalism and Regionalism I*, Springer, Heidelberg, 2014, pp. 281-306; and, with a focus on Swiss cross-border cooperation, OECD Territorial Reviews, *Switzerland*, OECD, Paris, 2002, spec. pp. 79-83.

3 www.regioinsubrica.org.

4 Framework conditions for cross-border cooperation between the employment services and the employers' organisations of Tyrol and South Tyrol were signed in 1997 and renewed and extended to other organisations in May 2000 within the *EURES TransTirolia* partnership. In November 2002, Grisons joined the TransTirolia with the *Kantonales Amt für Industrie, Gewerbe und Arbeit (KIGA)* (Cantonal Office for Industry and Labour). The partnership covers the Federal State of Tyrol, including the districts of Landeck, Imst, Innsbruck (city and State), Schwarz and Lienz in Austria; the Autonomous Province of Bolzano-South Tyrol in Italy; and the Canton of Grisons in Switzerland.

2 Relationship between Switzerland and the European Union, being Switzerland a member of the European Free Trade Association but not adhering to the European Economic Area

On 4 January 1960, Switzerland together with six other European countries (Austria, Denmark, Norway, Portugal, Sweden and the United Kingdom) signed in Stockholm the convention establishing the European Free Trade Association (EFTA) as a framework for the liberalisation of trade in goods amongst its member States and an economic counterbalance to the EEC. Iceland, Finland and Liechtenstein subsequently acceded the association in 1970, 1986 and 1991, whilst Denmark, the United Kingdom Portugal, Austria, Finland and Sweden left upon their accession to the EEC/European Community (EC) in 1973, 1986 and 1995 respectively. The current remaining four EFTA countries (Switzerland, Norway, Iceland and Liechtenstein) States undertook the obligation to remove customs duties on industrial products in trade among its members, thus creating a free trade area. The free trade area implies that goods originated in any of the contracting countries can freely circulate and be marketed in any other EFTA country without facing any restriction or discrimination and without being subject to any custom duties or measure of equivalent effect[5].

As Switzerland did not enjoy the benefit of the Community internal market, in order to promote trade between Switzerland and EEC member States, on 22 July 1972 the European Economic Community and the Swiss Confederation entered a bilateral free trade agreement (FTA), aiming at progressively eliminate the obstacles to trade in industrial goods, as well as on certain processed agricultural products, between the Community and Switzerland, by banning the introduction of new customs duties or charges having an equivalent effect on imports and the progressive abolition of the existing ones[6].

Further to the free trade umbrella agreement which entered into force on 1 January 1973 all industrial products have been traded free of duties between the parties. As it was sharply noted, the 1972 free trade agreement, "*although rather limited and unspectacular, ... helped to introduce an era of*

---

5 For a more comprehensive analysis of the origin and the goals of the EFTA system, see H. Corbet, D. Robertson (Eds.), *Europe's Free Trade Area Experiment. E.F.T.A. and Economic Integration*, Pergamon, Oxford, 1970.

6 D. Frei, *Switzerland and the EEC: Facts and Trends*, in *Journal of Common Market Studies*, 1973, vol. 12, n. 3, pp. 248-264.

trade stability during the 1970s and the 1980s, a period otherwise marked by great economic tension"[7].

When, some twenty years later, in 1985, the EU launched its project to complete the European internal market, Switzerland was involved in an intensive discussion on how to best frame its future role and position in Europe.

In 1989, it then occurred that the EU proposed to establish a European Economic Area (EEA) aimed at offering to the EFTA countries that did not wish to join the EU a tool intended to promote a closer relationship with the EU member States through an extensive access to the European internal market. Switzerland was then provided with a viable alternative to the accession to the EU, having the opportunity to strengthen its relationship with the EU without any political affiliation. Actually, the Swiss government moved even further, as it both signed the EEA agreement[8] and simultaneously lodged a request in Brussels to begin negotiations for membership of the EU. Nevertheless, as a consequence of the outcome of the *referendum* held on 6 December 1992, Switzerland accession to the EEA was rejected by 50,3% to 49,7% of the Swiss electorate and 18 of the 26 Cantons[9].

Hence, Switzerland is the only EFTA country not being part of the EEA agreement, which currently groups the 28 European Union member States and the other three EFTA countries: Norway, Iceland and Liechtenstein. By adhering to the EEA, Norway, Iceland and Liechtenstein committed to comply with EU legislation irrespective of not being EU member States. The latter does not apply to Switzerland, which shares negative integration (i.e., removal of barriers in trade between EFTA countries) but not positive integration stemming from European Union secondary legislation (Regulations and Directives), not being obliged, as EEA countries are, to mirror European Union rules in their domestic legislation[10]. This leaves room to and a need for

7 R. Schwok, *Switzerland-European Union: An Impossible Membership?*, Peter Lang, Brussels, 2009, p. 25.

8 The EEA agreement was signed in Oporto on 2 May 1992 by the European Communities, their member States and the then seven members of the EFTA. The most updated (14 October 2014) consolidated version of the EEA agreement is available at www.efta.int/legal-texts/eea.

9 To better understand the reasons behind the negative aptitude of Swiss electorate to support governmental initiatives aimed at fostering a strenghtened cooperation with the EU, see T. Christin, A.H. Trechsel, *Joining the EU? Explaining Public Opinion in Switzerland*, in *European Union Politics*, December 2002, vol. 3, n. 4, pp. 415-443.

10 For an overview of the EFTA and the EEA systems, see N. Fenger, M. Sanchez Rydelski, T. Van Stiphout (Eds.), *European Free Trade Association (EFTA) and the European Economic Area (EEA)*, Kluwer, Alphen aan den Rijn, 2012.

ad hoc negotiations between Switzerland and EU to agree on common rules applicable to selected matters only[11].

It is nevertheless worth mentioning that in its 2012 conclusions on the relationship between the EU and EFTA countries, the Council of the European Union, despite describing the relations between Switzerland and the EU as close and intensive, noted, however, that the system of bilateral agreements in effect to that point had reached its limits and that cooperation between Switzerland and the EU was in need of a new institutional framework.

The legal context outlined above has driven the Swiss Federal Council, to adopt, on 18 December 2013, a negotiating mandate concerning institutional issues. On the EU side, the Council of Ministers adopted a negotiating mandate for an EU-Switzerland framework agreement on 6 May 2014. The negotiations then started on 22 May 2014. Once concluded, the agreement is expected to be submitted to the Swiss Parliament for approval and, most likely, to the Swiss electorate in the event of a referendum.

Nonetheless, the running of the concerned negotiations and the launch of any further negotiations concerning additional agreements, aimed at establishing closer cooperation, has currently been suspended and remains subject to a more comprehensive assessment of the relations between Switzerland and the EU, further to the popular initiative "Stop mass immigration" and the follow up to the Swiss referendum held on 9 February 2014[12].

3 The Switzerland-EU bilateral agreements "packages"

In order to fill the gap generated by the Swiss electorate vote rejecting the perspective of an EEA membership, Switzerland and the EU then opted for a "*bilateral path*" to strengthen their economic and political relationship, through negotiations and adoption of several bilateral sectoral agreements, to extent the scope of the 1972 FTA on industrial goods by addressing additional selected matters[13].

A first set of seven agreements, commonly referred to as the "Bilateral Agreements I" package, were concluded on 1 June 1999 and subsequently

11 M. Vahl, N. Grolimund, *Integration without membership. Switzerland's bilateral agreement with the European Union*, CEPS, Brussels, 2006.

12 See, *infra*, C. Sanna, *The implementation of the initiative "against mass immigration" and the future of relations between Switzerland and the EU.*

13 An updated list of bilateral agreements between Switzerland and the EU is retrievable from the European Union External Action Service Treaties Office database at www.ec.europa.eu/world/agreements.

approved by 67,2% of the Swiss electorate through a referendum held on 21 May 2000[14].

A couple of years later, in June 2001, Switzerland and the EU agreed to launch a second round of bilateral negotiations. These resulted in eight further agreements, which formed the "Bilateral Agreements II " package, covering various policy areas in addition to the predominantly traditional market liberalisation agreements contained in the first set of agreements. The second set of bilateral agreements was signed on 26 October 2004. So far, Switzerland and the EU have concluded more than 120 sector-specific agreements, covering a wide range of EU policies including Swiss participation in many areas of the EU's internal market[15].

It has to be noted that bilateral agreements between Switzerland and the European Union concluded in the framework of the first package (Bilateral I) are linked, meaning that failure to fulfil relevant obligations, suspension or termination of one of them will automatically reflects on all the others. This is foreseen by the so-called *guillotine* clause[16], which stipulates that if one party terminates (or, by extensive interpretation, fails to fulfil any relevant obligation set by) one of the agreements, all the other agreements will cease to apply.

Looking more closely at the matters covered by the bilateral agreements, the seven ones included in the first package (1999) apply to the sectors of free movement of persons, air transport, carriage of passengers and goods by road and rail, trade in agricultural products, mutual recognition of conformity assessment (i.e. removal of technical barriers to trade), government procurement (i.e. rules of purchasing by public authorities), scientific and technological cooperation.

The nine agreements grouped in the second package (2004), which are not subject to the *guillotine* clause, cover taxation of savings, fight against fraud, association to the Schengen and Dublin agreements, processed agricultural products, statistical cooperation with Eurostat, pension, participation in the activities of the European Environment Agency, participation in the MEDIA

---

14 C. Sanna, *Gli accordi bilaterali tra la Svizzera e l'Unione europea*, in *Dir. comm. int.*, 2000, pp. 547-551.

15 For a more detailed analysis of the bilateral relationship between Switzerland and the European Union, see B. Nascimbene, *I rapporti tra la Svizzera e l'Unione europea. Gli accordi bilaterali e la politica europea della Svizzera*, in M. Condinanzi (a cura di), *Unione europea e Svizzera tra cooperazione e integrazione*, Giuffrè, Milano, 2012, pp. 3-22; M. Marescau, *EU-Switzerland: quo vadis?*, in *Georgia Journal of International and Comparative Law*, 2012 (39), pp. 727-755; C.H. Church (Ed.), *Switzerland and the European Union. A close, contradictory and misunderstood relationship*, Routledge, New York, 2007.

16 See, Art. 25 of the Agreement on the Free Movement of Persons.

programme[17], participation in EU programs aiming to encourage cross-border mobility of students, trainees and young people[18].

Deferring for a more in-depth analysis of the content and of the impact of the free movement of persons agreement to the next chapter[19], the principles set in the bilateral agreements (I and II) imply, *inter alia*, reduction of customs duties and quotas on certain agricultural products (with the exception of fresh meat, wheat and milk), free circulation of trucks subject to the payment of an heavy vehicle fee (HVF) for heavier trucks, the possibility for EU member States airlines companies to hold a majority share in Swiss airlines companies (and the other way round), the possibility for Switzerland to grant an income tax exemption for the pensions of retired EU officials living in Switzerland, to reduce customs duties on processed agricultural products (such as chocolate, instant coffee, soups, etc.) and to impose a withholding tax on all income accruing from the EU residents' savings[20].

With regard to the association to the Schengen area and cooperation regime, Switzerland agreed to remove identity checks on individuals at borders inside the Schengen area, although still maintaining customs controls on goods in Switzerland. As far as asylum and immigration policy is concerned, Switzerland accession to the Dublin/Eurodac[21] system was quite uncontentious.

Apart from those included in the bilateral packages, quite a large number of additional sectoral agreements have been signed between the EU and Switzerland over the last decade.

Thus, Switzerland cooperates with Europol and Eurojust in the field of criminal prosecution and judicial cooperation, based on two distinctive agreements entered into force on 1 March 2006 and on 22 July 2011 respectively.

Amongst other agreements, aimed at strengthening cooperation between Switzerland and the EU, it is worth mentioning that Switzerland takes part in the Erasmus+ exchange programme and in the Horizon 2020 research programme as a non-EU country without associate status. Switzerland also participates in the EU satellite navigation programmes Galileo and EGNOS and cooperates with EU institutions and bodies in the field and competition

---

17 The MEDIA programme comprises a series of support measures for the European audiovisual industry.

18 Socrates (incuding Erasmus), Leonardo da Vinci and Jeunesse programs.

19 See, *infra*, V. Salvatore, *The Agreement on the Free Movement of Persons (Fmp): genesis and content.*

20 For a sharp analysis of the Swiss-EU bilateral agreements approach, see, R. Schwok, *Switzerland's Approximation of its Legislation to the EU Acquis. Specificities, Lessons and Paradoxes*, in *European Journal of Law Reform*, 2007, vol. 9/3, pp. 449-465.

21 EURODAC is the EU wide fingerprints database to facilitate identification of applicants seeking asylum.

(exchange of confidential information between the European Commission and the Swiss Competition Commission) and defence (European Defence Agency). A working arrangement has also very recently (1 March 2016) entered into force, allowing Switzerland to participate in the European Asylum Support Office (EASO) activities and to be entitled to receive support from EASO.

Switzerland takes also part under *ad hoc* agreements in some EU missions and operations for civilian crisis management (such as EULEX in Kosovo, EUFOR ALTHEA in Bosnia and Herzegovina and EUTM in Mali)[22].

Finally, on 27 May 2015, the EU and Switzerland signed a historic new tax transparency agreement, which will significantly improve the fight against tax evasion. Under the agreement, as of 2018, both contracting parties will automatically exchange information on the financial accounts of each other's residents. The 2015 EU-Swiss agreement, which is consistent with the new OECD/G20 global standard for the automatic exchange of financial account information, stipulates that EU member States will receive, on an annual basis, the names, addresses, tax identification numbers and dates of birth of their residents with accounts in Switzerland, as well as other financial and account balance information[23]. This will put an end to bank secrecy, and as highlighted by the European Commission, "*the new transparency policy aims at not only improving EU member States' ability to track down and tackle tax evaders, but it will also act as a deterrent against hiding income and assets abroad to evade taxes*"[24].

4 Sectoral bilateral agreements between Switzerland and Italy

In addition to the agreements entered between Switzerland and the European Union, we have quite a substantial bunch of international agreements governing, on a bilateral basis, the relationships between Switzerland and its neighbour countries on a vast array of subjects[25]. The matters addressed by these agreements are mainly related to tax issues, bank regulations, administrative and judicial cooperation but, limiting the scope of the search

---

22 For a recent survey of the EU common security and defense policy operations, see B. Pohl, *EU Foreign Policy and Crisis Management Operations. Power, purpose and domestic politics*, Routledge, New York, 2014.

23 See, *infra,* M. Pierro, *Administrative Cooperation between Switzerland and the EU: the Exchange of Information.*

24 European Commission, *Fighting tax evasion: EU and Switzerland sign historic tax transparency agreement*, Press release, Brussels, 27 May 2015, IP/15/5043.

25 For an exhaustive and updated list of multilateral and bilateral international agreements concluded by Switzerland, see the *Treaty database* of the Swiss Federal Department of Foreign Affairs (FDFA) at: www.eda.admin.ch/eda/en/fdfa/foreign-policy/international-law/internationale-vertraege/datenbank-staatsvertraege.html.

to the relationship between Italy and Switzerland[26], you may, just by cherry picking, list bilateral agreements dealing with environmental protection[27], fisheries[28], water navigation[29], repatriation of cultural property[30], recognition of diplomas[31] or mutual recognition of conversion of driving licences[32].

Most recent negotiations between Italy and Switzerland have concentrated on automatic or on request exchange of information between competent authorities with regard to tax matters or cross-border assets[33]. Further efforts have been devoted to the renegotiation of the double taxation treaty and to the review of the taxation of income of cross-border workers.

Considering that at the EU level there are no rules defining the notion of cross-border workers in the field of taxation nor governing the division of powers between EU member States (or between EU member States and third countries) with regard to taxing rights, it becomes crucial for neighbour countries affected by cross-border relations to agree on which rules to apply to taxation of cross-border workers' incomes[34] and to the social security system.

---

26 For an historic survey of the evolution of bilateral relationship between Italy and Switzerland, see A. De Guttry, N. Ronzitti, *I rapporti di vicinato tra Italia e Svizzera*, Giuffrè, Milano, 1989.

27 Convention concerning the protection of Italo-Swiss waters against pollution signed on 20 April 1972 and entered into force on 7 August 1973.

28 Convention between the Swiss Confederation and the Republic of Italy on Fisheries in Italo-Swiss waters, signed on 19 March 1986 and entered into force on 1 April 1989.

29 Convention between the Swiss Confederation and the Republic of Italy concerning the navigation on the Lake Maggiore and on the Lake of Lugano, signed on 2 December 1992 and entered into force, further to exchange of notes, on 1 June 1997.

30 Agreement between the Swiss Federal Council of the Swiss Confederation and the government of the Republic of Italy on the import and repatriation of cultural property signed on 20 October 2006 and entered into force, further to exchange of notes, on 27 April 2008.

31 Swiss-Italian bilateral agreement on the mutual recognition of higher education qualifications, signed on 7 December 2000 and entered into force on 1 August 2001.

32 Agreement between the Swiss Federal Council of the Swiss Confederation and the government of the Republic of Italy on the mutual recognition of conversion of driving licences, signed on 4 December 2015, not yet entered into force.

33 See, *infra*, M. Pierro, cit.

34 See, *infra*, G. Ragucci, *Tax Treatment of Cross-border Commuters and Effects of the ALC.*

Vincenzo Salvatore*

The Agreement on the Free Movement of Persons (FMP): Genesis and Content

Abstract: Starting from the principles enshrined in the 1999 free movement of persons agreement, the author identifies and analyses the rules applicable to the movement of cross-border workers, also in the light of the evolving scenario that will be defined by the ongoing process of revision of the legal framework governing free movement of persons between Switzerland and the European Union.

1 The principles enshrined in the 1999 free movement of persons agreement

The agreement on the free movement of persons (FMP) between Switzerland and the EU was signed in 1999 as part of the "Bilateral Agreements I" package[1]. Based on the agreement European Union citizens on one hand and Swiss citizens on the other are free to establish their domicile and choose their place of work with no restrictions in the territory of the contracting parties, pursuant to the same principles and rules set by EU law governing free movement of persons between EU member States[2].

It has to be noted that the FMP agreement has been concluded in the form of a mixed agreement, having been signed by both the European Community and the then fifteen EC member States of the one part and by Switzerland of the other, as the responsibilities on the subject matter were not exclusive of the EC but shared between the EC and its member States[3].

---

* Professore Ordinario di Diritto Internazionale, Università degli Studi dell'Insubria, Varese (Italy).

1 *Agreement between the European Community and its Member States, of the one part, and the Swiss Confederation, of the other, on the free movement of persons*, done at Luxembourg on 21 June 1999, in *OJEC*, L 114/6 of 30 April 2002.

2 The agreement consists of 25 articles setting the main principles, three annexes containing detailed provisions applicable to free movement of persons, coordination of social security, mutual recognition of professional qualifications, three protocols, nine joint declarations and a final act.

3 For a comprehensive and up to date analysis of the legal implications of mixed international agreements, see C. Hillion, P. Koutrakos (Eds.), *Mixed Agreements Revisited: The EU and its Member States in the World*, Hart Publishing,

The agreement is managed by a Joint Committee, composed of representatives of the contracting parties, that coordinates administration and supervises the implementation of the provision set by the agreement, ensuring also a proper forum for discussion, exchange of information and settlement of disputes which may arises amongst the contracting parties.

The FMP agreement came into effect on 1 June 2002 and its applicability has been then progressively extended to all the 27 EU member States but Croatia[4] by subsequent Protocols, signed respectively in 2006 (I) and 2009 (II). It has been fully applicable to Italy, France, Finland, United Kingdom, Germany, Spain, Portugal, Greece, Austria, Denmark, Netherlands Sweden, Ireland, Belgium, Luxembourg, Malta and Cyprus since 1 June 2007. Freedom of movement of persons have been extended to Poland, Czech Republic, Estonia, Latvia, Lithuania, Hungary, Slovakia, Slovenia as of 1 May 2011. For Bulgaria and Romania, the transitional period will expire on 31 May 2016 at the latest. The agreement empowers contracting parties to invoke a safeguard clause[5] for a limited period of time, as it is will be the case with regard to Bulgaria and Romania, whose national workers may be affected by the reintroduction of work permit quotas until 31 May 2019[6].

Oxford, 2010; N.A. Neuwahl, *Joint participation in international treaties and the exercise of power by the EEC and its member States: mixed agreements*, in *Common Market Law Review*, 1991, pp. 717-740; D. O'Keefe, H.G. Schermers (Eds.), *Mixed Agreements*, Kluwer, Deventer, 1983.

4 The most recent amendments to the Swiss federal constitution delayed the signature of Protocol III extending the applicability of the FMP agreement to Croatia until 4 March 2016 (see, *infra,* § 3 of this chapter). Pending the ratification and the entry into force of Protocol III, access of Croatian nationals will remain subject to separate quotas pursuant to the provisions of the Swiss Federal Act on Foreign Nationals (outside quotas for third country nationals). These consist of 50 one-year B permits and 450 short term L permits.

5 The safeguard clause is foreseen by Art. 14(2) of the FMP agreement that enables the contracting parties, "*in the event of serious economic or social difficulties*", to request the Joint Committee to examine appropriate measures to remedy the situation. According to the same provision, "*the scope and duration of such measures shall not exceed that which is strictly necessary to remedy the situation*" and preferences shall be given to measures that "*least disrupt*" the wording of the agreement.

6 In recent years the safeguard clause was provisionally invoked for one year against the citizens of Poland, Czech Republic, Estonia, Latvia, Lithuania, Hungary, Slovakia and Slovenia with a Swiss B residence permit. Further to a decision of the Swiss Federal Council, the safeguard clause may be extended for a further period of time (one year) or to make it applicable to additional EU member States, as it was the case in 2013.

With regard to the duration, the FMP agreement has been concluded for an initial period of seven years and then it has been renewed indefinitely.

The main scope of the agreement is to accord to nationals of contracting parties the right of entry, residence, access to work as employed persons, establishment on a self-employed basis and the right to stay in the territory of another contracting parties. Right of entry into, and residence in, the territory of the contracting parties shall be granted also to persons without an economic activity in the host country.

An additional objective of the FMP agreement is to facilitate the provision of services in the territory of the contracting parties with particular regard to the liberalisation of the provision of services of short duration.

According to the principle of national treatment and non-discrimination, rights shall be granted by contracting parties at the same living, employment and working conditions as those accorded to nationals and nationals of one contracting party who are lawfully resident in the territory of another contracting party shall not be subject of any discrimination on grounds of nationality[7].

Namely, pursuant to Art. 7 of the agreement, in relation to the free movement of persons, the contracting parties undertake the obligation to make provisions to guarantee the right to equal treatment with nationals in respect of access to, and the pursuit of, an economic activity, and living, employment and working conditions; the right to occupational and geographical mobility in order to enable nationals of the contracting parties to move freely within the territory of the host state and to pursue the occupation of their choice; the right to stay in the territory of a contracting party after the end of an economic activity; the right of residence and the right to pursue an economic activity for family members, irrespective of their nationality; the right to acquire immovable property in so far as that is linked to the exercise of rights conferred by the agreement.

In order to make the rights conferred by the FMP agreement effective, the contracting parties commit also to adopt provisions to coordinate social security system, with the aim in particular of securing equality of treatment; determining the applicable legislation; aggregation, for the purpose of acquiring and retaining the right to benefits and of calculating such benefits, all periods taken into consideration by the national legislation of the countries concerned; paying benefits to persons residing in the territory of the contract-

7 For a recent survey of the principles governing the relationship between Switzerland and the EU, see K. Eisele, *The External Dimension of the EU's Migration Policy. Different Legal Position of Third-Country Nationals in the EU: A Comparative Perspective,* Brill Nijhoff, Leiden, pp. 218-224.

ing parties and fostering mutual administrative assistance and cooperation between authorities and institutions.

Another tool introduced by the FMP agreement to facilitate the free movement of persons between Switzerland and the EU in order for nationals of the contracting parties to gain access and pursue activities as employed and self-employed persons and to provide services is the obligation placed upon the contracting parties to take the necessary measures concerning the mutual recognition of diplomas, certificates and other qualifications, and the coordination of provisions governing access to and pursuit of activities as employed and self-employed persons and the provision of services.

The FMP agreement foresees that the number of new residence permits issued by Switzerland to employed and self-employed persons of the European Community may not be limited to fewer than 15000 per year valid for a period equal to, or exceeding, one year and 115500 per year valid form more than four months and less than one year. Nonetheless, pursuant to art. 10 (7), no quantitative limits may be applied to frontier workers.

The agreement also allows Switzerland and any contracting party to introduce more favourable provisions to govern their mutual relations.

Conversely, bilateral agreements linking Switzerland, of the one part, and one or more EU member States, of the other part, such as those concerning private individuals, economic operators, cross-border cooperation or local frontier traffic shall comply with the requirements set by the FMP agreement, implying that, in the event of incompatibilities, the FMP agreement will prevail.

Looking at the detailed provisions set by annex I to the agreement, it has to be noted that nationals of a contracting party have the right to reside and pursue economic activities in the territory of the other contracting party and, to make this right effective, they are entitled to the be granted a residence permit, or in case of cross-border workers, to a special permit. A person who has the right of residence and is a national of a contracting party is additionally entitled to be joined by the members of his family.

In case nationals of the contracting parties are not pursuing an economic activity in the host country, and do not have a right of residence pursuant to other provisions of the agreement (*e.g.* because members of family of an employed or self-employed worker), they have the right to receive a residence permit for them and the members of their family provided that they can prove to the competent authorities that they have sufficient financial means and full health insurance coverage.

In order to the make the freedom of movement effective Switzerland acknowledges the European Union system of mutual recognition of diplomas whilst organisation and functioning of social security systems, including provisions governing workers' rights to social benefits remain within the responsibility of each EU member State, which can therefore enter bilateral agreements with Switzerland at this regard.

2 The rules applicable to cross-border workers

Freedom of movement, equal treatment and social protection are paramount values that member States of the European Union are committed to protect and guarantee with regard to frontier workers[8].

Nonetheless, the notion of "*frontier workers*" (also called "*cross-border workers*") has not been clearly and unequivocally defined and it may vary significantly whether social securities rather than taxation related legal issues are taken into consideration[9]. The FMP agreement itself clarifies that its provisions do not affect the double taxation agreements' definition of "*frontier workers*".

A definition of "*frontier worker*" is provided by Regulation (EC) n. 883/2004 of the European Parliament and the Council of 29 April 2004 on the coordination of social security systems, as amended by Regulation (EC) n. 988/2004 of 16 September 2009, to be read in conjunction with implementing Regulation (EC) n. 987/1989 adopted on the same date, as follows: "*any person pursuing an activity as an employed or self-employed person in a Member State and who resides in another Member State to which he/she returns as a rule daily or at least once a week*".

European Trade Unions Confederation defines a cross-border worker in a much more detailed way as "*an employee who works in one Member State (State of employment) and lives in another (State of residence). It is essential that he retains his normal place of residence outside the State of employment. If the cross-border employee moves to the State of employment, he becomes a migrant worker. A resident who moves to a neighbouring State but continue to work in his original State of employment (migrant resident), is also a cross-border or frontier worker. The term "normal" place of residence does not*

8 European Parliament, Directorate General for Research, *Frontier Workers in the European Union*, Working Paper, Social Affairs Series, W 16A.

9 For a more in-depth analysis of the phenomenon of frontier work see the *Paper on "Cross-border work in the EU labour market"*, drafted by Fondazione Giacomo Brodolini jointly with Pancrazio Raimondo and Graziella Di Stefano from UIL Frontalieri and Michel Berti from UIL FVG, in the framework of InArco (Information Actions for Cooperation regarding Cross border workers in Alpine Arch countries). The project InArco is co-financed by the European Commission, DG Employment, Social Affairs and Inclusion under the Call for proposals VP/2012/004.

exclude the possibility that the cross-border employee, for practical reasons, also has temporary accommodation in the State of employment"[10].

A specific definition of frontier worker is also often included in bilateral double taxation treaties. When a taxation treaty does make particular provisions for frontiers workers, the definition applied for the concerned scope is generally stricter: a few tax agreements consider cross-border workers as persons living and working in a border area (*e.g.* within 10, 20 or 30 km from the border, depending on the agreement).

It is also preliminarily important to highlight that, pursuant to the FMP agreement, most EU/EFTA citizens do not need a permit to work in Switzerland for short-term employment, up to three months or 90 days per calendar year, but they are required to register with the cantonal employment authorities. If EU/EFTA citizens are seeking employment longer than three months, a residence permit is then needed required. Restrictions temporarily affect nationals of Bulgaria, Croatia and Romania who, pursuant to transitional provisions, currently need a work permit. Nonetheless, it has also to be mentioned that if and when foreign workers apply for welfare benefits, they then lose the right to remain in Switzerland.

As a supplement to the FMP agreement and further to a trade unions' initiative, job market measures (also known as "*flanking measures*") were introduced in 2002 and came into force on 1 June 2004 to protect both the Swiss working population and foreign employees sent to Switzerland from efforts to undercut salaries and the working conditions that apply in Switzerland.

Inter alia, according to the said measures, foreign companies that post workers must respect the minimum Swiss working conditions[11], such as rest periods and length of leave; the main contractor is liable for his subcontractors to respect the Swiss rules applicable to Swiss workers, collective contracts on the applicable minimum wages can be legally extended to specific sectors or areas to avoid repeated undercutting of minimum wages in the concerned sectors or areas.

These flanking measures were then progressively strengthened in 2006, 2009 and 2013.

With regard to social security, as a basic rule, an individual is subject to the legislation of the country where he actually works as an employed or a self-employed person, independently of where he lives, so that the compe-

10 European Trade Union Confederation, *Guide for mobile European workers*, 2011, available at: https://www.etuc.org/sites/www.etuc.org/files/Brochure_Guide_travailleur_mobile_EN-2_1.pdf

11 Federal Act of 8 October 1999 on the minimum employment and salary conditions for workers posted to Switzerland and accompanying measures, SR 823.20.

tent institution for the provision of social security benefits is the one of the country of work.

One of the most relevant problems faced by frontier workers working in Switzerland concerns social protection.

With regard to sickness insurance, frontier workers residing in a European Union country and employed in Switzerland have to subscribe to the compulsory system laid down by the Swiss Confederation for all residents. According to applicable legislation, sickness insurance for frontier workers ends on retirement or in the event of total unemployment and in any event of termination of gainful occupation in Switzerland. This means that the status of former frontier worker no longer exists: as soon as a frontier worker loses his job, he will automatically lose the benefit of his Swiss insurance and will have to take steps in his State of residence to secure new insurance cover.

Another difficulty relates to total unemployment of frontier workers who have paid contribution in Switzerland as the level of benefits is not calculated directly from actual earnings but on the basis of a reference amount corresponding to the pay for equivalent employment in the county of residence. This produces a figure which is substantially less than the worker's real pay, despite having been the basis of his contribution. This problem is particularly acute for Italian and French workers.

As far as Swiss invalidity pension is concerned, frontier workers receive social benefits and refunds only for disorders associated with the disability (ordinary pensions). For the rest (special pensions, to which residents are entitled), individuals must secure their own social insurance cover with a private mutual association, either in Switzerland or in their country of residence. In addition, a disability which arises a year after any employment in Switzerland has ceased does not give any entitlement to benefits. Finally, with regard to the old-age survivors' insurance, despite the former scheme did not take into account the spouse's place of residence, the current care allowance are eligible only for subject who are resident in Switzerland. On top of that, a frontier worker who has paid less than a year's contribution in Switzerland is not entitled to an old-age pension, nor to a refund of the contributions paid to the Old-age and survivor's insurance (OASI)[12].

Finally, attention has to be paid to the key role played by the European Employment Services (EURES).

EURES is a co-operation network founded in 1993 between the EU (European Commission) and EFTA countries to provide information, advice and recruitment/placement (job matching) services for the benefit of workers and employers as well as any citizen wishing to benefit from the principle of the

12 Information reported in this page is quoted from European Parliament, Directorate General for Research, *Frontier Workers in the European Union*, Working Paper, cit.

free movement of persons. By adhering to the EURES network since 1 June 2002, Switzerland supports employees and professionals in getting relevant information and advice on living and working in Switzerland, monitors employment areas in the cross-border regions and offers assistance to frontier workers, representing a valuable contact point amongst employment administration, both regional and national, and the social partners.

EURES is also one of the primary sources of information and statistics on cross-border labour market relationships.

3 An evolving scenario: the ongoing revision of the legal framework governing free movement of persons between Switzerland and the European Union

On 9 February 2014 the majority of the cantons and 50,3% of the Swiss electorate voted in favour of the initiative "*Against mass immigration*". The declared aim of the initiative was the introduction of quotas to "immigration", including in the notion cross-border commuters, asylum and job seekers either from the EU or from third countries. Therefore, the Swiss Federal Council and the Swiss Parliament have been respectively mandated to "renegotiate" the FMP agreement with the EU and to pass new legislation in order to comply with the outcome of the referendum. The revision process will have to be finalized within three years from the popular vote, *i.e.* by February 2017.

Nonetheless, as an immediate consequence of the outcome of the referendum, the introduction of quantitative limits to immigration required an amendment to the Federal Constitution, whose new Art. 121a, headed "*Control of immigration*", reads as follows[13]:

1.*Switzerland shall control the immigration of foreign national autonomously.*

2.*The number of residence permits for foreign nationals in Switzerland shall be restricted by annual quantitative limits and quotas. The quantitative limits apply to all permits issued under legislation on foreign nationals, including those related to asylum matters. The right of permanent residence, family reunification and social benefits may be restricted.*

3.*The annual quantitative limits and quotas for foreign nationals in gainful employment must be determined according to Switzerland's general economic*

13 As English is not an official language of the Swiss Confederation, the concerned constitutional provision has been quoted according to the translation provided by the Federal Council of the Swiss Confederation (and available on its institutional website: www.admin.ch for information purposes only).

interests, while giving priority to Swiss citizens; the limits and quotas must include cross-border commuters. The decisive criteria for granting residence permits are primarily a application from an employer, ability to integrate, and adequate, independent means of subsistence.

4.*No international agreements may be concluded that breach this Article.*

5.*The law shall regulate the details.*

The new constitutional text is patently not compatible with the obligations undertaken by the contracting parties in the FMP agreement, and as required by the transitional provision set by Article 197, clause 11 of the Swiss Federal Constitution:

1.*International agreements that contradict Article 121a must be renegotiated and amended within three years of its adoption by the People and Cantons.*

2.*If the implementing legislation for Article 121a has not come into force within three years of its adoption by the People and the Cantons, the Federal Council shall issue temporary implementing provisions in the form of an ordinance.*

On 20 June 2014, the Swiss Federal Council approved the concept for implementing the new article of the Federal Constitution and, on 7 July 2014, the Swiss Federal Office for Migration submitted to the EU a formal request to renegotiate the FMP agreement. Despite the EU immediate and firm objection to it[14], a mandate to negotiate with the EU on the amendments to the FMP agreement was approved by the Federal Council on 8 October 2014.

A few months later, on 11 February 2015 the Federal Council approved the draft of the new legislation on foreign nationals and additional measures to make better use of the potential workforce within Switzerland.

The admission of EU citizens will continue to be regulated by the FMP agreement, but it will have to be amended in line with the constitutional requirements. For citizens of third countries, the draft legislation being submitted for consultation provides for quotas and the prioritisation of existing Swiss residents, as it was previously the case[15].

---

14 In her letter dated 24 July 2014 (A(2014)2725295), addressed to the President of the Swiss Confederation, the EU High Representative clearly stated that "*Renegotiating these principles with the objecting of introducing quantitative limits and quotas combined with a preference for Swiss nationals would be in fundamental contraction to the objective of the Agreement of the free movement of person*".

15 For a crisp outline of the current discussion on the new immigration regime, see S. Carrera, E. Guild, K. Eisele, *No Move without Free Movement: The EU-Swiss controversy over quotas for the free movement of persons*, in CEPS Policy

Pending the approval of the new legislation and the revision of the FMP agreement, on 4 December 2015, the Federal Council invoked the safeguard clause provided by Art. 14.2 of the FMP agreement itself to make (at least temporarily) legitimate the introduction of quantitative limits and quotas on the free movement of persons with the EU[16].

Briefs, Brussels, April 2015, n. 331 (available for free downloading from the CEPS website at www.ceps.eu).

16 For a more in-depth analysis of the initiatives undertaken by the Swiss federal government to address the consequences of the revision of the constitutional provisions concerning immigration, see, *infra*, C. SANNA, *The implementation of the initiative "against mass immigration" and the future of relations between Switzerland and the EU.*

Cecilia Sanna*

The Implementation of the Initiative "against mass immigration" and the Future of Relations between Switzerland and the EU

Abstract: As a consequence of the "against mass immigration" initiative, the Swiss Federal Council took several actions to implement the outcome of the popular vote. In the context of relationships between Switzerland and the EU, the mandate to renegotiate the Free Movement of Persons (FMP) agreement, the revision of the law on Foreign Nationals (FNA), the introduction of additional measures pursuant to the FMP and the "bottom up" clause are thoroughly assessed by the author.

1 The initiative "against mass immigration" in the context of relationships between Switzerland and the EU

Switzerland is not a EU Member State, but still maintains with it intense bilateral relations, currently consisting of over 100 agreements. Fundamental are the so-called "Bilateral Agreements I" of 1999, which cover for the domains of free movement of persons, air transport, land transport, technical barriers to trade, public procurement, agriculture, science and technology cooperation agreements, and the so-called package of "Bilateral II" agreements as of 2004, covering the association to Schengen and Dublin, the taxation of savings, the fight against fraud, processed agricultural products, statistics, media, pensions, education[1].

The Agreement on the Free Movement of Persons (ALC), in force since 2002, is undoubtedly the most complex agreement, and the one that Switzerland has agreed with more difficulties, to the extent that the EU imposed that bilateral

* Ricercatore confermato di Diritto Internazionale e Europeo, Università degli Studi di Milano.

1 On the relations between Switzerland and the EU, cf. M. Condinanzi (Ed.), *Unione europea e Svizzera tra cooperazione e integrazione*, Giuffré, Milano, 2012; C. Kaddous, M. Jametti Greiner, *Accords bilatéraux II Suisse-UE et autres accords récents/BilteralAbkommen II Schweiz-UE und andereneueAbkommen*, Bâle-Genève-Munich-Bruxelles-Paris, 2006; D. Felder, C. Kaddous (Eds.), *Accords bilatéraux Suisse-UE: (commentaires), BilateraleAbkommenSchweiz-Eu: (ersteAnalysen)*, Bruylant, Bruxelles, 2001.

agreements I had to be simultaneously traded, signed and implemented all at once, and also imposed the introduction of the "guillotine clause", meaning that the extinction of one of the seven agreements would determine the forfeiture of all the others[2]. The clause was not included in subsequent agreements but it is again contained in the Association Agreement of Switzerland to the Horizon 2020 package, signed on 5 December 2014. In addition, although distinct, are closely associated with the ALC, agreements on the association to Schengen and Dublin (AAS and AAD) to which the application of the guillotine clause could be extended.

The initiative "against mass immigration", approved on 9 February 2014, imposes to Switzerland a review of these relations. We recall that popular initiative is one of the tools provided by the Swiss political system to encourage the participation of citizens in the government of the State. Precisely, citizens, numbering not less than 100,000, may request to submit to the vote of the entire electorate a proposal for full or partial amendment of the Federal Constitution (Fed. Const.), in accordance respectively with Art. 138 and Art. 139 Fed. Const. The approval of the abovementioned initiative has thus determined the introduction of artt. 121a and 197 n. 11 in the Fed. Const., requiring the federal government the fixation of maximum ceilings and annual quotas, to be applied to all permits to foreigners including EU citizens, «*established depending on the global interests of the Swiss economy and in compliance with the principle of preference for Swiss citizens* [...] *and also to renegotiate and adapt international treaties that contradict this principle within three years from the acceptance of that article by the Population and Cantons*». Although this initiative was approved by 50.3% of the votes, the turnout was up to 56%, which means a much higher participation compared to other voting to which Swiss people is frequently called. The reasons for voting can be explained by looking at the geography of the results. Foreign workers are considered at special risk by the Ticino (68.2% yes) where the Italian frontier workers exceeds 60000 units, and cantons notoriously intransigent (Appenzell, Schwyz, Uri, Glarus). The city of Basel, Neuchâtel, Geneva, Fribourg, Jura and Vaud are the cantons that, instead, have rejected the initiative with the largest number of votes, thus deeming foreign workers as a resource. The most delicate point in the approved initiative is that it re-

2 Agreement as of 21 June 1999 between the Swiss Confederation, on one side, and the European Community and its Members, on the other, concerning the free movement of persons (RS 0.142.112.681). The provisions contained in the ALC, it is recalled, apply to the citizens of the European Free Trade Association (EFTA), Norway and Iceland and their relatives, and also to workers posted on behalf of companies established in one of those States (FF 2001 4435). Hereinafter, reference will be made only to ALC.

quires the federal government to renegotiate the ALC, in the view of making it consistent with the new constitutional provisions, or to denounce it within three years. The matter, already difficult because of the importance covered by this Agreement in bilateral relations, is amplified by the fact that if the negotiations should not lead to a successful conclusion, and the agreement terminated, after six months, the other agreements embodied in the so-called Bilateral I would automatically decay on the basis of the aforementioned guillotine clause[3]. The outcome of this initiative, legally, does not affect the effectiveness of the bilateral agreements II but the reaction of the European Commission after the vote was clear: the approval of the new constitutional provisions call into question the totality of bilateral relations between the EU and the Confederation. On the other hand, the ALC, which for the EU is a mixed agreement (shared competence between the Union on the one hand and its Member States on the other) has been extended to States, which since 1999 have entered the Union, not automatically but by negotiating each time additional protocols, submitted to the vote of the Swiss population[4]. The new constitutional provisions of the initiative “against mass immigration” exclude the conclusion of new agreements that are not consistent with the introduction of quotas for immigrants. It is a directly applicable provision, which does not require implementation at the legislative level. Therefore, in the immediate, the Federal Council has been unable to sign the Protocol III, which contains the provisions on extending ALC to Croatia, EU Member State from 1 July 2014. The EU’s reaction was immediate, suspending the participation of the Confederation to the Horizon 2020 Program. The Swiss executive managed to resolve the stalemate through the grant to the Croatian citizens of quotas similar to those that would have entered into force with an extension of the free movement, which in any case in the early years would have been

3 On this please accept reference to *Gli accordi bilaterali tra la Svizzera e l’Unione europea*, in *Dir. comm. internaz.*, 2000, fasc. 2, p. 547 ss.

4 Cf. the Protocol to the Agreement between the Swiss Confederation, on the one hand, and the European Community and its Member States on the other, on the free movement of persons, regarding the participation, as contracting parties, of the Czech Republic, the Republic of Estonia, the Republic of Cyprus, the Republic of Latvia, the Republic of Lithuania, the Republic of Hungary, the Republic of Malta, Republic of Poland, the Republic of Slovenia and the Slovak Republic, pursuant to their accession to the European Union, RU 2006, 993; Protocol to the Agreement between the Swiss Confederation, on the one hand, and the European Community and its Member States on the other, on the free movement of persons, regarding the participation, as contracting parties of the Republic of Bulgaria and Romania pursuant to their accession to the EU, in the RU in 2009, 2421.

limited[5]. On 5 December 2014, the Minister Johann Schneider-Ammann was able to sign an agreement that reintroduces Horizon 2020, although partially (only applies to edge research and not for the industrial one) and only for a transitional period until 31 December 2016. As said in the statement released by the EU if, by that date, Switzerland will have not clarified its position on the free movement of persons, in particular by ensuring "non-discrimination of Croatian citizens and researchers" the agreement will decay.

The outcome of the federal elections of 18 October 2015, preceded by a substantially single-issue campaign, all focused on refugees emergency and relations with the EU, confirms an "euroscepticism" majority among the Swiss population and, therefore, the difficulties for the Swiss government to continue the bilateral way. The renewal, to recall, was about the Federal Assembly or the 200 seats in the House of People (National Council), and 45 of the 46 seats in the House of cantons (Council of States) as the new senator from Appenzell canton had already been elected in April by the assembly of citizens (Landsgemeinde). Nearly 30% of the vote has been collected by the Union of the Democratic Centre (UDC), the conservative right party, promoter, among other things, of the initiative "against mass immigration", winning 11 additional seats in the National Council compared to 2011's elections. On 9 December 2015, the two joined chambers have elected the seven members of the Swiss government (Federal Council), two of which, meeting the needs of democratic representation, are UDC exponents. The new government will undoubtedly have an effect on the position that Switzerland will take in the relations with the EU, having to convey the views of the electoral will.

The "euroscepticism" expressed by the Helvetic people is however prevailing but not absolute. In the same year in which the initiative "against mass immigration" was accepted, it was rejected the initiative to "Stop overpopulation – ensure the conservation of the natural foundations of life", to amend the Federal Constitution (Fed. Const.) aimed at curbing population growth by limiting immigration[6]. The "no" was expressed by 74% of voters (about 50%, and then on average) and has been consistent in all cantons, with percentages ranging from 63% in Ticino, to 83% in Canton of Vaud[7]. The initiative, known as "Ecopop" from name of the promoter association (Ecology and Population), called for the introduction in the Fed. Const. of two

5 Art. 91 of the Ordinance of 24 October 2007 on admission, residence and gainful employment, Introduced by n. I of the O dated 18 June 2008 (RU 2008 2737). Amended n. I of the O dated 29 November 2013, in force from 1 July 2014 (RU 2013 4371, 2014 997).

6 http://www.ecopop.ch/it/initiative-it. Voting was held on 30 November 2014.

7 Results can be found on the web page http://www.admin.ch/ch/i/pore/va/20141130/det588.html.

new articles (the 73rd and 197 n. 9) that would have imposed to Switzerland to activate "so that in Switzerland resides a population compatible with the long-term conservation of the natural basis of life" and to promote this goal also «in other countries, notably in the framework of international development cooperation»[8]. For this purpose the permanent resident population in Switzerland could not grow as a result of migration of more than 0.2 percent per year over three years[9] and the Federal government would have had to invest «*in measures to promote voluntary family planning, at least 10% of the funds allocated to development cooperation*», and that in order to reduce the birth rate in the countries concerned and so the immigration pressure on Switzerland. The result therefore clarifies the willingness of the Swiss people who surely asks for more control on immigration, though by identifying as a tool no strict quotas, fixed in the Constitution, but rather variable interventions according to the economic needs in order to protect indigenous work.

On the same day of the vote, the Group Out of Dead End (RASA) launched Federal popular initiative "*Out the dead end! We waive for the re-introduction of immigration quota*" to repeal Art. 121a and 197 n. 11 of the Fed. Const. Unlike most of the initiatives, the promoters are not parties but ordinary citizens who come from the world of education, labour and culture. They have proposed the initiative as a plan B wanting to give the people a chance to rule again on the item related to the quotas and thus decide on the fate of the bilateral agreements between Switzerland and the EU. In the fastest time and several months ahead of the deadline (6 February 2016) have been collected 109,089 signatures of which 108,640 declared valid by the Federal Court, which on 11 November 2015 who expressed the success of the initiative[10]. The vote is scheduled for the end of 2016 beginning of 2017: last chance to keep the bilateral path open, in case Switzerland is unable to renegotiate the ALC.

---

8 For an examination of the proceedings of the initiative, cf. http://www.admin.ch/ch/i/pore/vi/vis406.html.

9 Whereas in 2013 net migration was 87,000, could have immigrate about 17,000 people a year – that is, three-quarters less than net migration in recent years (the number of immigrants deduced that the emigrants).

10 FF 2015 6833.

2 Actions taken forward by the Federal Council to implement the initiative "against mass immigration": the mandate to renegotiate the ALC, the revision of the Law on Foreign Nationals (FNA), the introduction of additional measures in accordance with ALC. The "bottom up" clause.

In June 2014 the Federal Council approved the plan for the implementation of the new Art. 121a Fed. Const. It dealt with the decisions of 11 February 2015, namely by putting in consultation a draft amendment to the Law on Foreign Nationals (FNA), taking the mandate to negotiate the ALC adjustment with the EU and proposing a series of measures in the fields of social insurance, taxation, health, infrastructure and security, aimed at mobilizing the potential working force on the territory, while respecting ALC. This third point is not imposed by the constitutional provision but it is considered as complementary to the same.

The consultation procedure for implementation of Art. 121a Fed Const. in the FNA was held from 11 February to 28 May 2015 and had as its object two preliminary drafts: a review of the Foreign Nationals Act for the implementation of Art. 121a Fed. Const. and adjustment of the draft amendment to the Foreign Nationals Act referred to by the Parliament Federal Council (so-called integration project). The results of the consultation were announced in December 2015[11]. Taking into account the results of the consultations, the Federal Council instructed the Federal Department of Justice and Police (DJP) to develop, in collaboration with the Federal Department of Foreign Affairs (FDFA) and the Federal Department of Economic Affairs, training and research (DEFR), a relevant legislative proposal. On 4 March 2016 it has therefore been presented a message regarding the amendment of the Foreign Nationals Act (laying down provisions relating to immigration control and improvements in the execution of the agreements on free movement), an additional message on the integration project of the Foreign Nationals Act and a message on the ALC extension to Croatia[12].

The fulcrum of the proposals is the establishment of a safeguard clause that would allow to limit the free movement where specific threshold values were to be exceeded. The hope of the Federal Council is that the consent clause will be processed with the EU and integrated in the ALC. If, however, the negotiations with the EU will fail, Art. 121a Fed. Const. might be imple-

---

11 Cf. doc https://www.sem.admin.ch/dam/data/sem/aktuell/gesetzgebung/teilrev_aug_integration/ve2-ber-aig-i.pdf and https://www.sem.admin.ch/dam/data/sem/aktuell/gesetzgebung/teilrev_aug_art-121a/ve-ber-ums-121a-i.pdf.

12 Cf. documents on the following webpage http://www.ejpd.admin.ch/ejpd/it/home/aktuell/news/2016/2016-03-04.html.

mented through a unilateral safeguard clause that meets the requirements of the new constitutional provision that autonomously regulate even the immigration from EU countries, by introducing temporary restrictions and targeted residence permits, to be only issued to foreigners who are gainfully employed. The unilateral safeguard clause would be enshrined in the Foreign Nationals Act. The legislative message provides for the following mechanism: the Federal Council, by order, sets the rate of immigration from EU countries; federal caps (so-called limit values) shall be determined from this rate. In the case of exceeding the limit values, the Federal Council shall heighten those measures aimed in particular at promoting the potential of indigenous work force and integration of foreigners. Furthermore, if necessary, the Federal Council shall also adapt the enforcement of the law on foreigners. It is moreover planned the possibility to share federal caps on cantonal contingents (as is already the case for third-country nationals with gainful employment). If, in the course of a given year, the defined limit values were to be reached (reference date is on June 1 according to the message), ceilings and quotas to be applied to the issuance of permits to EU shall be established for the following calendar year. If the immigration control should require so, the Federal Council may extend the application of those ceilings and quota for an additional calendar year. The definition of these limits and the application of the same to residence permits will be defined by order; numerically, they may be different in type (i.e. immigration on asylum, with or without gainful employment or as part of family reunification). It also provided for the possibility to introduce restrictions even for short-term residence permits and permits for cross-borders workers (starting from 4 months) in order to avoid any circumvention. The recommendations of the new Immigration Commission will be considered at the time of the definition of limit values, ceilings and quotas, and competent parliamentary committees will also be heard.

The respect of the Swiss priorities and of conditions of pay and work, is verified within the definition of caps and quotas, as well as the accompanying measures relating to the free movement of persons. There shall be no examination of the individual case.

The message on the amendment of the Foreign Nationals Act also contains some modifications in order to ensure uniform implementation of the ALC in relation to social security payments. Specifically, in the event of loss of employment during the first twelve months of residence in Switzerland, the holder of a EU permit to short-stay, or an EU residence permit, retains its right of residence for the six months following the involuntary loss of employment, or until the expiry of the payment of unemployment benefits; during that period, however, it is excluded from social aid. In the event of loss of employment after the first twelve months of residence in Switzerland, the holder of a EU residence permit retains its right of residence during the six months following the cessation of the gainful employment or during the six months following the deadline for the payment of unemployment benefits. The legislative proposal also excludes the provision of social aid to foreigners (including EU citizens) staying in Switzerland in the exclusive view of seeking employment and to the members of their family, by standardizing the different cantonal regulations currently in force. Foreign citizens without a residence also will no longer have access to supplementary benefits.

It should be recalled that on 1 April 2015 came into force an amendment to the introduction of free movement of persons (OLCP), according to which EU citizens wishing to travel to Switzerland in search of a job, can receive a permit of short duration (of the validity of three months) only on condition of being self-sufficient (Art. 18, § 2 OLCP)[13].

This provision and the changes to the RTA provided in the message presented by the Federal Council on 4 March 2016, are to be considered compatible with the legal framework and case law developed by the EU, which admits clear exceptions to the general principle of equal treatment with nationals in relation to social assistance benefits. Directive 2004/38/EC, in particular, stipulates that the latter may be denied in the first three months of residence if the citizen is economically inactive or has entered the State for the purpose of looking for a first job[14].

Permanence is then granted for six more months if the person is able to demonstrate that he is actively looking for a job. At the end of six months he shall leave the State, unless he has the financial means to support himself and a health insurance[15]. In the event of loss of job, the host Country is obliged to analyze the specific situation, to decide whether or not to grant the aid and for this purpose shall be deemed the length of stay, age, state of health, the degree of integration the temporary nature of the difficulty, the contributions and rights acquired in the country[16]. The Court of Justice has interpreted those provisions on strict terms. We recall the *Reyes* case[17], in which the judges noted that the right to family reunification of EU citizens are still subject to control by the Member States, on the existence of economic dependency

13 RU 2015 849.

14 Directive 2004/38/CE of the European Parliament and the Council, dated 29 April 2004, concerning the right of EU citizens and their relatives to move and reside freely within the territory of Member States, amending Regulation (CEE) n. 1612/68 and repealing Directives 64/221/CEE, 68/360/CEE, 72/194/CEE, 73/148/CEE, 75/34/CEE, 75/35/CEE, 90/364/CEE, 90/365/CEE and 93/96/CEE, GU L 158 of 30 April 2004, p. 77.

15 Judgment 15 September 2015, C-67/14.

16 On topic, recently, C. Morviducci, *I diritti dei cittadini europei*, Giappichelli, Torino, 2014, p. 159 ss.

17 Judgment of 16 January 2014, C-423/12.

requirements, in chief to dependent family members who want to enter the territory of host Country. In the case *Dano*[18], a case of "social tourism", the Court considered lawful a national provision excluding nationals of other Member States from the benefit of certain "special cash benefits of non-contributory benefits" within the meaning of Art. 70, § 2, of the Regulation n. 883/2004, where these citizens do not benefit of a right to reside under Directive 2004/38 in the host Member State. The strict interpretation was confirmed in the recent judgment *García-Nieto*[19], which confirmed the possibility to exclude the access to non-contributory social benefits for citizens of other EU Member States, during the first three months of stay.

The Foreign Nationals Act modification Message also provides for the introduction of a legal basis that imposes on the competent authorities for the payment of supplementary benefits, the obligation to notify the competent authorities in the area of migration payments of annual supplementary benefits and reimbursement of expenses sickness and disability in cases of a certain gravity. If a cantonal authority competent in the field of migration receives these data, it will spontaneously communicate to the body responsible for establishing and paying the additional service, the possible non-renewal or the possible revocation of the residence permit.

An alternative to unilateral safeguard clause, presented in Bern on 7 March 2016, known as "Bottom up", is the work of the former Secretary of State Michael Ambühl: a model that primarily focuses on regional work markets, while closely monitoring wages and unemployment. The scheme respects the principle of free movement of persons, specifying rules for the application the ALC, referring in particular to the provisions laid down in Art. 14, § 2 ALC[20]. In some very exceptional cases, defined by precise socio-economic indicators, it would be possible to adopt different types of measures, limited in their scope and in their duration. In the absence of an exceptional situation, the principle of free movement of persons would be applied just as it does today. The new proposal also adopts a bottom-up approach, simply called "bottom-up". It includes the two dimensions of the free movement included in Art. 121a Const., namely frontier workers and immigration. It provides for

18 Judgment of 11 November 2014, C-333/13.

19 Judgment of 25 February 2016, C-299/14.

20 That provision states that "*In the event of serious economic or social difficulties, the Joint Committee shall meet, at the request of either Contracting Party, to examine appropriate measures to remedy the situation. The Joint Committee may decide what measures to take within 60 days of the date of the request. This period may be extended by the Joint Committee. The scope and duration of the measures are limited to what is strictly necessary to remedy the situation. The measures chosen should minimize interference with the functioning of this Agreement.*".

taking external safeguard (ALC) and internal action (not relevant to the ALC) and consists of three levels (sector – 48 regional branches of the economy; – 7 large regions Swiss national; – 32 EU / EFTA). The distinction between frontier workers and migration is linked to the requirement that frontier workers, who are usually resident in countries with lower living costs and less favourable economic dynamics, can generate effects more pronounced on the labour market than resident migrants. External measures for frontier workers imply preference for natives, measures less intrusive than a quota system and therefore more manageable. For migrants, the external measures will not however mean a preference for natives but an immigration brake. With regard to the internal measures, the study only outlines at a general level the measures that might be taken. These, such as the strengthening of the accompanying measures at local level, fall within the competence of the Swiss domestic politics and beyond the scope of this study. The upward logical provides for taking measures at the lowest possible degree, meaning less intrusive, before getting to the top level. It is therefore easier to work within sectors, rather than regional or national level[21].

The model has received good consents at the parliamentary level and most likely will be discussed in parallel to the safeguard clause proposed by the Federal Council.

As mentioned above, Art. 121a Fed. Const. requires renegotiation of the ALC, by introduction of the caps and annual quotas for all types of permits, regardless the purpose of the stay, and the priorities of the Swiss for gainful activity, or in the event of failure of the negotiations the termination of the Agreement by February 9, 2017.

Art. 18 ALC provides that a Contracting Party may submit to the Joint Committee a proposal for amendment of the ALC. Under that provision, after the drafting of the implementation plan of the Federal Council, Switzerland presented the EU with a request to change the ALC (letter of 4 July 2014 of the Director of the Federal Migration to the Director of EU delegation in the Joint Committee the ALC). On 24 July 2014, in a response to the president of the Confederation agreed with EU Member States, Mrs. Catherine Ashton, the then EU Commissioner for Foreign Affairs, informed Switzerland that negotiations designed to introduce quotas, caps and national priority are contrary to the principle of free movement. Moreover, while declaring the EU Commission and the European Foreign Service's availability to discuss the problems posed by the implementation, she stated that for the EU the non-discrimination, the right to gainful employment and to reside on the territory of another State party, and the stand-still clause are essential and

21 https://www.admin.ch/gov/it/pagina-iniziale/documentazione/eventi.event-id-6073.html.

non-negotiable points of the ALC. Despite this statement, the Federal Council adopted a negotiating mandate for adapting the ALC to Art. 121a Fed. Const. and established the objective it intends to pursue during negotiations, which is immigration control while assuring the bilateral path in relations with the EU. The approval of the final negotiating mandate from the Federal Council coincided the start of consultations on the draft project FNA, in February 2015. The EU has still not given any mandate to this effect, instead. Until Art. 121a. Fed. Const. will not be implemented, the provisions of the ALC remain in force. It is in compliance with such rules, in addition to the draft project of law and to the ALC negotiations, that the Federal Council has developed, as a third pillar, a number of accompanying measures to make better use of the potential work force on the territory (priority of indigenous workers), as well as to reduce the demand for foreign workers and improve the integration of those already present in Switzerland. These are measures which, according to several members of the political and economic world, should have been introduced long ago, and that might have prevented the popular approval of the new constitutional provision.

First, using the leeway at its disposal to curb immigration, the Federal Council adopted a partial revision of the Ordinance on admission, residence and gainful employment (OASA), entered into force on 1 January 2015[22]. The changes reduce the quotas for workers from non-EU third countries and not belonging to the EFTA countries. The short-term residence permits (L) and the residence permits (B) are decreased each of 1000 units. The short-term residence permits available went from 5000 to 4000, 2000 of which are attributed to the cantons, while the remaining 2000 shall remain in federal reserves. Residence permits for 2015 have been reduced from 3500 to 2500, half of which (1250) is assigned to the cantons, while the other half remains with the Confederation (1250). The Federal Council has also fixed the quotas for the admission of service providers from the EU for stays of more than 90 or 120 days a year. The quotas apply to service providers excluded from the ALC and the EFTA Convention. The residence permits in accordance with Art. 20a OASA halved, raising to 250. The quotas shall be made available to the cantons quarter. There is a separate Federal Reserve.

The Federal Council also approved two amendments to the Ordinance on the Value Added Tax (OIVA), came into force on 1 January 2015[23]. The Federal Council also approved two amendments to the Ordinance on the Value Added Tax (OIVA), came into force on 1 January 2015. They are concerned in particular foreign companies making in Switzerland jobs in the building sector civil engineering and finishing industries. Remain exempted from being

22 https://www.admin.ch/opc/it/classified-compilation/20070993/index.html.
23 https://www.admin.ch/opc/it/classified-compilation/20091866/index.html.

imposed the foreign firms that provide services subject to the tax on the purchase exclusively, even if in doing so achieve a turnover in Switzerland of over 100,000 francs a year. The intent is to reduce the competitive disadvantages of the national enterprises over foreign companies. The standard is applied on a transitional basis until the entry into force of the partial revision of the Law on the Value Added Tax (VAT Act) under which the Swiss and foreign enterprises will be subject to VAT from the first franc of turnover in Swiss territory, if their annual turnover achieved in the world exceeds 100,000 francs.

Alongside these interventions, so to say restrictive, it must be reported a legislation proposal to promote the principle of equal treatment provided by the ALC. Specifically, the Federal Council, the 28 November 2014 approved the dispatch on the revision of the Federal Law on taxation of the income from gainful activity. In Switzerland are taxed at source approximately 760,000 people gainfully employed employee without a permanent residence permit, of which about 490,000 have tax domicile or residence in Switzerland and are considered residents. About 270,000 people have no tax domicile or residence in Switzerland and are considered non-residents. On 26 January 2010, the Federal Court (ATF) has verified for the first time, that the taxation at source, infringes ALC where the subjected to withholding tax, who are not resident in Switzerland and will achieve more than 90% of their worldwide income (the so-called almost-residents) are entitled to the same deductions of taxed people in Switzerland in the ordinary way. With the revision, all persons subject to withholding tax residents will be able to ask for additional ordinary taxation. From an amount of earned income, which has yet to be established, they will be compulsorily subject by office's authority, to the procedure of the ordinary taxation. The almost residents (*i.e.* in particular frontier workers) will be able to choose between the withholding tax or the ordinary taxation. The regulatory action, however, does not innovate in the practice, since it codifies a situation that was already admitted by practice, following to the abovementioned judgment of the FT: up to now, however, it was only sporadically used. The change in law was received with concern by the local authorities detecting possible difficulties of application and the additional burden on the cantonal administrations Tax.

3 Conclusions

The future of relations between Switzerland and the EU will be clearer at the end of 2016, so that the federal government can meet the deadline of 9 February 2017 for the implementation of Art. 121 Fed. Const. Very unlikely the EU will agree to renegotiate the ALC by placing limits to the entry of EU citizens: this may in fact represent a precedent evocable by those EU Member States that have already introduced restrictive practices on the free movement and sought to introduce further limits[24]. Emblematic is the case of the UK, where the problem of immigration and the Country's future within the EU are two main points on the agenda of British Prime Minister David Cameron's policy. The British government, from 2013 onwards, has introduced several measures to combat illegal immigration and to prevent "*the social tourism*", the arrival in the British Isles with the explicit aim of exploiting the welfare system[25]. The measures mainly developed to control the mobility of Bulgarian and Romanian are also applicable without distinction to all EU nationals[26]. Undoubtedly even more significant is the referendum on the permanence of the United Kingdom to the EU scheduled for June 2016 and the issue of immigration is one of the reasons that could lead to the so-called *Brexit*. In this view it was signed 19 February 2016 the agreement with the European Council as an alternative to exit of the United Kingdom from the EU, which also provides for an "emergency brake" to the migration of EU citizens seeking work in the UK: the proposed Tusk provides an opportunity for London to limit migrants' access to welfare (*i.e.* to housing or income support) for the first four years of residence. Objective of the government would thus be a disincentive to the so-called "tourism of benefit"[27]. The UK however is not the only Member State who wants to pursue a restrictive immigration policy inside the common market: together with Netherlands, Austria and Germany, has sent a letter to the Commission asking for tough sanctions to counter the arrival within its territory of Romanians and Bulgarians. The letter was discussed at the European Council of June 2013 which invited the Commission to examine the implementation of the rules on free movement, including guidelines for combating the abuse of these rules, and to submit to the Council Justice and Home Affairs an interim report by October 2013 and a final report in December 2013[28]. The Commission adopted in November

---

24 On topic, please allow a reference to author's, *La crisi economica impone restrizioni alla libera circolazione delle persone?*, at www.eurojus.it.

25 https://www.gov.uk/government/collections/immigration-bill. The Immigration Bill 2015 provides that owners can evict illegal immigrants without recourse to a court, once received by the Interior Ministry, communication that they no longer possess a valid residence permit, and therefore the right to rent in UK. But not only. Before renting the house or part of it, they will have to check the status of the applicant, by checking their passport and residence permit, and reject it if not "regular". Who fails to fulfil these measures, it could face up to five years in prison. Only if the tenant refuses to leave the house, the owners will be forced to go to court, https://www.gov.uk/government/collections/immigration-bill-2015-16.

26 http://www.gov.uk/government/speeches/david-camerons-immigration-speech.

27 http://www.consilium.europa.eu/it/press/press-releases/2016/02/19-tusk-final-remarks-european-council/.

28 www.consilium.europa.eu/uedocs/NewsWord/it/jha/138874.doc.

2013 a Communication on free movement of EU citizens (COM (2013) 837) highlighting the lack of «a statistical relationship between the generosity of social security systems and the flows of European citizens», but at the same time exposing five actions which will support Member States to apply the rules and instruments made available to the EU even in terms of the use of structural funds and investment. 13 January 2014, the same institution has published a guide on the determination of the habitual residence to help Member States to correctly implement the rules on coordination of social security for EU citizens who have moved to another Member State[29].

Certainly the possibility of renegotiating the ALC and therefore the future of relations between Switzerland and the EU are closely linked to the development of these internal tensions, which currently characterize the integration process, and incisive will be the outcome of the referendum on the possible Brexit, pending which, at the time, any interim activity between Berne and Brussels it is essentially frozen.

29 http://europa.eu/rapid/press-release_IP-14-13_it.htm.

Giulio Peroni*

Economic and Monetary Union and Switzerland: Two Models Compared in the Light of the Economic Crisis

Abstract: Looking at the origin and the reasons behind and considering the impact of the 2007 economic crisis in the EU countries and in Switzerland, the author describes the initiatives taken and the key role played by the European Central Bank to mitigate financial and monetary risks within the Eurozone, and compares it to the Swiss approach, namely addressing the set of measures adopted by the Swiss National Bank to tackle the economic crisis.

1 Preliminary remarks

Recent economic data, as processed and disclosed by the Organization for Economic Cooperation and Development (OECD), the International Monetary Fund (IMF) and the Statistical Office of the European Union (Eurostat), seem to indicate that the Crisis that started from Summer 2007 and affected severely the entire international economy, is about to be basically overcome, especially with regard to the situation of the 'Old continent': one of the economic and trade area most severely affected by this phenomenon, considered as the worst recession ever occurred in contemporary economic history[1], especially, for

* Ricercatore confermato di Diritto Internazionale, Università degli Studi di Milano.

1 The current international economic and financial situation has been compared to another well-known event that shocked the world in the early decades of the twentieth century, the Crisis of 1929. Both phenomena would result from a lack of liquidity, suffered mainly by the US credit system, by an excessive liberalism, from a monetary policy too lax by the US Federal Reserve, by a heavy fall in the value of commodities and industrial production levels. However, the current crisis, unlike that of 1929 concentrated mainly in the US and Europe, has affected, though in different ways, all of the economic areas of the Globe. Moreover, it should be noted such as right on the basis of the mistakes made during the Crisis of 1929, in order to ensure liquidity to the market, it has seen in recent years a strong intervention by central banks (Federal Reserve, European Central Bank and Bank of England) to support the banking and credit system to boost the real economy, to allow greater circulation of money and facilitate access to credit by companies and individuals in general. For a comparison between the two

the devastating impact produced at social level[2]. It is sufficient to peruse the data on unemployment, particularly among the youth, or on higher rates of poverty and social exclusion, to realize how the years that passed until now, from the beginning of the crisis in 2007, have been so dramatic to be able not only to strain the Eurozone and the Euro resistance, but the entire European Union (EU) still nowadays under discussion, both at political, cultural and economic level[3].

The solution of the nodes listed above, despite the – however still weak – recovery occurred, will necessarily take a long time, resulting in the definition of new models of welfare, production and labor policies. The reform of these specific sectors has been, many times, the answer that various European governments have tried with the aim of overcoming the crisis. Their action has been primarily based on the adoption of economic measures based on principles of strict austerity, measures that in most of the cases were functional to the containment of the social spending, traditionally considered as unproductive. This is a choice that, however, did no more than exacerbate tensions within the different European countries, considering that during these years, the demand for social services and income support has inevitably been increased from a growing number of people who found themselves deprived of sources of income, and therefore of sustenance, because of the fact that the crisis passed from a purely financial crisis to a real economic one, with the result of tens of thousands of active people expelled from the world of work.

There was a perverse effect, if not paradoxical[4]. Just when solidarity and social protection systems were most needed both at European level and for

---

crises, see M. ALMUNIA, A.S. BÉNÉTRIX, B. EICHENGREEN, K.H. O'ROURKE, G. RUA, *From Great Depression to Great Credit Crisis: Similarities, Differences and Lessons,* National Bureau of Economic Research, Inc, Cambridge MA, 2009; P. KRUGMAN, *The Return of Depression Economics and the Crisis of 2008*, Norton Publications, London-New York, 2009; G. SAPELLI, *La crisi economica mondiale: dieci considerazioni,* Bollati Boringhieri, Torino, 2008.

2 On this point, see A.M. VITERBO, F. COSTAMAGNA, *L'impatto sociale della politica di condizionalità nel contesto della crisi dell'euro,* in N. NAPOLETANO, A. SACCUCCI (EDS.) *Gestione internazionale delle emergenze globali. Regole e valori*, Editoriale Scientifica, Napoli, 2013, p. 167 ss; G. PERONI, *L'azione dell'Unione europea in campo sociale e la crisi economica*, in G.P. MILANO, L. DANIELE, C. MALINCONICO, M.C. CICIRIELLO (EDS.), *Il Trattato di Lisbona due anni di applicazione. Atti della Giornata di studio in ricordo di Francesco Caruso (Roma, 7 ottobre 2011)*, Editoriale Scientifica, Napoli, 2013, pp. 409-424.

3 Consider, for example, the question of the possible Brexit, in other words, the exit of United Kingdom from the European Union, on which British citizens will be called to express themselves, it seems, by 2017.

4 Cf. G. PERONI, *Il difficile equilibrio tra austerità e solidarietà nell'Unione economica e Monetaria,* contributo *in corso di pubblicazione* in Raccolta degli Atti del

each Member States, under strong pressure of the European institutions (mainly the Commission and the European Central Bank - ECB) and the IMF[5], national governments intervened to reduce social spending: on the one hand, to meet the budget imposed by strict budgetary constraints requirements that characterize the Economic and Monetary Union (EMU), and on the other hand, to reassure international financial markets worried about a possible default of any of the most exposed European countries to the crisis; particularly, the so-called PIGS (Portugal, Ireland, Greece, Spain and Italy)[6].

It happens thus, that an ever-increasing slice of European citizens point at the European Union as the responsible for the significant deterioration of their living conditions, rather than to their political classes, not seeing any longer the integration process as an opportunity for economic, cultural, political and social growth, but rather as a brake, if not even an obstacle to the legitimate expectations of helping to build a better society.

Obviously, the economic crisis also hit Switzerland, one of the world countries with among the highest per capita income and one of the most industrialized economies. However, negative impact on the Swiss Confederation was less significant than what happened in the EU, both in terms of the decline in unemployment, both on the reduction of the gross domestic product (GDP), the index that measures the ability to produce wealth by each country[7].

The above-mentioned difference, in the opinion of the writer, is due to several factors, starting from the most basic such as, above all, the different territorial dimension and population. However, the profiles that appear to better distinguish the effectiveness of the reaction of the EU and Switzerland with respect to the current economic crisis seem to be two, even closely intertwined. I refer, first, to the fact that, despite several reform measures that

---

Convegno AUSE, *The European Economic Union: Economic, Social and Institutional Aspects,* Venezia, 17-19 Luglio, 2015.

5 On the IMF's role in the solution of the financial crisis with specific reference to the European case, see G. Adinolfi, *Il sostegno congiunto UE-FMI: è necessario un ripensamento della politica di condizionalità?*, in G. Adinolfi, M. Vellano (eds.), *La crisi del debito sovrano degli stati dell'aerea euro. Profili giuridici*, Giappichelli, Torino, 2013, pp. 3-27.

6 Acronym with a clear depreciatory value, also used as a technical term for a group of European States which, despite the diversity of their economies, are united by their inability to comply with the so-called Maastricht criteria included in Art. 140 TFEU, and by the fact that financial speculation has severely hit the prices of their sovereign bonds, especially in the period 2011-2013.

7 With regard to Switzerland's economic position in the current global economic context, see in particular the 107th of the Swiss National Bank 2014 Annual Report, available on the web page www.snb.ch/it/mmr/reference/annrep_2014.../annrep_2014_komplett.it.pdf

have occurred in recent years, the EU tax policy is still a prerogative of the Member States, unlike the monetary policy, which was devolved for exclusive title to the ECB and the European System of Central Banks (ESCB); on the other hand, the presence of central monetary authority does not have the same range of tasks and tools, which instead have other central monetary institutions, such as the Swiss one[8]. The latter, however, operates in a political and economic context in which fiscal sovereignty, unlike what happens at EU level, is not only shared between 'Berne' and the individual cantons and municipalities that compose the Swiss Confederation[9], but, also, strongly participated by the Swiss citizens through referendums and laws by popular initiative.

2 The root causes of the crisis

To understand the reaction to the economic crisis by both the EU side and the Swiss side, it is appropriate to carry out some considerations about the reasons by which the phenomenon under investigation was originated, appropriately taking into account that the crisis is the result of a very complex mix of causes, not only of economic nature but also political and legal.

Under the first point of view, we observe the intervention of several factors, such as: a strong increase in commodity prices since 2008, especially oil, whose price has reached a record level of $ 147 per barrel in June of that year[10]; the emergence of a heavy food crisis caused by the sharp rise in wheat prices, favored by the adoption of de-coupling policies[11], the unresolved fi-

8 On this point, compare in particular Art. 3 of the Protocol 4 on the Statute of the European System of Central Banks and of the European Central Bank concerning the duties of the 'Eurotower' with Art. 5 of the Federal Act on the Swiss National Bank.

9 It is worth remembering how Switzerland was born in 1291 under an alliance intervened between the different cantons and then evolved from Confederation in effective federal state in 1848, when it was approved the first Constitution, federal and liberal. In 1874, came into force a new Constitution (reformed, then, in 1999) that determined the transition from a representative democracy to a semi-direct democracy, in which the popular vote, with, above all, the implementation of the referendum instrument still plays today a decisive role in the assumption of the most significant decisions of the Swiss policy. A smooth study on institutional and Swiss political, economic cultural model is in the volume of S. GEROTTO, *Svizzera*, Il Mulino, Bologna, 2011.

10 Consider that in January 2016, oil prices are around $ 35. On this point, see the constantly updated data of the respective prices on the site *www.borsaitaliana.it*

11 It is an agrarian policy instrument through which the state aids are granted independently from production. In other words, farmers are free to produce or not to produce, receiving, however, the relevant assistance in the form of a single

nancial crisis generated by the speculative bubble of the 'Internet values'[12] that began in 2001 and, finally, the excessive ease for individuals to obtain credit, resorting to the instrument of sub-prime mortgages for the purchase of properties in the United States, which was followed by the failure of several insurance companies and banks, of which it should be mentioned the most striking case related to the default of Lehmann Brothers; entities all heavily exposed to the securitization linked to the granting of that type of loans.

The reasons behind the crisis, however, as noted above, are not only economic[13]. You can not fail to observe how, perhaps with rare exceptions, current political classes are characterized by the absence of charismatic figures, able not only to 'take head' and face with determination the events occurred, but, in particular, also able to know how to make real 'operation truth' towards their respective citizens. In other words, it seems that the current European political *élites* have not yet had the courage to explain the reasons of the crisis and why proves necessary to adopt specific measures, rather than others. In other words, the European Union and their respective Member States have not appeared to be capable, so far, to describe what future they imagine for the current generation and the next one, in the light of the current recession and the sacrifices imposed to date by a large part of the Old Continent's population.

The absence of a genuinely shared EU-wide strategy on how to deal with the phenomenon under consideration is evident also regarding at the plurality of tools created to tame it by the European Union during these years (think, just to name a few, to the Euro Plus Pact, the Six Pack, the European stability Mechanism – ESM and the treaty on Fiscal Compact)[14]. The feeling one gets is one for which both the European and national political classes have not been able to deal with the crisis, using solutions sometimes confused that favored,

---

payment. On this specific profile, see G. Peroni, *Il commercio internazionale dei prodotti agricoli nell'accordo WTO e nella giurisprudenza del Dispute settlement Body*, Giuffrè, Milano, 2005, pp. 87-115.

12 Speculative bubble means a particular situation of the market where there is a considerable and unjustified increase in the prices of certain goods and services, due to a sudden increase in demand and limited in time. For further information, please refer to J.E. Stiglitz, *I ruggenti anni Novanta. Lo scandalo della finanza e il futuro dell'economia*, Einuadi, Torino, 2004; nonché N. Roubini, M. Uzan, *International Financial Crisis and the New International Financial Architecture*, Edward Elgar Publishing, Cheltenham-Northampton, 2005, pp. 56-130.

13 On this specific issue, please refer to the considerations set forth in the following paragraph.

14 On the nature and operation of these tools, please refer to G. Peroni, *La crisi dell'euro: limiti e rimedi dell'unione economia e monetaria*, Giuffrè, Milano, 2012, pp. 151-199.

faultlessly, the clear affirmation of populist movements with strong anti-European traits, especially within the most affected countries, such as Greece.

A way of partially acquitting the confusion that has characterized the action of the various European political leaders, is undoubtedly the absence of supranational institutions capable of effectively managing the economic and monetary effects of the globalization of trade, mainly realized thanks to the introduction in 1994 of the Agreement establishing the World Trade Organization (WTO)[15].

The globalized world today is, in truth, devoid of real international centers of political-economic power[16], capable to effectively govern such epochal phenomena as the present one and that are, by now, far beyond the intervention capacity of individual states and, in particular, of the United States, which has traditionally been seen as the only true "Super Power" existing economic in the world.

Besides, effective regulatory reform at the base of the governance of the international economy, introduced in July 1944 in Bretton Woods, has not yet been realized, and this in spite the obvious fact that the macroeconomic sce-

---

15 From a legal and economic perspective, globalization is based on the process of progressive integration of markets by virtue of the gradual liberalization of trade. it is worth pointing out that economic globalization is not, as has sometimes been led to believe, a recent phenomenon, but even dating back to the first half of the nineteenth century, when the liberal ideas of Adam Smith and David Ricardo, expressed respectively in *the Inquiry into the Nature and Causes of the Wealth of Nations* (1776) and *On the principles of political economy and taxation* (1817), have begun to be reflected into a systematic policy of relaxation of protectionist measures, first in United Kingdom and then in the other major industrialized countries of that time. Only with the establishment of *World Trade Organization* (WTO), which took place during 1994 with the signing of the Marrakesh Agreements, whose task is to liberalize international trade, in the widest possible way, globalization began to be extensively discussed. In fact, economic activity has taken precisely during these last years thanks to this set of international treaties, increasingly a supranational level under the influence also of other different factors, such as the movement of capitals, the dominance of exclusively financial exchanges on those of the real economy, the advent of new information and telecommunication technologies, like internet.

16 The response to the crisis by international economic organizations, especially the International Monetary Fund and the World Bank, is not particularly effective, due to the limitations that characterize them, both at the level of functioning of its governing bodies, both for the not always appropriate legal instruments to which they can have recourse for the effective implementation of the decisions taken. As meaning that the role of international institutions has been enhanced, but the statement of an effective global economic governance is still far from being realized, see G. Napolitano (Eds.), *Uscire dalla crisi. Politiche pubbliche e trasformazioni istituzionali*, Il Mulino, Bologna, 2012.

nario has completely changed. Today there are new economic realities as the countries of the BRICS area, especially China, as well as other new economic actors such as credit rating agencies and, above all, sovereign wealth funds and hedge funds capable, in the first case to address the choices investment of economic and financial operators; while, in the second and third case of earn profits equal to the GDP of medium-sized industrialized countries and therefore able to move up in their cheap money supply, choices that might be capable to destabilize any financial balance so far achieved.

To all that has been up to now described, it must be added the absence of international rules governing the movement of capitals and the financial services to avoid financial turmoil such as those that occurred recently. On this point, it is enough to remember the reduced regulation, moreover reached with difficulty, existing in the context of GATS, which is deputy to the regulation in the field of the services within the framework of WTO system. The existing legal vacuum at international level has inevitably favored the financial speculators including the various hedge funds[17] private equity funds[18], and sovereign wealth funds[19], who have benefited of finding an open field in their

---

17 Hedge funds are a special category of mutual funds, which owe their name to the fact that managers can use all the financial instruments that the market has, and therefore, from derivatives, to shares, bonds and debt securities in general. They usually are made according to the laws of countries considered off-shore and, as such, as well as subjected to a very favorable tax regime, even on a dimly stringent discipline in prudential terms and protection to the private investor. With regard to off-shore markets see A. Zoromè, *Concept of Offshore Financial Centers: in Search of an Operational Definition,* in *IMF Working Paper* (WP/07/87), April 2007; V.T. Canova, *The Transformation of U.S. Banking and Finance: from Regulated Competition to Free Market Receivership,* in *Brooklyn Law Review,* 1995, pp. 1295-1354; with reference to the *hedge funds* see V. Lazzeri, *Economia e finanza degli hedge funds*, in *Banca, Impresa e Società*, 2000, pp. 383-414; T.A. Paredes, *On the Decision to Regulate Hedge Funds: the Sec's Regulatory Philosophy Style and Mission*, in *University of Illinois Law Review,* 2006, pp. 975-1027.

18 These are investment vehicles that employ the money of their lenders for the acquisition of companies or equity interests in companies under special conditions (in the process of setting up, developing or even in the course of insolvency) in order to grow their own asset value with a view to their subsequent sale to other parties, with the aim of profiting from the initial purchase price and that of sale. On this point, see R. Kulms, *Capitale privato ed investimenti: Governance d'impresa attraverso il diritto societario?,* in *Rivista di Diritto Societario*, 2009, pp. 433-455.

19 The Sovereign Funds are basically public investment instruments, directly controlled by the State to which they belong, and are used to engage in financial instruments (shares, bonds, real estate) and other activities, tax surpluses or foreign exchange reserves, resulting, above all, from the sale of raw materials (mainly oil

constant quest for maximized profits, taking advantage of the lack of rules to establish effective mechanisms for the management of the crisis.

3 The eurozone crisis and the possible dusk of the irreversibility of the euro.

Also the crisis of the Eurozone falls within the complicated framework herein disclosed, or more properly, the crisis of the EMU and, consequently, of the single currency (Euro), which is its most important expression. All this is a direct result of the strong speculative movement that has affected, especially in the period 2011-2012, the trend of stock prices of the public debt of the PIGS which entailed the emersion of the issue of the sovereign debt crisis for the first time in Europe.

In other words, was revealed the real possibility that some of these countries were no longer able to meet the strict European budget constraints and basic assumptions of EMU, and so compelled to terminate from the Euro or even expelled[20]; undermining, thus, not only the existence of Economic and Monetary Union[21], but above all, the supposed irreversible nature of the single

---

and gas). Among the most important Sovereign Funds by size, should be mentioned those of Abu Dhabi, Norway, Saudi Arabia, China, Singapore, Kuwait, Russia, Libya and Qatar. They represent the rise of a new form of capitalism, which poses particular problems precisely in the light of the current crisis. In fact, they are among the few liquids investors, taking advantage of 'low prices' of the shares of many European and US companies. In this way they are able to acquire more and more significant investments in strategic sectors of the different national economies and, inevitably, in the future this fact could lead them to modify the low profile from them so far held, consisting in systematic waiver to elect its representatives to the governance of companies in order to reassure the shareholders as the stakeholders and the various national policy makers on purely financial purposes and non-strategic policies of their investments. For a debate of the different profiles indicated see F. Bassan, *The Law of Sovereign Wealth Funds*, Edward Elgar Publishing, Cheltenham-Northampton, 2011; Id., *Una regolazione per i fondi sovrani,* in *Mercato concorrenza e regole*, 2009, pp. 95-132; A Gigante, A. Ligustro, *Il diritto internazionale degli investimenti alla sfida dei fondi sovrani*, in *Diritto pubblico comparato ed europeo*, 2010, pp. 1179-1221.

20 On the trends of conflicting currency euro in 2007-2011, please refer to the web page http://www.ricerca24.ilsole24ore.com/piucercati/PAGES/storico+cambio+euro+dollaro.html.

21 Cf. P. De Grauwe, *Crisis in the Eurozone and How to Deal with it*, in *CEPS Policy Brief, No. 204*, 2010, February; B. Hall, Q. Peel, *Paris and Berlin at Odds over Default System*, Financial Times 2010, October, 26; R. Canale, O. Napolitano, *The Recessive Attitude of EMU policies: Reflections on the Italian Experience, 1999-2008*, in *MPRA Paper No. 20207*, 2009.

currency[22]. In the opinion of those who admit it[23], such a character would derive from art. 140 TFEU, which replaced artt. 120 (§ 1), 122 (§ 2) and 123 (§ 4) TEC, with which have been set the relevant parameters or macroeconomic convergence criteria, with respect to which a State, once he has met them, would be obliged to assign the respective monetary sovereignty to the EU and, consequently, to adopt the euro without any 'way out', according to the so-called *all or nothing* approach, with the only exception of those countries provided with a specific opt-out clause[24].

On this point, it is worth remembering as in another study[25] it has been tried to demonstrate, in truth, how this irreversible nature does not exist so much as in terms of primary EU law, as under international law of treaties, by which the first is originated. It is possible to leave the single currency willfully, with the termination mechanism, or being eventually deported if no longer able to meet the conditions at the base of its adoption, although this is an option of strong and currently unpredictable economic, political and legal consequences.

In fact, it should be remembered how Euro is not just the end result of a long historical and political process that started from the beginning of the communitarian phenomenon[26], manifesting itself only with its actual adop-

---

22 Cf. C. Proctor, *The Future of Euro. What Happens if a Member State Leaves?*, in *European Business Law Review*, 2006, pp. 909-937; P. Athanassiou, *Withdrawal and Expulsion from The EU and EMU: Some Reflections, ECB Legal Working paper Series n. 10*, December, 2009, pp. 1-43.

23 Cf. *ibidem*; M. Lorca Susino, *The Euro in The 21 Century: Economic Crisis and Financial Uproar*, Routdlege, London, 2013, pp. 1-31; P. Bagus, *The Eurosystem: Costs and Tragedies*, in D. Howden (Ed.), *Institutions in Crisis: European Perspectives on the Recession*, Routdlege, London, 2011, pp. 117-141; H. Hofmeister, *Goodbye Euro: Legal Aspects of Withdrawal from the Eurozone*, in *Columbia Journal of European Law*, 2011, pp. 111-134; J.C. Dammann, *The Right To Leave the Eurozone*, in *Texas International Law Journal*, 2013, pp. 125-155.

24 Opting out is the exception that, in order to prevent a general stalemate in the European integration process, it is given to Member States not wishing to join the other Member States with regard to a specific sector of Community cooperation. Under this principle, the United Kingdom asked not to participate in the third stage of EMU and similar treatment was granted to Denmark. Similarly, it has happened with regard to the Schengen acquis subject to partial adoption agreements, as Ireland, the United Kingdom and Denmark can decide, case by case, whether to participate in whole or in part to the measures provided for therein.

25 See G. Peroni, *Il recesso dall'euro: una via percorribile, ma non auspicabile,* in *Studi sull'integrazione europea*, 2015, vol. 1, pp. 85-108.

26 When the European Economic Community (EEC) was established in 1957, the theme of monetary cooperation among the Member States was absent from the

tion on January 1, 2002, but, above all, Euro represents the first form of real European federalism, with which some EU Member States have decided to forgo one of their own specific and typical sovereign function: the power to issue currency[27]. Give up the Euro means, in other words, to abdicate the idea that, in the future, it may be realized the project, supported by Churchill first[28], of building the United States of Europe, of which the Economic and Monetary Union is, at the time, in a federalist perspective, the most significant element hitherto reached, despite the limitations that characterize it.

---

respective political agenda, because the attention of those countries was aimed at, above all, the creation of a commercial area of free trade, which is then manifested in the most evolved form of a customs union. However, it was already clear at the European level, the need to define a set of rules that would be able to ensure some form of monetary cooperation in order to more effectively regulate the payment system in the view of reaching itself a full realization of trade between the EEC member countries. On the long path that led to the adoption of the Euro, see M.G. Tenaglia Ambrosini, *La moneta e l'Europa: da Bretton Wodds a Maastricht e oltre,* Giappichelli, Torino, 1996.

27 Monetary sovereignty consists in the possibility of emitting metal and paper currency, decide the cut, the size, the *nomen*, the legal tender, its possible substitution to another, determining the conversion rate, as well as the circulating amounts thus influencing both the internal value as the external one and the resulting inflation rate, up to get power to impose the restriction on relative movement to affect the free circulation of capitals as much of the payments. For a detailed reconstruction of the concept of monetary sovereignty see T. Treves, *Il controllo dei cambi nel diritto internazionale privato*, Cedam, Padova, 1967, pp. 14-20; D. Carreau, *Souveraineté et Coopération Monétaire Internationale*, Editions Cujas, Paris, 1971, pp. 52-54; M.R. Shuster, *The Public International Law of Money*, Clarendon press, Oxford, 1973, pp. 9-12; G. Burdeau, *L'Exercice des Competences Monetaires par les Etats*, in *Recueil des cours de l'Académie de droit international de La Haye*, 1988, pp. 236-237; C. Proctor, *Mann on the Legal Aspects of Money*, Clarendon press, Oxford, 2005, pp. 500-503; R.M. Lastra, *Legal Foundations of International Monetary Stability*, Oxford University Press, Oxford, 2006, pp. 16-17.

28 In the popular "*Speech to the academic youth*" held at the University of Zurich in 1946, Churchill formulated the conclusions he had drawn from the lessons of history: "*Yet all the while there is a remedy which (...) would in a few years make all Europe (...) free and (...) happy. (...) It is to re-create the European Family, or as much of it as we can, and to provide it with a structure under which it can dwell in peace, in safety and in freedom. We must build a kind of United States of Europe*". The extract of Churchill's speech is widely available online.

4 The role of the European Central Bank to safeguard the single currency: a discussed but necessary intervention

Until now, in the management of eurozone' crisis, the action undertaken by the European Central Bank (ECB) has been crucial[29] both in trying to prevent the gap between the interest rates on government bonds of different European countries from reaching unsustainable levels (the so-called *spread*), and to prevent the European financial banking system from being affected by a dangerous liquidity crisis, that might have generated a real credit crunch, shorting, thus, the whole continental banking system.

On this point, among the various measures taken by the 'Eurotower' deserve to be remembered, in addition to the repeated and strong reduction in the official discount rate (which was brought on November 7, 2013 at a level never before reached 0.25%)[30], also the *Security Market Program* (SMP), the *Long Term Refinancing Operation* (LTRO), the *Outrights Monetary Transaction* (OMT) and, finally, the latest *Quantitative easing* (QE). In particular, it should be emphasized how through the SMP has in fact started, beginning in 2010, the buyback program on the secondary market for debt securities of those European countries (Italy, in particular) who have found themselves at the center of speculative action by the international financial markets. Subsequently, with the ECB's LTRO program, the 'Eurotower' intervened in support of the Italian and Spanish banking systems by ensuring very low rate loans to supply continuous liquidity to the banking industry in these countries

---

29 On the European Central Bank, see A. Malatesta, *La Banca centrale europea, Gli aspetti istituzionali della banca centrale della Comunità europea*, Giuffrè, Milano, 2003; S. Ortino, *La Banca centrale nella costituzione europea*, in *Quaderni costituzionali*, 1993, pp. 33-69; *La cooperazione internazionale e transfrontaliera in materia di vigilanza bancaria. Il ruolo della Banca centrale europea*, in AA.VV., *Istituzioni, mercato e democrazia.* Liber amicorum *per gli ottanta anni di Alberto Predieri*, Giappichelli, Torino, 2007; A. Predieri, *Euro poliarchie democratiche e mercati monetari*, Giappichelli, Torino, 1998. On Economic profiles, please refer, on all, T. Padoa Schioppa, *La lunga via per l'euro*, Il Mulino, Bologna, 2004; Id., *L'euro e la sua banca centrale. L'Unione dopo l'unione*, Il Mulino, Bologna, 2004; C. Giannini, *L'età delle banche centrali. Forme e governo della moneta fiduciaria in un prospettiva istituzionalista*, Il Mulino, Bologna, 2004.

30 On this point, it is worth observing G. Contaldi, voce *Politica economica e monetaria (Diritto dell'Unione europea)*, in *Enc. dir.*, Annali VII, Giuffrè, Milano, 2014, p. 826, according to which: the operations on the interest rate, although falling within the monetary policy instruments pertaining to the ECB, if are such as to determine an extremely low percentage of the cost of money, such that the costs for banks to obtain loans from central institution are practically eliminated, in practice we witness "... an exceptional use of powers" attributed to the monetary Authority.

in order to maintain adequate circulation of money among the banking and financial institutions themselves and between them and the companies.

Through the OMT instrument it has been permitted, on paper at least, to the ECB to buy unlimited secondary market of short-term bonds (1-3 years) from the Member State interested in receiving the necessary financial support, on condition that this last agree to adopt a specific structural economic reform program, worth failure to deliver the applied aid program.

Finally, it should be mentioned the QE, an extraordinary measure that aims to boost the eurozone economy, bringing down the cost of government debt and the interest rates of the respective government bonds, reviving the credit market and stopping deflation, in other words, the decline in consumer prices that exists today throughout Europe. It is a measure by which the Central Bank carries out the planned purchases of financial securities (in particular, government bonds) traded in the market. In addition to give the benefits to public finances of governments, which would then have a bit more resources to address towards economic growth, quantitative easing may be deemed to have positive effects on the banking system. The Central Bank, in fact, buying the government securities held in European banks, would stimulate them to expand lending to households and businesses, encouraging, in this way the economic recovery, averting the risk that deflation will become increasingly affective[31].

The measures briefly described before, have been currently defined as unconventional as they do not find their direct legal bases in the primary provisions of the Treaties.

It has, moreover, been claimed that these tools are poorly compatible with the prohibition set forth in art. 123 TFEU to provide credit facilities to the Member states and to local governments. The activism of the ECB would, therefore, not only resulted in a deviation from its mandate, clearly expressed in the Treaties, but, indeed, a change in one of its material tasks.

On this point, it should be noted that the ECB, together with the ESCB, has, as its main task, to ensure price stability, objective clearly stated in art. 127 TFEU and reaffirmed by art. 282 TFEU. A theme, that of price stability, which is also found in other primary rules in the European Union; in particular, art. 3, § 2, TEU and art. 119, § 2, TFEU, becoming a real 'value' that somehow all European policies that involve spending, should strive. This fact derived primarily from reading art. 119, § 2, TFEU, where it establishes a real

31 A phenomenon considered even more dangerous than an even sensitive increase in inflation, as in economics it is believed that falling prices generate an expectation of additional future losses, bringing individual traders to continually postpone purchases and, thus, leading to a sharp decrease of economic activities and consumption block.

hierarchy between the above mentioned objective and the one subordinate to it, of contributing to realization of all those functional economic policies to create an open market economy based on the principles of free competition.

Price stability, in short, was elevated to essential condition, so that other economic policies could be more effective.

However, there have been immediately criticism against this approach[32], as it would deprive the ECB, in contrast to every other central banks, of any form of discretion in the conduct of monetary policy, making it impossible to put such a policy at the service of more general aims of economic policy.

In fact, the discretional power would not be excluded, but limited[33]. In other words, the objective of price stability would be so pervasive that only when two monetary policy measures are equally able to ensure the said stability, then the ECB will be able to give priority to the policy that best realizes the support for economic action; otherwise, if there are several options available, it should always chosen the one that ensures the stability of prices, regardless to its impact on the economy[34].

From the reasoning briefly carried out, one senses why the extraordinary measures taken by the ECB in the course of the economic and financial crisis have undergone of heated debate, so much that on several occasions even the EU Court of Justice was called to rule on the legitimacy of the cited measures.

Trying to synthesize the positions intervened, it seems possible to say, on the basis of the assessments made by the Court of Luxembourg[35], that in

---

32 See A. Malatesta, cit., p. 31; G. La Malfa, *L'Europa legata. I rischi dell'Euro*, Rizzoli, Milano, 2000, p. 90 ss.

33 See R. Smits, *The European Central Bank Institutional Aspects*, Lunner Law International, The Hague-London-Boston, 1997, p. 187.

34 The stability to which we refer is the internal one of the currency, while the external one, or exchange rate stability, is not considered. It has been defined by the Governing Council of the ECB as '*an increase in the twelve months of the Harmonised Index of Consumer Prices - HICP - for the euro area of below 2%*', to be maintained in the medium term. On this point, see ECB Monthly Bulletin June 2003, p. 85 ss. Moreover, the internal stability should not be understood in absolute terms, in the sense that a modest increase in the total inflation rate is acceptable in the view of avoiding a dangerous flare-deflationary.

35 Cf., in particular, the recent case Gauweiler Case C-62/14, judgment of the Court (Grand Chamber) of 16 June 2015 on the request for a preliminary ruling by the Federal Constitutional Court (BVerfG) of the Federal Republic of Germany (FRG) on the legitimacy of the OMT program (Outright Monetary Transaction). For a comment, see L. Scipione, *Prime riflessioni sulla legittimità delle OMT e sul ruolo della BCE alla luce di una recente sentenza della Corte costituzionale tedesca*, in *Dir. banca e mercato fin.*, 2014 pp. 183-235; E. Mostacci, *Dal 'dialogo' al decalogo: le OMT nel primo rinvio pregiudiziale del 'Bundesverfassungsgericht'*, in *Diritto pubblico comparato ed europeo*, 2014, pp. 36-43. The case is part of

case of extreme economic situations, the conduct of monetary policy can not be detached from the overall economic environment. In other words, it can not be prevented to the ECB opportunity to practice temporarily expansionary monetary policy in order to counteract the dangers of large entities that threaten the stability of the currency[36]. Besides, the ultimate purpose and *raison d'être* of any central bank is to support confidence in the currency. A purpose that justifies the adoption of any actions that will allow the survival of the currency, because a central institution exists as long as there is a currency that is called to be issued and its circulation to be governed[37].

It can so be explained, even resorting to the theory of the implied powers[38], how the measures taken to 'Eurotower' meet the criterion of the practical effect. Saving the Eurozone and, therefore, the single currency is a *sine qua non* for the achievement of all the other economic and social objectives that the European Union stands for, beginning with its existence as a political, economic and commercial entity, within the international community[39].

5 Switzerland and its economic model in front of the crisis.

Switzerland, like already partially observed at the beginning of this paper, is traditionally perceived as a 'happy island' from an economic and social viewpoint[40]; just to name a few, think of the level of average wages, the low level of taxation or even the high rate of internationalization of its manufac-

---

the OMT jurisprudential trend on the ECB's monetary policy started with the leading case *Pringle* C-370/12; E. GAMBARO EDOARDO, F. MAZZOCCHI, *Le regole dell'Unione europea alla prova della crisi dei debiti sovrani: il caso Pringle*, in *Dir. comm. Inter.*, 2013, pp. 545-569.

36 Cf. C. WALDHOFF, *Art. 127*, in SIEKMANN (Ed.), *Kommentar zur Europaisschen Wahrungsunion*, Tubingen, 2013, p. 287.

37 On this profile see G. NAPOLETANO, *Il ruolo delle banche centrali nella gestione della crisi dell'eurozona: osservazioni su alcuni aspetti istituzionali*, in G. ADINOLFI, M. VELLANO (Eds.), *La crisi del debito sovrano*, cit., p. 69 ss.

38 It is a theory developed with regard to the phenomenon of international organizations that an international tribunal may use all means at its disposal to achieve the aims of the organization's founding treaty itself, even when these resources are not expressly provided for in the text of the Treaty. In the TFEU, there is a specific provision such as art. 352 TFEU which recalls the above theory.

39 Cf. G.L. TOSATO, *L'integrazione europea ai tempi della crisi dell'euro*, in *Riv. Dir. Inter.*, 2012, p. 689; M. RUFFERT, *The European Debt Crisis and European Union Law*, in *Common Market Law Review*, 2011, p. 1787 ss.; ECB Monthly Bulletin June 2009, p. 9 ss and October 2012, p. 7 ss.

40 On this point, see the report published by *Il Sole 24 ore* on April 24, 2015, p. 14 in which Switzerland is appointed to be the best country in the World to live in.

turing base[41]. It is, moreover, a purely liberal economy, therefore with limited presence of the State in the economy, supported by a banking system among the most developed and solid in the world, at the extent that the major Swiss banks control a sizable share of the market global asset managed abroad, this way making the Swiss Confederation and, in particular, Zurich one of the major international financial centers.

The economic strength of Switzerland is, in truth, also the effect of a marked political stability; result, in its turn, of a quite peculiar institutional system and a traditionally based fiscal policy on international tax competition and the preservation of a high level of secrecy in the banking and in financial sector[42]. These aspects, together with the fact that the Swiss economy appears scarcely integrated with the European one[43] although its high level of internationalization, have undoubtedly helped to mitigate the negative effects of the crisis in the Swiss Confederation.

However, in recent years the country, under pressure both from the United States, both from different European countries and on all France, Germany and Italy, had to make considerable efforts in particular to adapt to international standards in the area of fiscal transparency, also because of the financial nature of the ongoing recessionary phenomenon that has affected even national giants of finance, such as the *Union de Banques Suisses* (UBS). In the reports produced by OECD related to this aspect, Switzerland has moved from the list of financial centers that had not yet reached such standards to the list of the fully compliant countries[44].

---

41 See S. Gerotto, cit., pp. 16-21, which shows that the average salary of an employee in Switzerland in 2007 was € 46,058, against 23,206 of an Italian equivalent; while taxation in 2005 according to OECD data represented 29.7% of GDP against 41.6% in Italy. Always on the basis of OECD in 2000, Switzerland exported 46.8% of its GDP, while importing 41.6 of the respective GDP with a positive net balance of 4.15. A figure that would highlight the strong internationalization of the Swiss economy.

42 The international comparison of the total tax rate (TTR), that is the overall tax burden, shows that Switzerland is a tax system that is constantly very competitive compared to other highly developed countries. The TTR measures the amount of all taxes and the compulsory social security contributions borne by the business as a percentage of commercial profits. For an evaluation of the tax burden in the various European countries, please consult the website http://www.doingbusiness.org.

43 On several occasions, the Swiss electorate has expressed the wish not to integrate within the European Union system, so that the Swiss authorities have been forced to conclude a whole series of bilateral agreements with the EU to remedy the lack of integration.

44 See, on this point, the Federal Department of Finance report on the results of the consultation procedure on the approval and implementation of the Council of Europe and OECD Convention on Mutual Administrative Assistance in Tax

It marks a change in pace that the federal government wanted to achieve, especially for international image: deleted, or at least mitigated, the collective that Switzerland is merely a tax haven, and not a significant economic and industrial power at global level, instead. An economic force that is based a lot, as mentioned above, on tax competition over other European (and others) legal systems, so much so that Switzerland became the headquarters for various multinational companies[45]. The competition on the side of taxes and fees is a profile that is a real feature of the liberal conception that underpins the economy of the Swiss Confederation; so much to be enshrined in the Constitution itself and be fully implemented, in particular, internally, between the twenty-six Swiss cantons and, within each canton, between any individual municipalities of which it is composed[46].

Tax competition is, therefore, a structural feature of the Swiss economy, where all the cantons have full liberty in matters of taxation, in relation to the quantitative aspects of taxation, in particular concerning the determination of the applicable rates. Each canton is, therefore, free to experiment with novel solutions and tax, and then, depending on the results, those solutions can be adopted, maintained and possibly imitated by others. In summary, we are seeing a form of fiscal sovereignty shared between the federal government, cantons and municipalities, which is itself essential precondition for that tax competition which, undoubtedly, has allowed Switzerland to cushion much more the effects of the economic crisis compared to other European countries, both in terms of contraction of gross domestic product both of the unemployment rate growth, thereby maintaining in time attractiveness to foreign investment and foreign capital: an actual "engine" of the economy in general[47].

Nevertheless, the broad fiscal freedom, left to the individual cantons and municipalities, is balanced by an equalization system that revolves around the balance budget rule in art. 126 of the Swiss Constitution, where, in terms of financial management, it is established that "*The federal government balances in the long term, its exits and entrances*". The said disposition continues by establishing, in the second paragraph, that "*the maximum amount of total expenditure to be allocated in the budget depends on the estimated total revenue, taking into account the economic situation*". Therefore, the expenses can only be increased if their financing is secured by additional revenue or

Matters, of June 2015, drawn up by Secretary of State of Finance, available on the web page https://www.admin.ch/documents.

45 Cf. the data reported by www.dirittosenzafrontiere.ch.

46 Cf. artt. 126 to 135 of the Swiss Constitution, available on the web page https://www.admin.ch/opc/it/classified-compilation/19995395/index.html.

47 Cf. econometric data reported by the Swiss National Bank in the 107th of the 2014 Annual Report referred to in the preceding note 7.

corresponding waivers and any tax cuts should be matched by a proportional reduction in expenses.

The constitutional rule of a balanced budget grants freedom to the cantons in deciding which tax policy to pursue, but it is a freedom that can not result in a debt out of control, which could still undermine the economic stability of the Swiss Confederation. The equalization system provides, then, the reduction of inequalities between the different geographical areas; in other words, it provides for the transfer of resources from the richer cantons to weaker ones, according to a model known as 'burden compensation', assessed according to two criteria: the geo-topographical (which usually incur peripheral cantons) and socio-demographic (relative to population density)[48].

These are rules that the European Union endorsed only in part and recently. I refer to the provision on the so-called balanced budget laid down by the well known *Treaty on the Fiscal Compact*[49], according to which, pursuant to art. 3, § 1, letter *a*, it is imposed a balance on surplus in public accounts on EU Member States, only admitting temporary deficits and at the presence of negative economic cycles or of serious economic crisis, to the extent that this exception does not undermine the maintenance of accounts and therefore, the sustainability of public debt in the long run. Beyond the criticism concerning the manner in which it was adopted within the European Union and individual Member States respective jurisdictions[50], that is a rule that, if

---

48 Cf. B. Regazzoni, *L'esperienza del federalismo in Svizzera*, in www.federalismi.it, 2011, Id., *Dieci anni di freno all'indebitamento in Svizzera*, in www.federalismi.it, 2012.

49 The fiscal compact formally the Treaty on Stability, Coordination and Governance in the Economic and Monetary Union, also referred to TSCG, is an intergovernmental treaty that introduced a new stricter version of the Stability Growth Pact. It was signed on 2 march 2012 by all EU member States with the exception of Czech Republic and the United Kingdom. On this subject see L.S. Rossi, *Fiscal Compact e conseguenze dell'integrazione differenziata nell'UE,* in P. Bonvicini, F. Brugnoli (Eds.), *Il Fiscal Compact* Roma, 2012, p. 29 ss; G.L. Tosato, *Il Fiscal compact,* in G. Amato, R. Gualtieri (Eds.), *Prove di Europa unita. Le istituzioni europee di fronte alla crisi,* Passigli Editore, Firenze, 2013, p. 27 ss.; G. Peroni, *La Crisi dell'euro*, cit., pp. 171-185.

50 Cf. G.L. Tosato, *Qualche riflessione sul nuovo trattato europeo*, in *Affari internazionali, Rivista on line di Politica, strategia ed economia*, as of 21 December 2011; id., *Il nuovo trattato europeo e le Istituzioni dell'Ue*, in the same *Rivista*, as of 3 January 2012; L.S. Rossi, *Quattro opzioni per il futuro dell'UE*, in the same *Rivista*, as of 20 December 2011; A. Brancasi, *L'introduzione del principio del c.d. pareggio di bilancio: un esempio di revisione affrettata della Costituzione*, in www.forumcostituzionale.it; D. Cabras, *Il pareggio di bilancio in Costituzione: una regola importante per la stabilizzazione della finanza pubblica, ibidem*. For a comparative comment F. Fabbrini, *Il pareggio di bilancio nelle Costituzioni euro-*

it was adopted before the crisis, it might have helped to make more consistent the economic situations of the eurozone countries, reassuring in doing so most of the financial markets.

The EU, however, has not yet provided any form of tax burden sharing, as any community or union should somehow predict internally. In truth, the one just mentioned is a very complex issue, since it is known that the European Union, in several points of its founding treaties, recalls the value-principle of solidarity, in order to foster the construction of a social market economy[51]. However, this solidarity will evaporate entirely when it comes to establish forms of financial solidarity between Members; in these terms, it is absolutely clear art. 125 TFEU which prohibits any form of mutualisation of public debt.

In the case of Switzerland, moreover, it was not only the particular system of fiscal policy on which the Swiss economy rests that allowed to cushion the effects of the crisis, but also the specific action of the respective Central Bank who led a currency policy, especially in the period 2011-2014, aimed at maintaining over time the exchange rate between the Swiss Franc and the Euro stable. The parity between the two currencies was fixed at the rate of 1 Franc and 20 cents for one Euro, so that the national currency would not valorize to much against the Euro, fact that would have lent to obvious repercussions on Swiss exports, already hit by the global crisis[52].

---

pee, in *Quaderni costituzionali*, 2011, pp. 933-935 R. Perez, *La nuova disciplina del bilancio in Germania*, in *Giornale di dir. amm.*, 2011, pp. 95-99.

51 Cf. G. Peroni, *Il difficile equilibrio ...*, cit.

52 To maintain the minimum threshold in the exchange rate, in fact, the SNB undertook in recent years to buy massive amounts of euro to offset the demand for Swiss francs, enough to lead some to question this policy. Over the past three years, moreover, the budget of the SNB has risen far over 500 billion francs dangerously approaching to the total value of federal GDP with about 45% of the reserves consisting of euro, in continuous devaluation against the dollar. It explains in doing so, the decision of 15 January 2015 by which the Central Bank, surprising the currency markets and stock exchange, has announced the immediate abandonment of the minimum exchange rate of CHF 1.20 per euro rate. The Central Bank justified its decision by pointing out that his '*exceptional and temporary measure has protected the economy of Switzerland that was likely to suffer serious damage.*'. Communicating the end of the minimum threshold, the SNB has also led to -0.75 percent the interest rate that is applied to banks' funds that are deposited at the same SNB. The main policy rate on the franc, Libor, has been adjusted downwards and is now at -1.25 and -0.25 per cent (up to now had been -0.75 and +0.25 percent). These are measures which, according to the main economic observers would have the advantage in the medium term to cushion the negative effects of the free currency fluctuation involving for many companies to adopt cost-cutting measures involving in turn possible wage reductions, increased

This set of measures adopted by the Swiss National Bank (SNB) (such as the progressive reduction in the official discount rate, the opening of credit to financial institutions and credit residents, the purchase and sale of securities in foreign currency) have been instrumental in the pursuance of the main objective of its mandate, which, as in the case of the ECB, is to ensure price stability.

However, it can not do without observe how this objective for the Central Bank should be measured on the Swiss cyclical economic situation, implying that the monetary policy should not only not to be considered with priority over the economic, but it can not be separated from this last, in order to ensure the stability of the Swiss economic system[53].

Therefore, Switzerland can teach much to the European Union. First, it shows how the monetary and economic policy can not be decided at different levels. It is unlikely, in other words, to transfer the monetary policy, such as so far occurred, to the European institutions, in particular the ECB and the ESCB, without providing for a transfer of power, at least partial also from a fiscal policy point of view. Otherwise, as repeatedly stressed in the literature[54], it creates a dangerous asymmetry capable, sooner or later, to undermine the building of any monetary union[55]. Also, it can not be built a union of this type without providing the respective authorities who chairs, of all those powers and resources which traditionally have all central banks to deal with crisis situations of extreme gravity that might impair the existence of the currency and the authority that controls it.

The crisis should have taught that no set of rules for monetary policy even if very stiff and difficult to modify, such as those laid at the basis of the ECB, is able, to prevent the development and functional transformation of the same central monetary authority, when the estate of the currency for the defense of which have been established is in danger. This is in fact what happened thanks to a 'useful' interpretation made by Eurotower and supported by the Court of Justice, of the primary provisions of the treaties governing

---

time of work, transfer of jobs overseas to low-value added activities and need to re-think and innovate production systems goods and supply of services.

53 See, in this regard, the Federal Act on the Swiss National Bank, in particular artt. 5, 9 and 11 on the tasks and relations with the operators of the financial market and with the federal government.

54 Over all, Robert Mundell, theorist of the so called 'optimum currency monetary areas' with the related paper *A Theory of Optimum Currency Areas*, in *American Economic Review*, 1961, pp. 657-665.

55 See G. Peroni, *The failure of the Latin Monetary Union: a Forerunner of Euro Crisis?*, in R. Leboutte, S. Aprile (eds.), *Un Europe de papier: projets et programmes européennes au milieu du XIX siècle*, Editions du Septentrion - Universitè de Lille, Lille, 2015, pp. 235-247.

the monetary policy. Both institutions, probably aware that this policy is not an 'exact science', but rather variable and changeable depending on the economic situation, have, properly, provided that it could adopt other more effective tools, awaiting sooner or later to be given greater flexibility in its conduction starting from a profound reform of the primary rules contained in the European treaties.

Luca Calzolari and Maria Grazia Buonanno*

The relations between the European Union and the Swiss Confederation in the Antitrust Field: between Extraterritoriality and the Recent Agreement concerning Cooperation on the Application of their Competition Laws

Abstract: The study provides an in-depth and thorough analysis of bilateral cooperation between the European Union and the Swiss Confederation in the antitrust field, addressing, inter alia, the recently signed agreement by the Swiss Confederation and the EU. The essay mainly focuses on the international nature of competition infringements, law and enforcement and on the different systems and strategies of international antitrust enforcement, analysing them from the 'single economic entity' and the 'implementation' doctrines perspectives up to the recent endorsement of the 'effects doctrine'.

1 The international nature of competition infringements, law and enforcement: between positive and negative conflicts of jurisdiction

Antitrust offences are international by their very nature. For example, multinational corporations often hold a dominant position throughout the world, so that their abusive behaviours may affect the markets in several jurisdictions. In the same vein, a cartel involving only foreign companies may easily harm competition[1] on a given domestic market as much as one formed solely

---

* §§ 1 to 8 have been written by Luca Calzolari, PhD in European Law (Università di Milano), LL.M in European Law (University of Aberdeen), while §§ 9 to 13 have been written by Maria Grazia Buonanno, PhD candidate in European Law (Università di Trieste).

1 *I.e.*, may have negative effects on the structure of the market and/or on consumer welfare. Indeed, although one of the most significant judgments of the ECJ relating to the extraterritorial application of competition law deals also with the complex issue of the purposes of competition law (cf. GC, 12 June 2014, case T-286/09, *Intel Corp.* v *European Commission*, NYR; see *infra* note 103), this is not the place to discuss such much debated topic. Therefore, also any attempt to provide the reader with a definition of "competition harm" falls outside the scope of the present article. Moreover, the literature on the matter is very extensive; among the most

by national undertakings. The same holds true for operations of concentration: the market power of the new entity may well reduce competition in

---

recent works, and also for further references to the "classic" and most influential readings, see R. VAN DEN BERGH, A. GIANNACCARI, *L'approccio più economico nel diritto comunitario della concorrenza. Il più è troppo o non (ancora) abbastanza?*, in *Mercato concorrenza regole*, 2014, p. 393; S. BASTIANON, *Il carattere speciale (pro-integrazionista) del diritto antitrust alla luce del Protocollo n. 27*, in M. FRIGESSI DI RATTALMA, P. DE CESARI, *Nuove sfide in tema di concorrenza e aiuti di Stato nell'Unione europea*, Editoriale Scientifica, Napoli, 2013, p. 23; G. GHIDINI, E. AREZZO, *L'assalto fallito? Riflessioni sulla proposta rivisitazione in chiave «più economica» dell'abuso di dominanza?*, in *Mercato Concorrenza Regole*, 2010, p. 115; G. COLANGELO, *T-Mobile Netherlands e GlaxoSmithKline. La giurisprudenza comunitaria torna indietro*, in *Mercato Concorrenza Regole*, 2010, p. 527; F. DENOZZA, *Il progetto teorico dell'analisi economica del diritto antitrust e il suo fallimento*, in P. BARUCCI, C. RABITTI BEDOGNI (EDS.), *Vent'anni di antitrust. L'evoluzione dell'autorità garante della concorrenza e del mercato*, Giappichelli, Torino, 2010, p. 137; A. PERA, *Le relazioni pericolose: antitrust e interesse dei consumatori*, in P. BARUCCI, C. RABITTI BEDOGNI (EDS.), *op. cit.*, p. 1165; S.C. SALOP, *Question: What is the Real and Proper Antitrust Welfare Standard? Answer: the True Consumer Welfare Standard*, in *Loyola Consumer Law Review*, 2010, p. 336; E. BUTTIGIEG, *Competition Law: Safeguarding the Consumer Interest. A comparative Analysis of US Antitrust Law and EC Competition Law*, Kluwer Law International, Alphen aan den Rijn, 2009; L. PARRET, *Do we (still) know what we are protecting?*, TILEC Discussion Paper 2009-2010; G. BRUZZONE, M. BOCCACCIO, *Identifying Infringements of Competition Rules: The Role of Economic and Legal Thinking*, in E.A. RAFFAELLI (EDS.), *Antitrust tra diritto nazionale e diritto dei consumatori*, Giuffrè, Milano, 2009; D. DE SMET, *The diametrically opposed principles of US an EU antitrust policy*, in *European Competition Law Review*, 2008, p. 356; A. PERA, *Changing Views of Competition, Economic Analysis and EC Antitrust Law*, in *European Competition Journal*, 2008, p. 127; F. CINTIOLI, *The interpretation of competition law between the legal method and the economic approach*, in *Dir. Un. Eur.*, 2007, p. 873; K.J. CSERES, *The Controversies of the Consumer Welfare Standard*, in *Competition Law Review*, 2007, p. 121; F. DENOZZA, A. TOFFOLETTO, *Contro l'utilizzazione dell'«approccio economico» nell'interpretazione del diritto antitrust*, in *Mercato Concorrenza Regole*, 2006, p. 563; A. PERA, V. AURICCHIO, *Consumer Welfare, Standard of Proof and the Objectives of Competition Policy*, in *European Competition Journal*, 2005, 153; D. HILDEBRAND, *The European School in EC Competition Law*, in *World Competition*, 2002; C.D. EHLERMANN, *The modernization of EC Antitrust Policy: a Legal and Cultural Revolution*, in *Common Market Law Review*, 2000, p. 537. With regard to the EU perspective, see also the recent ECJ, 6 October 2015, case C-23/14, *Post Danmark A/S* v *Konkurrencerådet*. NYR. With regard to the Swiss perspective, the Federal Cartel Act of 1995 clarifies that competition law aims at "*impedire gli effetti nocivi di ordine economico o sociale dovuti ai cartelli e alle altre limitazioni della concorrenza e di promuovere in tal modo la concorrenza nell'interesse di un'economia di mercato fondata su un ordine liberale*" (cf. Legge federale del 6 ottobre 1995, *sui cartelli e altre limitazioni della*

markets different from those where the merging companies are established. In other words, markets know no national boundaries[2], and national competition law (and national enforcers) must face this challenge. This is even truer in the current ever-increasingly globalized world[3], where «*decisions reached in one corner of the world can reverberate around the globe in less time than it takes to tell the tale*»[4].

Two opposite outcomes may result from the fact that the negative effects of antitrust-relevant conducts usually spread across several jurisdictions, potentially leading to both over and under enforcement of competition law. On the one hand, it may happen that no State claims jurisdiction over a given conduct (so-called "negative conflict of jurisdiction")[5]. This may lead to under-deterrence, thus increasing the likelihood of antitrust infringements. On the other hand, several States may affirm their jurisdiction over a given matter (so-called "positive conflict of jurisdiction")[6]. This may lead to over-

concorrenza, in *RU*, 1996, p. 546; note that English is not an official language of the Swiss Confederation, while Italian is).

2 To quote E.M. Fox, *Can we solve the antitrust problems of globalization by extraterritoriality and cooperation? Sufficiency and legitimacy*, in *The Antitrust Bulletin*, 2003, p. 350.

3 It is a well-known fact that "[c]*ompetition problems have* [...] *become increasingly 'global' as firms compete in international markets in response to greater international competition*", mainly due to the fact that "[g]*lobalisation has increased multinational corporate expansion and greater international competition has in turn increased the risk of cross-border anti-competitive conduct*" (cf. L. Cejnar, R. Burgess, *Challenging the need for a "Global" Competition Law*, in *European Competition Law Review*, 2014, p. 461). See A.S. Grewlich, *Globalisation and Conflict in Competition Law*, in *Journal of World Competition*, 2001, p. 367; A. Kaczorowska, *International Competition Law in the Context of Global Capitalism*, in *European Competition Law Review*, 2000, p. 117.

4 Cf. *United States* v. *Nippon Paper Industries Co.*, 109 F. 3d 1, 8 (Cir. 1997), to quote one of the most famous decisions issued by the US Supreme Court with regard to the extraterritoriality of the Sherman Act.

5 For example, national antitrust enforcers may shift their responsibilities one to each other: competition authorities that could act against a given infringement affecting also markets falling under the jurisdiction of other authorities may decide not to tackle it, either because they prefer to rely on the enforcement activities of these other antitrust authorities, either because they lack incentives to act.

6 For example, if a cartel sells its products within different States, each antitrust authority of the concerned States may be willing to take measures against the cartelists, in order to protect national consumers. Similarly, if a merger involved companies based in two States, both national antitrust authorities usually demand to clear the operation, so that two (or more) national laws applies to the same conduct.

deterrence, as well as to a raise of undertakings' costs of compliance with competition law, and a symmetrical decrease in legal certainty.

2 The meaning and nature of jurisdiction in the context of international antitrust enforcement

Before going any further, a brief clarification of the meaning and nature of the term "jurisdiction" is required. The above examples already suggest that the notion should be interpreted extensively. Indeed, in public international law, the concept of "jurisdiction" represents a corollary of States' sovereignty[7]. Thereby, it does not refer only to the capacity of national courts to hear specific cases brought before them (so-called "adjudicatory jurisdiction"). Rather, it includes also the right of States to enact legislation and to define its scope of application with regard to persons, circumstances and territories (so-called "prescriptive jurisdiction"), as well as the States' authority to take actions to enforce compliance with the legislation adopted (so-called "enforcement jurisdiction")[8].

Although this is not the place to deal with this complex and classical topic of public international law, it suffices to recall that (no less than[9]) five bases

---

7 Indeed, "[j]*urisdiction is, essentially, the appointment of power, and in international law power affects national sovereignty*" (cf., *ex pluribus*, L. Brilmayer, *Justifying International Acts*, Cornell University Press, Ithaca-London, 1989, p. 15).

8 Simplifying, "'[j]*urisdicition' is the term that describes the limits of the legal competence of a State or other regulatory authority (such as the European Community) to make, apply, and enforce rules of conduct upon persons*" (cf. V. Lowe, *Jurisdiction*, in M. Evans (Ed.), *International Law*, Oxford University Press, Oxford, 2006, p. 335; C. Staker, *Jurisdiction*, in M. Evans (Ed.), *International Law*, Oxford University Press, Oxford, 2014, p. 309). In other words, such notion "*non può quindi essere fatta coincidere con quello che si esprime con il termine italiano 'giurisdizione'*"; indeed, the term jurisdiction includes, "*oltre la funzione giurisdizionale in senso proprio, anche tutto quanto la tradizione europeo-continentale esprime con la nozione di amministrazione, ricollegandosi con ciò, verosimilmente, alla nozione medievale di 'jurisdictio' intesa come comprensiva di ogni forma di potere pubblico. Con lo stesso termine di 'jurisdiction' la tradizione anglosassone indica spesso anche il potere legislativo dello Stato, designato allora come 'legislative jurisdiction' o 'jurisdiction to prescribe', contrapposta a ciò che si indica come 'jurisdiction to adjudicate' e 'jurisdiction to enforce'*" (cf. R. Luzzatto, I Queirolo, *Sovranità territoriale, "jurisdiction" e regole di immunità*, in S.M. Carbone, R. Luzzatto, A. Santa Maria, *Istituzioni di diritto internazionale*, Giappichelli, Torino, 2011, p. 235, spec. p. 237).

9 Indeed, "*this list is not exhaustive, as other bases of jurisdiction may be recognised in the future*" (cf. International Bar Association, *Report of the Task Force on Extraterritorial Jurisdiction*, 2009, p. 11).

of jurisdiction have emerged and developed, *i.e.* the nationality, territoriality, universality, passive personality and protective principles[10]. States may therefore claim jurisdiction over a given conduct relying on each of these grounds[11]. At least from a theoretical viewpoint, this holds true also in the perspective of the application of competition law to situations involving international elements. However, one should consider that such principles do not share the same degree of acceptance among States. In the general perspective, for example, the least controversial (and therefore most important) connecting factors are the ones based on nationality and territoriality. Indeed, the very idea of sovereignty implies that a State should be able to exercise power over its nationals (with whom the State has a so-called genuine link[12]) and within its territory[13].

The latter ground maintains its relevance also in the specific context of competition law, mainly because it allows States to exercise their jurisdiction not only over acts committed within their borders (so-called "subjective territoriality"), but also over acts committed abroad that have consequences within their borders (so-called "objective territoriality"). As we will see, this (also) means that States may apply their national competition law to affect conducts carried out outside their territory as long as such conducts produce harmful "consequences" on their domestic market. By contrast, the other bases of jurisdiction are in this sector far less important, if not virtually irrelevant[14].

---

10 Among others, cf. A. Abass, *International Law*, Oxford University Press, Oxford-New York, 2012, p. 525.

11 To be sure, the mentioned principles do not constitute public international rules aiming to limit the scope of national jurisdiction. Rather, they represent domestic rules developed by (several) States in order to establish the circumstances under which the exercise of their jurisdiction over situations involving transnational elements may be reasonable, in the light of sufficiently close legal connections (cf. F. Munari, *Il diritto comunitario antitrust nel commercio internazionale: il caso dei trasporti marittimi*, Cedam, Padova, 1993, pp. 194-195).

12 See ICJ, 6 April 1955, *Nottebohm (Liechtenstein* v. *Guatemala)*, in *I.C.J. Reports*, 1955, p. 4. *Ex plurimis*, see D. Harris, *The Protection of Companies in International Law in the Light of the Nottebohm Case*, in *International and Comparative Law Quarterly*, 1969, p. 295. More recently, see M. Andenas, *Jurisdiction, Procedure and the Transformation of International Law: From Nottebohm to Diallo in the ICJ*, in *European Business Law Review*, 2012, p. 127.

13 Cf. J.L. Brierly, *The Law of Nations: An Introduction to the International Law of Peace*, Clarendon Press, Oxford, 1963, p. 162.

14 For example, this is the case of the universality and the protective principles. On the one hand, the first principle allows every State to assert its jurisdiction over crimes that "*are regarded as so heinous that every State has a legitimate interest in their repression*", such as "*genocide, crimes against humanity, and serious war crimes*" (cf. C. Staker, *op. cit.*, p. 322). In these cases, regardless of the location

3 Different systems and strategies of international antitrust enforcement: the territorial approach to the application of competition law

At least from a theoretical perspective, there are three different ways to deal with the several issues arising from the inherent international nature of competition law and enforcement[15]. Each of these solutions solve some of the problems while creating others.

Firstly, it is possible to conceive a system where States have jurisdiction only and solely over those conducts performed by their nationals or physically carried out within their territory. As said, the nationality and (subjective) territoriality principles are indeed the oldest and most common grounds to govern the exercise of jurisdiction by States under public international law, far beyond the antitrust context. Therefore, it is not surprising that such approach was followed, over a century ago, in the very first case in which the issue of jurisdiction over anticompetitive foreign conducts came up for a decision before a national court, namely the US Supreme Court[16].

---

of the offense or the nationality of the offender and the victim, the main interest is to avoid that such crimes go unpunished. As is well known, however, antitrust offences are certainly not included within the group of such serious crimes: many States do not even qualified them as criminal offences. On the other hand, even if the offence is not particularly serious, the second principle allows every State to assert its jurisdiction "*when essential interest of the State are at stake*", and therefore "*vital issues are threatened, even if by non-nationals acting outside the territory of the State*" (cf. C. STAKER, *op. cit.*, p. 321). Although every State's right to protect its own trade has been considered as the proper base of jurisdiction in antitrust cases (for the references see W.L. FUGATE, *Foreign Commerce and the Antitrust Laws*, Aspen Publishers, New York, 1996, p. 57), the "vital interest" requirement actually makes unlikely that this ground of jurisdiction can be used to cover anticompetitive offences. Indeed, the general view is that the protective principle applies only if the restrictive practice targets and hinders the whole economy of the State, thus threatening its national security (cf. M. AKEHURST, *Jurisdiction in International Law*, in *British Yearbook of International Law*, 1973, p. 145, spec. pp. 206-207). On the scope of application of the passive personality principle, see *infra*.

15 In this vein, see for example A. TIZZANO, *Appunti sulla cooperazione internazionale in tema di concorrenza*, in *Dir. Un. Eur.*, 1999, p. 695; S. BASTIANON, P. M. FERRARI, *Gli strumenti di cooperazione internazionale in materia antitrust e i rapporti intercorrenti tra l'Unione europea e la Svizzera*, in M. CONDINANZI (ED.), *Unione europea e Svizzera tra cooperazione e integrazione*, Giuffré, Milano, 2012, p. 307, spec. p. 308; F. WAGNER VON PAPP, *Competition Law and Extraterritoriality*, in A. EZRACHI (ED.), *Research Handbook on International Competition Law*, Edward Elgar, Cheltenham, 2012, p. 21.

16 Indeed, in the well-known *American banana* case, the US Supreme Court held that "*the general and almost universal rule*" according to which "*the character of an*

While it is able to ensure the avoidance of multiple enforcement, such model is not – and cannot be – effective unless every State enacts antitrust legislation that is willing and capable to enforce. Nowadays, the first requirement does not pose particular problems, since the vast majority of States have adopted rules aiming at protecting competition[17]. However, not all of these States have also the resources and/or the political strength to apply such rules[18]. Moreover, national interests may alter the selection of cases and enforcement priorities. For example, there are conducts (such as export cartels) that are hardly investigated by competition authorities: the main reason is that their negative effects are borne by foreigners (*i.e.*, companies and consumers that buy from the cartel), while the profits are enjoyed domestically (*i.e.*, by the national undertakings involved in the cartel).

4 The extraterritorial approach to the application of competition law

In order to tackle such (and other) deficiencies, States tend to exercise jurisdiction outside their territory, *vis-à-vis* foreign conducts that have certain "consequences" within their national borders. In other words, they often try to apply their competition law extraterritorially to regulate foreign conducts that may affect their national market. This second scenario arises mainly because the political and economic aims pursued by national competition rules would be irremediably jeopardized if such rules could not cover conducts that take place outside the national borders. In 1945, recognizing that the anticompetitive consequences of a given conduct can be felt far from where they originate, the same US Supreme Court that previously denied the extraterritorial application of the Sherman Act, admitted that such piece of legislation covers "*overseas conspiracies*" (*i.e.*, agreements concluded outside the US) «*if they were intended to affect imports and did affect them*»[19]. This

---

act as lawful or unlawful must be determined wholly by the law of the country where the act is done" applies also to antitrust offences (cf. *American Banana* Co v. *United Fruit* Co, 213 US 347, 356, 29 S. Ct 511, 512 (1909).

17 Cf. M.M. Dabbah, *International and Comparative Competition Law*, Cambridge University Press, Cambridge, 2010, p. 3.

18 For examples, although having formally promulgated pieces of legislation to protect competition, many developing countries "*do not have the resource to enforce the law* [and p]*articularly, they do not have the resources and credible deterrence power to control the anticompetitive acts of multinational corporations*" (cf. E.M. Fox, *Can we solve the antitrust problems of globalization*, cit., pp. 359-360).

19 Cf. *United States* v. *Aluminum Co. of America*, 148 F2d 416, 444, (2nd Cir. 1945). As is well known, the *revirement* has been eased by the judgment handed down by the Permanent Court of International Justice (the "PCIJ") in the famous

soon came to be known as the "effects doctrine", since it basically provides States with jurisdiction over foreign conducts that have certain effects within their territory[20].

Besides influencing the level of enforcement (and possibly creating legal uncertainty[21]), this scenario triggers the question about its legitimacy[22]. Indeed, the fact that a State unilaterally demands to apply its antitrust rules to economic activities carried out within the territory of other States may be regarded by the latter as an intervention in their domestic affairs, and therefore as a violation of the general principle of the equality of States. In other words,

---

Lotus case, where the PCIJ clarified that, as a matter of principle, public international law does not prevent States from extending "*the application of their laws and the jurisdiction of their courts to persons, property and acts outside their territory*" (cf. Lotus Judgment, 7 September 1927, PCIJ Series A, No. 10 (1927). See, *inter alia*, L. CAVARÉ, *L'arrêt du "Lotus" et le positivisme juridique*, in *Travaux Juridiques et Economiques de l'Université de Rennes*, 1930, p. 144; G.W. BERGE, *Case of the S. S. Lotus*, in *Michigan Law Review*, 1928, p. 361; A.P. FACHIRI, *The Case of the S.S. Lotus*, in *British Year Book of International Law*, 1928, p. 131; G. SALVIOLI, *Il caso del Lotus*, in *Rivista di Diritto Internazionale*, 1927, p. 521; H. WALTHER, *L'affaire du 'Lotus' ou de l'abordage hauturier en droit pénal international*, Paris, 1928.

20 Indeed, in the *Alcoa* case, Judge Hand further clarifies that "*it is settled law* [...] *that any State may impose liabilities, even upon persons not within its allegiance, for conduct outside its borders that has consequences within the United States*".

21 Indeed, it is rather obvious that "*review by different antitrust authorities of anti-competitive conduct can lead to undesirable outcomes, such as divergent results*" (cf. D. GERADIN, M. REYSEN, D. HENRY, *Extraterritoriality, Comity and Cooperation in EC Competition Law*, in A. GUZMAN (ED.), *Cooperation, Comity, and Competition Policy*, Oxford University Press, Oxford, 2010, p. 21). With regard to the well-known case of some international mergers that have been assessed in different ways by the EU and the US authorities, see A. BAVASSO, *Boeing/McDonnel Douglas: Did the Commission Fly Too High?*, in *European Competition Law Review*, 1998, p. 243; B. BISHOP, *The Boeing/McDonnel Douglas Merger*, in *European Competition Law Review*, 1997, p. 417; A. BURNSIDE, *Ge, Honey I sank the Merger*, in *European Competition Law Review*, 2002, p. 107. E.M. FOX, *U.S. and European merger policy-fault lines and bridges*, in *Concorrenza e mercato*, 2002, p. 211; C. OSTI, R. PARDOLESI, *Falsi amici: le concentrazioni in Europa e negli Stati Uniti*, in *Giur. comm.*, 2002, p. 153.

22 In this vein, one of the basic concepts is that "*in the case of global markets, each nation that enjoins, conditions, or penalized conduct with cross-border effects is effectively enforcing antitrust law for the world without being authorized to do so by affected peoples; and it is doing so under a standard that is good for the enforcing nation*" (cf. E.M. FOX, *Can we solve the antitrust problems of globalization*, cit., p. 35).

States may considered such approach as an infringement of their – economic – sovereignty[23].

To be sure, from a legal viewpoint, there is by now a quasi-unanimous consensus that public international law does not preclude the (inbound[24]) extraterritorial application of competition law. Indeed, such approach is rooted in the (objective) territoriality principle[25], according to which, as said, jurisdiction over a given conduct should be ascertained by taking into consideration its "consequences", rather than the location of the infringer when the conduct was carried out. In line with this principle, as we will see below, both the (main) doctrines underlying the extraterritorial application of antitrust rules refer precisely to the market where the conduct has its "effects" or it has been "implemented".

However, going beyond a strictly legal perspective[26], it has to be noted that the extraterritorial application of national antitrust law has originated not only a legal but also an intense political debate[27], and actually represents

---

23 In other words, the application of competition law to foreign conducts on the ground of the territoriality principle could "*be contrary to international law because it might constitute an attempt to impose an alien economic policy on the State where the agreement was performed*" (cf. M. Akehurst, *op. cit.*, p. 193).

24 Indeed, "[t]*he days are gone when countries, such as the United Kingdom, opposed the very principle of extraterritoriality* [and] [n]*owadays, only outbound extraterritoriality is still perceived as a serious breach of sovereignty, and likely to be, in itself, a source of friction*" (cf. B. Zanettin, *Cooperation Between Antitrust Agencies at the International Level*, Hart Publishing, Oxford, 2002, p. 34; on the difference between inbound and outbound extraterritoriality see *infra*).

25 *Contra* see however D. Rishikesh, *Extraterritoriality versus Sovereignty in International Antitrust Jurisdiction*, in *World Competition*, 1991, p. 33, spec. p. 34, arguing that the effects doctrine (*i.e.*, one of the main theories on which the extraterritorial application of competition law is based), is "*unlike the objective territorial principle according to which the commission of at least part of the act must be within the territory*" of the State claiming jurisdiction over the conduct.

26 After all, it is well known that "*molti autori ritengono impossibile, "poco fruttuoso", o addirittura erroneo individuare nel diritto internazionale norme materiali limitative della giurisdizione degli Stati. L'esame della prassi, infatti, evidenzia come i problemi di extraterritorialità, piuttosto che a motivo della violazione di norme di diritto internazionale, sorgano per l'esistenza di concorrenti interessi "sovrani" riguardo alla medesima fattispecie, e perché l'applicazione extraterritoriale di norme da parte di uno di essi, a prescindere dalla legittimità di siffatta applicazione, può minacciare importanti interessi di altri ordinamenti. Il che, ovviamente, indipendentemente dalle tesi sostenute nei relativi giudizi dai soggetti (individui o Stati) parti ad essi o comunque a vario titolo interessati*" (cf. F. Munari, *op. cit.*, p. 203).

27 Indeed, although the debate about the extraterritorial enforcement of national competition laws "*can appear to be a dry debate about 'jurisdiction' and 'inter-*

one of the most controversial issues in post-war international trade[28]. The main reason is that, in fields such as antitrust, conflicts of jurisdiction, and especially the positive ones, are often political rather than legal in nature. Indeed, when a State claims to apply its competition law to foreign conducts, it is essentially demanding to regulate (part of) the economic life of the country on whose market those conducts were committed. In other words, the "regulating" State is interfering with the economic policy of the "regulated" State, as clearly highlighted – *inter alia* – by the Swiss Watchmakers case[29]. Being so sensitive to economic and political considerations, it is not surprising that the extraterritorial application of competition law has led to several and notable frictions between otherwise closely allied States[30].

Nevertheless, the phenomenon at stake seems tenable even under this different perspective. The ground of "political" justification is quite straightforward: if they decide to extend their economic activities abroad and operate in other markets, it seems fair that foreign undertakings accept the local rules of the game[31], including competition law. Therefore, if they decide to sell their products in a State where a provision similar in scope to art. 101 TFEU is in force, foreign undertakings shall avoid agreements, decisions and concerted practices having "*as their object or effect the prevention, restriction or distortion of competition*", even in the (rather hypothetical) case that their national law allows such practices.

---

national law' [i]*t is in reality about politics, about who can make and enforce rules governing competitive enterprises*" (cf. D.I. Baker, D.B. Ayer, *Anti-trust Imperialism*, in *European Competition law Review*, 1993, p. 3).

28 Cf. J. Coppel, *A question of Keiretsu: Extending the Long Arm of US Anti-trust*, in *European Competition Law Review*, 1992, p. 192.

29 Cf. *United States* v. *Watchmakers of Switzerland Information Center*, Inc. Trade Cas. 70600. In this case, the US authorities complained about a spare parts non-export agreement signed by Swiss undertakings active in the watch industry, on the ground that such agreement was damaging foreign (*i.e.*, US) companies active in the same market. Although probably legitimate, the concerns expressed by the US conflicted with the economic policy supported by the Swiss government, which explicitly considered such agreement "*an important element of Swiss economic policy for the maximising of export revenue*" (cf. D.E. Rosenthal, W.M. Knighton, *National Laws and International Commerce. The Problem of Extraterritoriality*, Royal Institute of International Affairs, London, 1982, p. 25; see also B. Zanettin, *op. cit.*, pp. 34-35).

30 Seg. A. De Mestral, *The extraterritorial extension of laws: how much has changed*, in *Arizona Journal of International & Comparative Law*, 2014, p. 43.

31 At least as far as "*these rules are applied in a non-discriminatory fashion*" (cf. M.J. Trebilcock, *Competition Policy and Trade Policy*, in *Journal of World Trade*, 1996, p. 71, spec. p. 100).

Two more observations are required. On the one hand, the current general acceptance of the extraterritorial application of competition law does not ensure that political conflicts cannot arise. The so-called blocking statutes represent a clear example of this scenario. As is well known, this term refers to domestic legislation adopted to hinder the application of foreign laws to national undertakings, as well as to obstruct foreign enforcement measures. One of the first examples of this kind of legislation is the Ontario Business Records Act issued in 1947[32], while one of the most famous is the Protection of Trading Interest Act[33] enacted by the UK in 1980 to react to the then particularly sensitive issue of the so-called US antitrust imperialism. However, the quite recent promulgation by the Russian President of an Order to protect Gazprom from the EU Commission investigation for an alleged breach of art. 102 TFEU shows that these instruments are not completely old-fashioned[34].

The mechanisms envisaged to prevent the extraterritorial application of other countries' competition law are manifold and their analysis falls outside the scope of the present article[35]. What matters here is that their activation

---

32 Ont. Rev. Stat., c. 44 (1960). See D.I. BAKER, *Antitrust Conflicts between Friends: Canada and the United States in the Mid-1970's*, in *Cornell International Law Journal*, 1978, 168.

33 Cf. An Act to provide protection from requirements, prohibitions and judgments imposed or given under the laws of countries outside the United Kingdom and affecting the trading or other interests of persons in the United Kingdom, Ch 11, 20 March 1980. See T.J. KAHN, *The Protection of Trading Interests Act of 1980: Britain's Response to U.S. Extraterritorial Antitrust. Enforcement*, in *Northwestern Journal of International Law and Business*, 1980, p. 476.

34 Cf. Decree of the President of the Russian Federation n. 1285 of 11 September 2012, on the Measures of Protection of Interests of the Russian Federation in Cases of Foreign Economic Activities. See S. BENNETT, *The European Commission v. Gazprom*, in *Wisconsin International Law Journal*, 2014, p. 886; M. MARTYNISZYN, *Legislation Blocking Antitrust Investigations and the September 2012 Russian Executive Order*, in *World Competition*, 2014, p. 103; P.S. MORRIS, *Iron Curtain at the border: Gazprom and the Russian blocking order to prevent the extraterritoriality of EU competition law*, in *European Competition Law Review*, 2014, p. 601; N. SARTORI, *The European Commission vs. Gazprom: An issue of Fair Competition or a Foreign Policy Quarrel?*, Istituto Affari Internazionali Working Papers n. 13/2013.

35 *Inter alia*, see J.R. ATWOOD, *Blocking Statutes and Sovereign Compulsion in American Antitrust Legislation*, in *Swiss Review of International Competition Law*, 1986, p. 5; L. COLLINS, *Blocking and Clawback Statutes: The United Kingdom Approach*, in *Journal of Business Law*, 1986, p. 372; S. APRIL, *Blocking Statutes as a Response to the Extraterritorial Application of Law*, in C.J. OLMSTEAD (Ed.), *Extraterritorial Application of Laws and Responses Thereto*, ESC Publishing, Oxford, 1984, p. 223; P.A. BATISTA, *Confronting. Foreign "Block-*

usually does not require any (alleged) violation of the grounds of jurisdiction recognized under public international law. Rather, the applicability of the protective instruments included in blocking statutes is normally triggered by the mere necessity to protect strategic undertakings and thus national interests. The above confirms the essentially political nature of conflicts of jurisdiction arising in the context of the international enforcement of antitrust legislation[36].

On the other hand, there are situations in which the extraterritorial application of competition law is questionable from both the legal and the political points of view. Indeed, two different forms of extraterritorial application exist: inbound and outbound extraterritoriality. So far, we have focused only on the first category, which in fact refers to those cases where States apply their competition law to conducts that, although carried out abroad, have effects within their territory. The second category concerns those cases where States try to use their domestic competition rules to open up foreign markets to the benefit of their national undertakings[37]. This means that competition law is applied extraterritoriality towards conducts that simply prevent the access of the undertakings of the "regulating" State to the market of the "regulated" State, *i.e.* towards conducts that not only are committed abroad, but also have no effects on the domestic market of the "regulating" States[38]. The only persons affected are the undertakings of the "regulating" State that are willing to export or invest in the "regulated" State.

A particularly clear example is the one of a cartel operating only in a given country whose legislation hypothetically does not prohibit such form of collusion, or even encourages (or compels) firms to join national cartels. By definition, the cartel reinforces the market power of its members, thus hindering the access of foreign undertakings into the cartelized market. The same holds true with regard to unilateral behaviours (such as refusals to contract

ing". Legislation: A Guide to Securing. Disclosure from Non-resident. Parties to American Litigation, in *Journal of International Law*, 1983, p. 61; D.A. Sabalot, *Shortening the Long Arm of American Antitrust Jurisdiction: Extraterritoriality and the Foreign Blocking Statutes*, in *Loyola Law Review*, 1982, p. 213.

36 Indeed, blocking statutes "*risultano applicabili non già previa la dimostrazione di alcuna violazione di norme internazionali in tema di giurisdizione, bensì semplicemente una volta che sia stata accertata l'esigenza di proteggere e regolare settori considerati importanti dell'industria nazionale*" (cf. F. Munari, *op. cit.*, p. 204).

37 See D. Liakopoulos, A. Marsilia, *The Regulation of Transnational Mergers in International and European Law*, Brill-Nijhoff, Leiden, 2010, p. 13.

38 See, for example, *United States* v. *Pilkington* plc, 59 Fed. Reg. 30604 (1994).

with potential exporters) as well as to other forms of horizontal and vertical cooperation (such as the well-known Japanese *keiretsu*[39]).

In these cases, the conflict between the "regulating" and the "regulated" State is particularly intense. From the legal perspective, outbound extraterritoriality is not covered by the territoriality principle, either in the subjective or objective form. The only basis of jurisdiction that the "regulating" State can invoke is the passive personality principle. This principle provides States with jurisdiction over any offence committed against their nationals (*i.e.*, national undertakings that cannot export or invest due to the restrictive practice committed in the foreign market), regardless of both the location and the seriousness of the offense, as well as of the nationality of the offender. As said, however, the passive personality principle has not found general acceptance in the international community, although sometimes advanced by States[40]. And even less certain is the possibility to apply such principle in the antitrust context[41].

But outbound extraterritoriality is controversial also from the political perspective. In this case, the idea that companies should accept the local rules of the game when they operate in foreign countries plays against the extraterritorial application of competition law, rather than justifying it. Indeed, saying that a State has jurisdiction over conducts committed abroad, that have no effect on its territory, and that only affect its national undertakings' chance to export or invest abroad, basically amounts to hold that such undertakings have the right to export their national competition law along

39 *I.e.*, those "*arrangements whereby families of Japanese companies are lined by, inter alia, cross-shareholding, interlocking directorates and exclusive supply arrangements*", thus allegedly producing, "*in practice, a market shared exclusively by certain domestic companies to the exclusion of all others, including, and especially, foreign exporters*" (cf. J. Coppel, *op. cit.*, p. 193). On such topic, *inter alia*, see also J. Davidow, *Application of U.S. Antitrust Laws to Keiretsu Practices*, in *World Competition*, 1994, p. 5; A. Helou, *The Nature and Competitiveness of Japan's Keiretsu*, in *Journal of World Trade*, 1991, p. 99; J.E. Johnson, *Keiretsu: Their Effect on Business and How American Government and Business Can Confront Them*, in *Brigham Young University Law Review*, 1992, p. 1155; G.K. Bader, *The Keiretsu Distribution System of Japan: Its Steadfast Existence Despite Heightened Foreign and Domestic Pressure for Dissolution*, in *Cornell International Law Journal*, 1994, p. 365.

40 For the references, see *inter alia* C. Staker, *op. cit.*, p. 326.

41 For example, from the fact that "[t]*he passive personality principle is a controversial and, many would argue, insufficient basis of jurisdiction*", it follows that "*a US claim of jurisdiction over Japanese companies on the basis that they had caused economic loss to US companies in Japan would be highly contentious and cannot be said to be a realistic possibility*" (cf. J. Coppel, *op. cit.*, p. 197).

with their goods and services[42]. An assumption whose legitimacy is far from obvious, given that local conduct on local markets with local consumer effects are paradigmatically entrusted to the regulatory choices of the locality[43].

5 The multilateral approach to the application of competition law

The above shows that a system where every single State can unilaterally apply its national rules extraterritorially is not much nearer to a solution to the complex questions posed by the international nature of antitrust enforcement than the model based only on their territorial application. Other ways have therefore been proposed.

Firstly, in several occasions courts have sharpened the theories upon which the extraterritorial application relies, and particularly the contents of the effects doctrine. As said, the US Supreme Court established this doctrine in the already mentioned *Alcoa* case. With the aim of lessening the room for conflicts between different States, the subsequent case law tried to limit the extraterritorial reach of the Sherman Act. On the one hand, the notion of "international comity" was thereby introduced[44]. This principle has a twofold dimension, consisting of a negative and a positive comity, and basically calls for a weighing-up exercise by national courts and authorities, requiring (*rectius*, suggesting, on the grounds of courtesy) to refrain from exercising their State's jurisdiction if this choice can impair other States' interests. On the other hand, only direct, substantial and reasonably foreseeable effects on the domestic market begun to be considered sufficiently "qualified" to support the applicability of national antitrust legislation to foreign conducts[45].

---

42 To quote F. Wagner Von Papp, *op. cit.*, p. 38.

43 To quote E.M. Fox, *Can we solve the antitrust problems of globalization*, cit., p. 367.

44 *Inter alia*, see *Timberlane Lumber Co.* v. *Bank of America*, 549 F.2d 597, 613, 615 (9th Cir. 1976); *Mannington Mills, Inc.* v. *Congoleum Corp.*, 595 F.2d 1287, 1296-98 (3d Cir. 1979). With regard to the ECJ case law, see for example GC, 18 June 2013, T-406/08, *Industries chimiques du fluor (ICF)* v *European Commission*, NYR, § 215-222.

45 *Inter alia*, see *Hartford Fire Ins. Co.* v. *California*, 509 U.S. 764, 796 n. 23 (1993), where it has been held that "*it is well established by now that the Sherman Act applies to foreign conduct that was meant to produce and did in fact produce some substantial effect in the United States*". With regard to the ECJ case law, see for example General Court, 25 March 1999, case T-102/96, *Gencor Ltd* v *Commission* [1999] *ECR* p. II-753, § 90.

Secondly, these criteria – and especially the comity principle – have been codified not only at the national level[46], but also and foremost in several international bilateral agreements. Since States did not always consider themselves strictly bound by positive and negative comity[47], the idea was to transpose such principles into the realm of international treaties, in order to foster their strength. The second part of the present article deals broadly with bilateral agreements, so that no further details are needed here.

However, it is clear that bilateral cooperation is – at its best[48] – suitable to lessen the problems raised by the territorial and extraterritorial application of national competition rules to supranational conducts, but it cannot eradicate them, due to their global nature. Therefore, the third (and last) line of action envisaged to pursue such aim has been the one based on multilateral cooperation. Indeed, several international bodies and institutions have tried to deal with this challenge, at least since the 1948. In particular, there have been many attempts to elaborate a common set of substantial rules, as well as to establish some sort of multilateral enforcement regime. For many years, the WTO represented the natural forum where these political discussions took place[49]. The 2001 Doha Round went as far as adopting a

---

46 See, for example, the US *Foreign Trade Antitrust Improvements Act of 1982*, 15 U.S.C. §§ 1 (note), 6a, 45(a) 1982. See D.T. MURPHY, *Moderating Antitrust Subject Matter Jurisdiction: The Foreign Trade Antitrust Improvements Act and the Restatement of Foreign Relations Law (Revised)*, in *University of Cincinnati Law Review*, 1986, p. 779; E.G. GARVEY, *The Foreign Trade Antitrust Improvements Act of 1981*, in *Law and Policy in International Business*, 1982, p. 1.

47 Among others, see L. BELLODI, *L'extraterritorialità rivisitata. Brevi riflessioni sulle recenti tendenze*, in *Diritto del Commercio Internazionale*, 2013, p. 1023.

48 After all, "[a]*lthough bilateral agreements may be arguably slightly easier to achieve form a policy perspective, it is unlikely that a series of bilateral agreements would be consistent. Negotiation between countries will inevitably lead to different agreements being reached, thus not moving the world any closer to an "international" competition law*" (cf. L. CEJNAR, R. BURGESS, *op. cit.*, p. 465). Indeed, "*a true global competition culture can only be attained when many countries are involved. If a certain degree of convergence could be attained, even if it is a superficial one, the geographical scope would be much broader than in a bilateral context. As the economy becomes more and more globally integrated, bilateral agreements do encounter their limitations. A proliferation of bilateral agreements in the long term might prove to be counter-effective and confusing*" (cf. V. DEMEDTS, *International Competition Law Enforcement: Different Means, One Goal?*, in *Competition Law Review*, 2012, p. 223, spec. p. 233).

49 Although it has been noted that the WTO is an international institution that "*concerns itself with public restraints of trade*", while competition rules regard "*private restraints of trade*" (cf. F.M. FISHER, *Transnational competition law and the WTO*, in *Journal of International Trade Law & Policy*, 2006, p. 42, spec. p. 44).

Declaration that included some basic dispositions on competition policy, as well as a call for more international cooperation, also foreseeing the creation of an international competition framework. However, such initiatives were dropped shortly after, mainly because of a lack of support from developing States emerged in the 2003 Cancun Round. The reasons of the dissent were manifold[50], and not all of them concerned the merit of the proposals[51].

Nevertheless, both the establishment of common rules and the creation of an international framework for their application are options that no longer seem to be on the table. Indeed, multilateral cooperation has followed a different pattern. The most significant developments (not to say, the only ones) have occurred within the framework of the so-called International Competition Network, *i.e.* an informal forum created in 2001 by the competition authorities of several States to foster mutual dialogue and cooperation. The contacts between those in charge of competition enforcement at the national level have led to the adoption of various documents and guidelines, thus enhancing convergence in competition policy around the world, although

---

50 Inter alia, "*developing countries expressed concern about the resources that would be needed to implement the proposals. Some could only see benefits to richer, capital-exporting countries; according to some poorer states, the benefits of an international competition law regime to them were less than clear. Some states were concerned about the possible impact on sovereignty, and their freedom to determine their own development priorities. Other states felt that there were more urgent priorities within the world trading system to address*" (cf. J.A. Zerk, *Extraterritorial Jurisdiction: Lessons for the Business and Human Rights Sphere from Six Regulatory Areas*, Harvard Corporate Social Responsibility Initiative Working Paper No. 59, 2010, p. 99).

51 So that it has been observed that "[t]*he idea of a multilateral competition framework was a victim of the spirit of the times*", mainly because such proposal was based on the conferral of new powers to the WTO in a moment when "[t]*he WTO, like the World Bank,* [was] *seen in many quarters as part of the problem, not the remedy*", as well as because at the time "*many developing countries had become unhappy with the concept of 'free trade' which seemed previously to have become universally accepted as the remedy for the world's ills*" (cf. A. Jones, B. Sufrin, *EU Competition Law: Text, Cases and Materials*, Oxford University Press, Oxford-New York, 2014, p. 1294). To be sure, the potential setting up of a global competition regime has been criticised also for reasons that are more specifically connected to the content of the proposal. For example, it has been affirmed that "[e]*stablishing a common set of rules will itself be challenging and ensuring that a common set of rules is applied in the same way in each country will be almost impossible. The creation of an international body to administrate those rules is unlikely to proceed as countries are concerned about losing their sovereignty over these issues*" (cf. L. Cejnar, R. Burgess, *op. cit.*, p. 467).

by means of soft law instruments[52]. So far, "recommended practices" have been issued with regard to competition assessment[53], merger analysis[54] and procedures[55], market power[56] and predatory pricing analysis[57], as well as with regard to the application of unilateral conduct rules to state-created monopolies[58]; a so-called "Anti-cartel enforcement manual" has been produced too[59].

There is no need to further discuss these aspects, or to analyse their positive impact on the context of international cooperation in the field of antitrust. What matters here is simply that the failure of all the attempts to develop a global strategy for international antitrust enforcement entails that the (unilateral and, at best, bilateral) extraterritorial application of national competition rules still represents "*the most important weapon in the arsenal of competition law enforcers*" against international anticompetitive conducts[60].

Before turning to bilateral cooperation, and particularly to the recently signed agreement by the Swiss Confederation and the EU[61], it seems therefore useful to recall how these countries deal with the extraterritorial application of their national competition law[62].

6 The extraterritorial application of Swiss …

To be sure, the Swiss approach can be described quite briefly. Despite the fact that the effects doctrine has been explicitly recognized by the Federal Court

52 See D.P. Wood, *Soft Harmonization Among Competition Laws: Track Record and Prospects*, in *Antitrust Bulletin*, 2003, p. 305.
53 See http://www.internationalcompetitionnetwork.org/uploads/library/doc978.pdf.
54 See http://www.internationalcompetitionnetwork.org/uploads/library/doc316.pdf.
55 See http://www.internationalcompetitionnetwork.org/uploads/library/doc588.pdf.
56 See http://www.internationalcompetitionnetwork.org/uploads/library/doc317.pdf.
57 See http://www.internationalcompetitionnetwork.org/uploads/library/doc966.pdf.
58 See http://www.internationalcompetitionnetwork.org/uploads/library/doc318.pdf.
59 See http://www.internationalcompetitionnetwork.org/uploads/library/doc756.pdf.
60 To quote F. Wagner Von Papp, *op. cit.*, p. 22.
61 Cf. *Agreement between the European Union and the Swiss Confederation concerning cooperation on the application of their competition laws*, in *OJ*, 2014, L 347/3.
62 It is worth dealing with both the countries also because, as explicitly recognized by the Swiss Federal Tribunal, the Federal Cartel Act is construed independently from EU competition law (cf. Tribunale Federale, 11 April 2011, Joined cases C-343 e C-344/2010, *Swisscom (Schweiz) AG*).

since 1967[63], the proverbially mild nature[64] of the Federal Cartel Act of 1962[65] led for many years national authorities to have a quite reluctant attitude towards its extraterritorial application[66]. In other words, until recently, there has been no or limited risk of conflicts with other States' jurisdiction, simply because the application of Swiss antitrust legislation to foreign conducts for the purposes of protecting the domestic economic order was not usually even sought. As seen above[67], Switzerland has rather been on the receiving end of this scenario, being quite often the target of other States' claims to apply their competition rules to economic activities carried out within the Swiss borders.

The perspective has changed over the last years. Firstly, the revision of the domestic competition rules, culminated with the adoption of the already mentioned Federal Cartel Act of 1995[68], led to the legislative endorsement of the effects doctrine[69]. Indeed, contrary to many other national antitrust

---

63 "*Bien que la loi du 20 décembre 1962 ne contienne aucune disposition explicite sur sa portée en matière internationale, elle s'applique également aux entraves à la concurrence commises à l'étranger et qui sortissent leurs effets en Suisse*" (cf. Tribunale Federale, 21 march 1967, *Hachette*, ATF 93 II p. 192, spec. p. 196). To be sure, it has to be noted that in such case the Federal Court has further clarified that "*adopting the effects doctrine to justify the application of substantive law did not necessarily imply the assumption of jurisdiction and the justification of a Swiss venue as a matter of public interest*" (cf. M. Haymann, *Extraterritorial Application of Antitrust Law. The Swiss Approach*, in *Revue Suisse du droit international de la concurrence*, 1981, p. 17, spec. p. 22).

64 To quote M. Haymann, *Extraterritorial Application of Antitrust Law*, cit., p. 18. It has to be noted that, under the Federal Cartel Act of 1962, even cartels were considered admissible as a matter of principle (cf. Id, p. 19).

65 See Legge federale del 20 dicembre 1962, *sui cartelli e le organizzazioni analoghe*, in *RU*, 1964, p. 49.

66 See C. Canenbley (Ed.), *Enforcing Antitrust Against Foreign Enterprises*, Kluwer, Deventer, 1981, p. 11.

67 See for example the already mentioned Swiss Watchmakers case (cf. *United States v. Watchmakers of Switzerland Information Center*, Inc. Trade Cas. 70600).

68 Cf. Legge federale del 6 ottobre 1995, *sui cartelli e altre limitazioni della concorrenza*, cit. See also the previous Legge federale del 20 dicembre 1985, *sui cartelli e le organizzazioni analoghe*, in *RU*, 1986, 874.

69 Although, as said, already "*bien reconnu en droit suisse*", the effects doctrine "*a finalement été consacre par le législateur Suisse* [...] [d]*ans la loi fédérale sur le droit international prive de 1987*", and "[e]n *ce qui concerne le domaine d'application du propre droit Suisse de la concurrence,* [dans] *l'article 2, alinéa 2, de la loi de 1995*" (cf. J. Basedow, *Souveraineté territoriale et globalisation des marchés: le domaine d'applications des lois contre les restrictions de la concurrence*, in *Recueil des cours – Académie de Droit International de La Haye*, M. Nijhoff, The Hague-Boston-London, 1997, p. 123).

legislations[70], this very same piece of legislation explicitly states that its provisions apply to all the practices that have an effect in Switzerland, even if they originate in another country[71]. The codification of the effects doctrine has in turn led to a stronger enforcement of national competition rules towards cartels and other agreements concluded abroad, as well as towards abusive unilateral conducts and concentrations that take place outside Switzerland.

This is particularly true with regard to foreign agreements amounting to vertical territorial restrictions, *i.e.* with regard to those contracts between a manufacturing company and its authorized dealers for countries other than Switzerland that prohibit the latter from importing into the Swiss territory. For example[72], in 2012 the Swiss Competition Commission (hereinafter, the "Comco") fined the Germany-based company BMW for having imposed on its authorised EEA dealers an export prohibition towards non-EEA countries, including Switzerland[73]. In other words, Comco fined a foreign undertaking for a vertical agreement concluded abroad with other foreign companies, on the ground that such agreement represents a territorial restriction having the effect of keeping BMW vehicles' prices on the Swiss market higher than those that would be obtained if foreign dealers were not prohibited from engaging in parallel imports, and thus could sell directly to (non-EEA and therefore also) Swiss customers. The Federal Administrative Court has recently dismissed the appeal brought by BMW against the decision, confirming that the protection of the effectiveness of the Federal Cartel Act requires that its

70 As we will see, although not "national", this include "[t]*he main articles concerning competition law in the* [TFEU], *Articles 101 and 101 TFEU,* [that] *do not mention whether they apply extraterritoriality*" (cf. V. Demedts, *op. cit.*, p. 229).

71 Cf. Article 2(2) of the Federal Cartel Act, which stipulates that «[l]*a presente legge si applica alle imprese di diritto privato e di diritto pubblico che fanno parte di un cartello o di altri accordi in materia di concorrenza, dominano il mercato o partecipano a concentrazioni di imprese*», and it is "*applicabile a fattispecie che esplicano i loro effetti in Svizzera, anche se si sono verificate all'estero*".

72 But, among the most recent cases, see also Tribunale Amministrativo Federale, 19 dicembre 2013, case B-506/2010, *Gaba International AG*; Tribunale Amministrativo Federale, 19 December 2013, case B-463/210, *Gebro Pharma GmbH*, with regard to an agreement between an Austrian (Gebro) and a Swiss company (Gaba), by which the former undertook not to export the products of the latter outside of Austria, so that such agreement essentially prohibits parallel imports from Austria to other countries, including Switzerland.

73 Cf. decision of the Comco, May 7 2012, im Untersuchungsverfahren 22-0408 betreffend die Bayerische Motoren Werke AG wegen unzulässiger Wettbewerbsabrede gemäss Art. 5 Abs. 1 i.V.m. Art. 5 Abs. 4 KG.

provisions apply to foreign conducts that produce economic effects inside the country[74].

7 … and EU competition law: from the "single economic entity" and the "implementation" doctrines …

The development of the extraterritorial dimension of EU competition rules has followed a windier path[75]. While, until very recently[76], the ECJ has not explicitly endorsed the effects doctrine, two other legal theories have been put forward to support the extraterritorial reach of artt. 101 and 102 TFEU: the so-called "single economic entity" and "implementation" doctrines.

The first theory was established in the very first occasion where the ECJ could deal with the extraterritorial application of EU competition law. The reference is to the famous *Dyestuffs* case[77], where a UK based company named ICI was involved in a price fixing cartel with several undertakings based in

74 Cf. Tribunale Amministrativo Federale, 13 November 2015, case B-3332/2012, *Bayerische Motoren Werke AG*.

75 *Inter alia*, see P. De Pasquale, *L'applicazione extraterritoriale delle regole antitrust*, in L.F. Pace (Ed.), *Dizionario sistematico del diritto della concorrenza*, Napoli, 2013, p. 144; A. Themelis, *The Internet, Jurisdiction and EU competition Law: The Concept of 'Over-territoriality'* in *Addressing Jurisdictional Implications in the Online World*, in *World Competition*, 2012, p. 325; V. Scordamaglia, *Merger Control Rules in the EU and their Extraterritorial Application*, in *Medjunarodni Problemi*, 2008, p. 47; P. De Pasquale, *La tutela della concorrenza oltre i confini comunitari tra applicazione extraterritoriale e cooperazione*, Editoriale Scientifica, Napoli, 2005; B. Nascimbene, *Aspetti internazionali della politica di concorrenza comunitaria*, in *Dir. comm. int.*, 2001, p. 309; C. Schepisi, *Le relazioni esterne in materia di concorrenza: gli accordi CE/USA e CE/Canada tra dimensione internazionale e dimensione comunitaria*, in *Dir. Un. Eur.*, 2001, p. 149; R. Adam, *Limiti esterni delle norme comunitarie sulla concorrenza*, in *Riv. dir. int.*, 1975, p. 254.

76 For example, yet in 2012, it has been noted that "*there has been no definitive statement from the Court of Justice on this issue*" (cf. R. Whish, D. Bailey, *Competition Law*, Oxford University Press, Oxford, 2012, p. 496). As we will see below, the situation has changed with the judgment issued by the General Court in the *Intel* case (cf. case T-286/09, *Intel*, cit).

77 Cf. ECJ, 14 July 1972, case 48/69, *Imperial Chemical Industries Ltd.* v *Commission (Dyestuffs)* [1972] *ECR* p. 619. See F.A. Mann, *The Dyestuffs Case in the Court of Justice of the European Communities*, in *International and Comparative Law Quarterly*, 1973, p. 35; K.E. Markert, *The Dyestuff Case: A Contribution to the Relationship between the Antitrust Laws of the European Economic Community and Its Member States*, in *Antitrust Bulletin*, 1969, p. 869; V. Korah, *The EEC Dyestuffs Case*, in *Journal of Business Law*, 1972, p. 319; A. Acevedo, *The EEC Dyestuffs Case: Territorial Jurisdiction*, in *Modern Law Review*, 1973, p. 317.

different Member States. Since the UK was not part of the (then) EEC, the Commission initially relied on the effects doctrine to include ICI among the undertakings condemned and fined for breaching art. 101 TFEU[78]. In its appeal against the decision, ICI contested – *inter alia* – the basis chosen by the Commission to assert its jurisdiction. Although Advocate General Mayras endorsed the adoption of the effects doctrine[79], the Commission considered "safer" to provide the ECJ with an alternative (and, at the time, far less controversial) solution to confirm its jurisdiction, rooted in the nationality principle.

The solution relies on the concept of "undertaking"[80]. Although artt. 101 and 102 TFEU are addressed to "undertakings", there is no definition of such concept in the Treaties or in secondary legislation. In *Dyestuffs*, the Commission argued for the first time that the term should reflect the economic reality, rather than the legal one. It follows that separate legal persons can be a sole "undertaking" (*i.e.*, a "single economic entity") for the purposes of competition law, if they are tied to each other from an economic and managerial perspective. This assumption was laid down as a general principle: it has therefore several consequences that go well beyond the context of the extraterritorial application of EU competition law[81]. For example, the theory of the single economic entity implies that intra-group agreements between different companies cannot breach art. 101 TFEU: although composed by several legal persons, an "undertaking" is free to choose how to organize itself.

What matters here, however, is that the theory at stake makes it possible to hold (and actually to presume) parent companies liable for competition law infringements committed by their subsidiaries over which they can exercise control. Indeed, if the subsidiaries do not determine their own conducts on the market, there is no doubt that they form a single economic entity with the holding company. Just as a given company is the only entity liable for antitrust offences committed by each of its departments, so too an "undertaking" is the only entity liable for the breaches of art. 101 and 102 TFEU committed by each of the legal persons by which it is possibly composed (so-called corporate group liability).

78 Artt. 101 and 102 TFEU are "*applicable to all restrictions of competition which produce within the Common Market effects set out in Article* [101(1) TFEU]" (Cf. § 28 of the Commission decision of 24 July 1969, IV/26.267 – *Dyestuffs*, in *OJ*, L, 1969, 195/11.

79 Cf. Opinion of Advocate General Mayras of 2 May 1972, case 48/69, *Imperial Chemical Industries Ltd.* v *Commission (Dyestuffs)* [1972] *ECR* p. 619.

80 See A. Jones, *The boundaries of an undertaking in EU competition law*, in *European Competition Journal*, 2012, p. 301.

81 See O. Odudu, D. Bailey, *The single economic entity doctrine in EU competition law,* in *Common Market Law Review*, 2014, p. 1721.

Although the presumption of joint liability raises several controversial and much-debated issues even when the subsidiary and the parent company are both based in the EU[82], it is here appropriate to focus only on the international perspective. The imputation of the subsidiary's infringements to the parent company entails that the place where the anticompetitive effects take place is irrelevant for the purposes of establishing jurisdiction. Indeed, even when the parent company is based abroad, the circumstance that the subsidiary is established in one of the Member States is enough for the Commission to assert its jurisdiction. What is more, since one of the companies forming part of the single economic entity is established within the EU, the jurisdiction over the whole entity is based on the nationality principle, *i.e.* on one of the

82 For example, especially in the light of the great difficulties that the parent companies encounter in order to rebut such presumption, it is notorious that the mechanism poses some problem of compatibility with Article 47 of the EU Charter of Fundamental Rights, as well as with Article 6 of the European Convention on Human Rights. See for example P. Hughes, *Competition Law Enforcement and Corporate Group Liability – Adjusting the Veil*, in *European Competition Law Review*, 2014, p. 68; N.I. Pauer, *The Single Economic Entity Doctrine and Corporate Group Responsibility in European Antitrust Law*, Alphen aan den Rijn, 2014; B. Leupold, *Effective enforcement of EU competition law gone to far? Recent case law on the presumption of parental liability*, in *European Competition Law Review*, 2013, p. 570; J. Joshua, J. Botteman, L. Atlee, *"You Can't Beat the Percentage" – The Parental Liability Presumption in EU Cartel Enforcement*, in *Global Competition Review*, 2012, p. 3; M. Bronckers, A. Vallery, *No longer presumed guilty? The impact of fundamental rights on certain dogmas of EU competition law*, in *World Competition*, 2011, p. 535; S. Thomas, *Guilty of A Fault One has not Committed. The Limits of the Group-Based Sanction Policy Carried out by the Commission and the European Courts in EU-Antitrust Law*, in *Journal of European Competition Law & Practice*, 2012, p. 11; L. La Rocca, *The controversial issue of the parent-company liability for the violation of EC competition rules by the subsidiary*, in *European Competition Law Review*, 2011, p. 68; A. Svetlicinii, *Parental liability for the antitrust infringements of subsidiaries: a rebuttable presumption or probatio diabolica? ("Arkema SA v European Commission", ECJ (Second Chamber), judgment of 29 September 2011, C-520/09 P; and "Elf Aquitaine SA v European Commission", ECJ (Second Chamber), judgment of 29 September 2011, C-521/09 P)*, in *European Law Reporter*, 2011, p. 288; A. Winckler, *Parent's Liability: New case extending the presumption of liability of a parent company for the conduct of its wholly owned subsidiary*, in *Journal of European Competition Law & Practice*, 2011, p. 231; K. Hofstetter, M. Ludescher, *Fines against Parent Companies in EU Antitrust Law: Setting Incentives for "Best Practice Compliance"*, in *World Competition*, 2010, p. 55; A. Montesa, A. Givaja, *When Parents Pay for Their Children's Wrongs: Attribution of Liability for EC Antitrust Infringements in Parent-Subsidiary Scenarios*, in *World Competition*, 2006, p. 555.

least controversial connecting factors recognized in public international law. This is precisely what the Commission proposed, and the ECJ endorsed, in *Dyestuffs*. ICI was involved in the cartel through one of its subsidiaries located in the (then) EEC. Such subsidiary enjoyed no economic independence: it merely carried out the instructions received by the parent company. Despite the separation of legal personality, ICI and the subsidiary constituted a single economic entity: therefore, the former could be held liable and fined for the participation of the latter in the cartel, without the need to either approve or disapprove the adoption of the effects doctrine in the (then) EEC legal order.

However, the single economic entity doctrine is inherently not suitable to broaden the extraterritorial reach of EU competition rules to such an extent that they can cover all the foreign conducts that may potentially distort competition within the internal market. For example, it is not possible to rely on such theory in order to apply art. 101 TFEU to a cartel or a concerted practice involving only foreign companies selling their products, or providing their services, in the EU directly from their third country of origin, without setting up any subsidiary in any Member State. This would provide undertakings with an easy way to evade competition rules and harm the internal market.

The willingness to fill the gaps caused by the limits of the single economic entity doctrine led the ECJ to develop a second theory, *i.e.* the implementation doctrine. This doctrine was established for the first time in the equally famous *Wood Pulp* case[83], although it was probably not necessary for the solution of the dispute[84]. The case concerned a concerted practice between several foreign wood pulp producers and two foreign trade associations. All the economic operators involved in the concentred practice contested the

83 Cf. ECJ, 27 September 1988, joined cases 89, 104, 114, 116, 117 and 125 to 129/85, *A. Ahlström Osakeyhtiö and others* v *Commission (Wood Pulp I)*, [1988] *ECR* p. 5193. See F.A. Mann, *The Public International Law of Restrictive Practices in the European Court of Justice*, in *International and Comparative Law Quarterly*, 1989, p. 375; D.F.G. Lange, J.B. Sandage, *The Wood Pulp Decision*, in *Common Market Law Review*, 1989, p. 137; E. Breibart, *The Wood Pulp Case: The Application of European Economic Community Competition Law to Foreign Based Undertakings*, in *Georgia Journal of International and Comparative Law*, 1989, p. 149; V. Lowe, *International Law and the Effects Doctrine in the European Court of Justice*, in *The Cambridge Law Journal*, 1989, p. 9; M. Friend, *The Long Arm of Community Law*, in *European Law Review*, 1989, p. 169.

84 Since all the companies involved in the concerted practices had subsidiaries or other establishments within the EEC, and therefore the Commission could probably assert its jurisdiction even on the ground of the single economic entity. Nevertheless, the ECJ held that "[i]*t is irrelevant* [...] *whether or not* [the producers] *had recourse to subsidiaries, agents, sub-agents, or branches within the Community in order to make their contacts with purchasers within the Community*" (cf. joined cases 89, 104, 114, 116, 117 and 125 to 129/85, *Wood Pulp I*, cit., § 17).

Commission jurisdiction since they all had their registered offices abroad. Once again, the ECJ was encouraged to adopt the effects doctrine, this time by Advocate General Darmon who passionately stated that this choice was compatible with public international law[85].

Although it did not follow the suggestion, the ECJ came up with a quite similar solution. Such solution relies on the observation that the anticompetitive practices that can trigger the application of art. 101 TFEU are composed by two elements: the formation of the practice and its implementation[86]. The ECJ held that the second element is the decisive factor in order to establish jurisdiction. It follows that art. 101 TFEU can be applied to all the anticompetitive practices that are implemented within the EU, regardless of the places where the cartelists are based, the anticompetitive agreement is formed, or the goods are produced. In this light, the affinity with the effects doctrine is quite evident. Even if in *Wood Pulp* the ECJ carefully avoided to use the term "effects", both the theories focus on the "consequences" of the antitrust offence, rather than on the location of the infringers when the anticompetitive practice was carried out, or the place where such practice was formed. Therefore, they are both based on the objective territoriality principle, and both provide with jurisdiction those States whose market is affected by a foreign anticompetitive practice.

Although similar, the two doctrines are quite obviously not identical[87]. The most important difference concerns their respective extraterritorial reach. In other words, the question is whether an anticompetitive conduct may have effects on a given market, while not being implemented in that market. The answer to such question requires a clarification of the term

---

85 In short, after a quite long review of the relevant case law and legal literature, Advocate General Darmon concluded that "*there is no rule of international law which is capable of being relied upon against the criterion of the direct, substantial and foreseeable effect*" (cf. Opinion of Advocate General Darmon, 25 May 1988, joined cases 89, 104, 114, 116, 117 and 125 to 129/85, *A. Ahlström Osakeyhtiö and others* v *Commission (Wood Pulp I)*, [1988] *ECR* p. 5214, § 57).

86 Cf. joined cases 89, 104, 114, 116, 117 and 125 to 129/85, *Wood Pulp I*, cit., § 16.

87 *Inter alia*, see J.P. Griffin, *Extraterritoriality in U.S. and EU Antitrust Enforcement*, in *Antitrust Law Journal*, 1999, p. 159; P. Torremans, *Extraterritorial Application of E.C. and U.S. Competition Law*, in *European Law Review*, 1996, p. 280; R.P. Alford, *The Extraterritorial Application of Antitrust Laws: The United States and the European Approaches*, in *Virginia Journal of International Law*, 1992, p. 1; J.J. Friedberg, *The Convergence of Law in an Era of Political Integration: The Wood Pulp Case and the Alcoa Effects Doctrine*, in *University of Pittsburgh Law Review*, 1991, p. 289; S.T. Gubner, *Wood Pulp – The European Economic Community and Effects Doctrine Jurisdiction: The Community's New Weapon*, in *Transnational Lawyer*, 1990, p. 759.

"implementation". In *Wood Pulp*, the ECJ held that the producers and the trade associations "*implemented their pricing agreement within the* [c]*ommon* [m]*arket*" since they were directly selling the products concerned by the price fixing practice to European customers[88]. Due to these direct sales, the concerted practice was "implemented" in the (then) EEC, and therefore caught by art. 101 TFEU.

In the recent *InnoLux* case[89], the ECJ[90] further clarified that an anticompetitive agreement is "implemented" into the EU even if the sales to EU customers do not directly concern the cartelised products, but rather only finished products that incorporate the cartelised products as an input. The case concerned a worldwide cartel among the major international manufacturers of LCD panels for computer and television monitors, all established outside the EEA. One of the particularities of the case was precisely that only a few of the cartelised products (the LCD panels) were directly imported into the EEA. Indeed, the manufactures usually sold almost all the cartelised products to their foreign subsidiaries, so that the latter could use them as input to produce other goods (televisions and computers). Only the transformed products were then imported into the EEA. According to the Commission, the sales of the finished products incorporating the cartelised products were enough to consider the cartel implemented in the EEA.

Being one of the vertically integrated companies involved in the cartel, InnoLux claimed that in so doing the Commission exceeded the limits of its territorial jurisdiction[91]. On the one hand, the direct sales of finished products could not be considered as direct sales of cartelised LCD panels into the EEA. On the other hand, art. 101 TFEU could catch the internal sales of the cartelised products within vertically integrated undertakings only if they occurred in the EEA[92], otherwise being purely foreign transactions between foreign companies.

Following an approach later confirmed by the ECJ[93], the General Court dismissed the appeal, confirming that the Commission had territorial jurisdic-

88 Cf. joined cases 89, 104, 114, 116, 117 and 125 to 129/85, *Wood Pulp I*, cit., § 17.
89 ECJ, 27 February 2014, case T-91/11, *InnoLux Corp.* v *European Commission*, NYR.
90 Within the meaning of Article 19 TUE, according to which the ECJ includes, at least, the Court of Justice and the General Court.
91 Cf. case T-91/11, *InnoLux*, cit., § 56.
92 Cf. case T-91/11, *InnoLux*, cit., § 72.
93 Indeed, although the point was not directly appealed by InnoLux, the ECJ has taken the chance to repeat that "*it is apparent from the case-law of the Court of Justice that when undertakings which are established outside the EEA, but which produce goods that are sold within the EEA to third parties, collude on the prices they charge to their customers in the EEA and put that collusion into effect by*

tion to proceed against the global cartel. It follows that a given cartel is "implemented" in the EU, within the meaning of *Wood Pulp*, even when "*the products to which* [it] *relates are – before they reach the internal market – first the subject of a transaction between two companies which are established outside the EEA and are part of the undertaking that has participated in the cartel*"[94].

Arguably, as highlighted in the opinion of Advocate General Wathelet[95], this wide interpretation of the implementation doctrine further reduces the

---

selling at prices which are actually coordinated, they are taking part in collusion which has the object and effect of restricting competition within the internal market within the meaning of Article 101 TFEU and which the Commission has territorial jurisdiction to proceed against" (cf. ECJ, 9 July 2015, case C-231/14 P, *InnoLux Corp.* v *European Commission*, NYR, § 72).

94 Cf. case T-91/11, *InnoLux*, cit., § 73. After all, "*when the cartelised LCD panels made by the applicant were incorporated into finished products by companies belonging to the same undertaking as the applicant and those finished products were sold in the EEA by that undertaking, the cartel must be considered to have affected the transactions which took place up to and including the moment of that sale*" (cf. case T-91/11, *InnoLux*, cit., § 70), either because the "*sales internal to that undertaking were made at higher prices because of the cartel*", either because "*the harmfulness resides in the competitive advantage enjoyed by the undertaking participating in the cartel by comparison with the other undertakings which make finished products incorporating cartelised LCD panels but which purchase those panels at a price that does not result from normal market conditions*" (cf. case T-91/11, *InnoLux*, cit., § 71).

95 Indeed, Advocate General Wathelet concluded that "*the only justification for the Commission's having jurisdiction with regard to the sales at issues must arise in this case from the application of the 'qualified effects' test*" (cf. Opinion of Advocate General Wathelet, 30 April 2015, case C-231/14 P, *InnoLux Corp.* v *European Commission*, NYR, § 48). The main reasons of this conclusion being that "[w]*hat triggers the EU's jurisdiction, in accordance with the criterion of implementation developed in* Woodpulp I, *is the sale in the EEA of the products which are the subject of the concerted action, being, in this case, LCD panels. Significantly, there is no finding in the contested decision of any concerted action relating to the finished products that incorporate the LCD panels manufactured by the cartel participants. Equally, the General Court failed to have regard to the criterion expressed in* Woodpulp I *when it stated* [...] *that sales of the finished products incorporating the LCD panels 'were harmful to competition within the EEA'. Suffice it to recall that the sales of the finished products were not made on the market within the EEA to which the infringement related, that is to say, the market for LCD panels. Finally, contrary to the General Court's assertion* [...], *it is not sufficient to identify the sales 'having [any] link [whatsoever] with the EEA' in order to establish the territorial applicability of EU competition law, in accordance with the criterion laid down in* Woodpulp I. *What needs to be shown is the sale, within the EEA, of the product in respect of which the infringement was committed, in this case, LCD panels. The sale of a different product, one which incorporates an LCD panel as a component*

distance with the effects doctrine[96]. However, differences resist and the scope of the former theory remains narrower. The literature suggests at least three scenarios where the implementation doctrine may lead to different outcomes than those that would be reached if the effects doctrine were applied[97]. Two of these scenarios concern foreign negative conducts (*i.e.*, cases where foreign companies refuse to deal with EU undertakings), while the latter pertains to behaviours that only indirectly affect the internal market. In the first scenario, foreign companies decide to "boycott" EU undertakings, refusing to buy their products. In the second scenario, foreign undertakings (likely, producers of raw materials) refuse to supply EU undertakings, for example because they are part of a market share agreement. In the third scenario, foreign cartelists do not import the cartelised products directly to the EU, but rather sell them to a foreign dealer (not involved in the price fixing agreement), well aware of the fact that the dealer will then sell the cartelised products to EU customers.

While these anticompetitive behaviours may quite certainly have "effects" within the EU, there are little doubts that they are not "implemented" in the internal market. Therefore, the implementation doctrine does not provide the Commission with jurisdiction over those conducts, not allowing the application of artt. 101 and 102 TFEU.

8 … to the recent endorsement of the "effects doctrine"

In the light of the above, one may understand why the Commission[98] and several Advocates General have recommended the ECJ to replace the imple-

---

that is not itself the subject-matter of the sale, does not fulfil that requirement" (cf. Advocate General Wathelet, case C-231/14 P, *InnoLux*, cit., § 65).

96 To be sure, it has even been argued that in the *InnoLux* case "*the Court of Justice was asserting jurisdiction over an entirely foreign conduct which had an effect on the EU market*", and that "[t]*he necessary link between the foreign conduct and the local effect, in the view of the Court of Justice, was a component-finished product relationship, meaning that the cartelised good is a component of a final product sold locally*" (cf. S.S.H. Chan, *InnoLux Corp v. European Commission: Establishment of the effects doctrine in extra-territoriality of EU competition law?*, in *European Competition Law Review*, 2015, p. 463, spec. p. 467).

97 See, *inter alia*, F. Wagner Von Papp, *op. cit.*, pp. 45-46; A. Jones, B. Sufrin, *op. cit.*, p. 1277; S.S.H. Chan, *InnoLux Corp v. European Commission*, cit., 466; J.P. Griffin, *Foreign Governmental Reactions to US Assertions of Extraterritorial Jurisdiction*, in *European Competition Law Review*, 1998, p. 68.

98 To be precise, the Commission has not always called for the substitution of the implementation doctrine with the effects doctrine. Rather, anticipating the approach that has been later followed by the General Court (cf. case T-286/09, *Intel*, cit.), it has sometimes asserted that the two theories are alternative ways for the purposes of establishing jurisdiction. In this vein, the Commission has for example affirmed

mentation doctrine by explicitly recognising the applicability of the effects doctrine within the EU legal order[99]. On the one hand, the implementation doctrine does not allow the Commission to assert its jurisdiction over some kinds of anticompetitive behaviours that may nonetheless harm the internal market. On the other hand, the implementation and the effects doctrines reach diverging outcomes only in a very limited number of cases; conversely, in the vast majority of circumstances, it makes no practical difference, for the purposes of establishing jurisdiction, whether the one or the other doctrine is applied. Therefore, having two theories, formulated in two slightly different ways, (only) occasionally leading to different solutions, does not seem to be the most effective method to deal with the complex issues arising from the extraterritorial application of domestic competition rules, but rather it appears just as a useless way to create legal uncertainty[100].

Nevertheless, until very recently, the ECJ has always refused to take an explicit stand in favour (or against) of the effects doctrine. To be sure, there are few cases where the Court stopped just short of doing so. For example, the judgments handed down quite some time ago in *Béguelin* and *Gencor* already gave hints in this direction[101]. More recently, the ECJ came close to

---

that artt. 101 and 102 TFEU "*apply irrespective of where the undertakings are located or where the agreement has been concluded, provided that the agreement or practice is either implemented inside the* [EU], *or produce effects inside the* [EU]" (cf. Guidelines on the effect on trade concept contained in artt. 81 and 82 of the Treaty (2004/C 101/07), in *OJ C*, n. 101, 27 April 2004, p. 81, § 100).

99 As seen, the endorsement of the effects doctrine was recommended, *inter alia*, by Advocate General Mayras (cf. case 48/69, *Dyestuff*, cit.), by Advocate General Darmon (cf. joined cases 89, 104, 114, 116, 117 and 125 to 129/85, *Wood Pulp I*, cit.), and finally by Advocate General Wathelet (cf. case C-231/14 P, *InnoLux*, cit.).

100 *Inter alia*, see F. Wagner Von Papp, *op. cit.*, p. 45.

101 The first case concerned a vertical agreement between a foreign manufacturer and one of its dealers established in a Member State. The ECJ held that "[t]*he fact that one of the undertakings which are parties to the agreement is situate in a third country does not prevent* [the] *application of* [Article 101 TFEU] *since the agreement is operative on the territory of the common market*" (cf. ECJ, 25 November 1971, case 22/71, *Béguelin Import Co.* v *S.A.G.L. Import Export* [1971] *ECR* 949, § 11). However, it has to be noted that one of the companies involved was established in the (then) EEC and that no actions or fines were envisaged against the foreign undertaking. In the second case, the Commission prohibited a merger between two companies incorporated in South Africa, stating that the application of EU rules on the control of concentrations between undertakings (then Council Regulation (EEC) n. 4064/89 of 21 December 1989, *OJ*, L 395, 30 December 1989, p. 1, now replaced by Council Regulation (EC) n. 139/2004 of 20 January 2004, *OJ L* 24, 29 January 2004, p. 1) was "*justified under public international law*" because it was "*foreseeable that* [the] *proposed concentration* [was going to] *have an immediate and substantial effect in the Community*" (cf. case T-102/96,

recognize the validity of the effects doctrine both in the *ICI* and in the *Nexans* cases[102]. However, the quoted passages were basically made as *obiter dicta*,

---

Gencor, cit., § 90). However, this statement is not conclusive as to the adoption of the effects doctrine, since the ECJ also clarified that "[t]*he Commission did not err in its assessment of the territorial scope of the* [merger] *Regulation by applying it in this case to a proposed concentration notified by undertakings whose registered offices and mining and production operation* [were] *outside the Community*", because, according to *Wood Pulp* (cf. joined cases 89, 104, 114, 116, 117 and 125 to 129/85, *Wood Pulp I*, cit.), "[t]*he criterion as to the implementation of an agreement is satisfied by mere sale within the Community, irrespective of the location of the sources of supply and the production plant*" (cf. case T-102/96, *Gencor*, cit., §§ 87-88). On the first case, see *Beguelin Import Company v. S.A. G. L. Import Export - Case 22/71*, in *Antitrust Bulletin*, 1972, p. 1125. On the second case, see U. Draetta, *The international jurisdiction of the E.U. Commission in the merger control area*, in *Revue de droit des affaires internationals*, 2000, p. 201; M.P. Broberg, *The European Commission's Extraterritorial Powers in Merger Control. The Court of First Instance's Judgment in Gencor v. Commission*, in *International and Comparative Law Quarterly*, 2000, p. 172; Y. Van Gerven, L. Hoet, *Gencor: Some Notes on Transnational Competition Law Issues - European Court of First Instance 25 March 1999, T-102/96, Gencor Ltd. v. Commission*, in *Legal Issues of Economic Integration*, 2001, p. 195.

102 In the first case, explicitly referring to the *Béguelin* judgment (cf. case 22/71, *Béguelin*, cit.) the ECJ affirmed that "*EU competition law is applicable to a cartel which produces effects within the internal market irrespective of the fact that one of the undertakings participating in an agreement is located in a third country*" (cf. T-406/08, *ICF*, cit., § 210). The most interesting aspect of the second case relates to the fact that, unlike all the others, it does not concern prescriptive jurisdiction. Indeed, what was at stake was whether or not, during the so-called dawn raids, the Commission could get access to information relating to transactions occurred outside the EU internal market, *i.e.* a matter of enforcement jurisdiction. While admitting that the Commission cannot perform a dawn raid if it suspects that the alleged offence produces effects only outside the internal market, the ECJ affirmed that the Commission can examine documents relating to foreign markets "*in order to detect conduct which is liable to affect trade between Member States and which has as its object or effect the prevention, restriction or distortion of competition within the common market*" (cf. ECJ, 25 June 2014, case C-37/13 P, *Nexans SA and Nexans France SAS* v *European Commission*, NYR, § 27). As better clarified by Adovate General Kokot, the main reason is that "*the existence of anti-competitive practices with potentially adverse effects on competition on the internal market may quite conceivably be drawn also from business records relating to local projects in third countries*". For example, this may happen when "*those documents shed light on the modus operandi of a globally-operated cartel or where, because of their links to transactions within the European Union, the projects concerned may themselves have an impact on the internal market*". And, "[f]*rom the point of view of international law, that connection is sufficient to justify the examination of such business records by the Commission in the course*

rather than clear statements, and are therefore not conclusive as to the acceptance of the effects doctrine by the Court.

The decisive step in this direction has been taken by the General Court in the famous *Intel* case[103], where the Court has entirely upheld the much debated Commission decision against such US based undertaking. As is well known, the case concerned Intel's abuse of its dominant position on the worldwide market for microprocessors. Microprocessors are an essential component of any computer, and therefore a necessary input for computer manufacturers. According to the judgment, Intel adopted an anticompetitive strategy aimed at foreclosing from such market its only significant competitor, AMD. The strategy was implemented by means of the commercial relations between Intel and its most important trading partners, *i.e.* the world's major computer manufacturers and the EU largest computer retailer. The strategy had a twofold dimension: Intel was involved in both exclusivity rebates[104] and

---

of a preliminary investigation" (cf. Opinion of Advocate General Kokott, 3 April 2014, case C-37/13 P, *Nexans SA and Nexans France SAS* v *European Commission*, NYR, § 70).

103 Cf. case T-286/09, *Intel*, cit. The deluge of comments already demonstrates the great importance of the judgment, which goes well beyond the realm of extraterritorial jurisdiction. *Inter alia*, see A.F. Özkan, *The Intel judgment: the Commission threw the first stone but the EU courts will throw the last*, in *European Competition Journal*, 2015 p. 69; N. Petit, *Intel, leveraging rebates and the goals of Article 102 TFEU*, in *European Competition Journal*, 2015, p. 26; B. Sher, *Keep Calm – Yes; Carry on – No! A Response to Whish on Intel*, in *Journal of European Competition Law & Practice*, 2015, 219; R. Whish, *Intel v Commission: Keep Calm and Carry on!*, in *Journal of European Competition Law & Practice*, 2015, 1; P. Ibáñez Colomo, *Intel and Article 102 TFEU Case Law: Making Sense of a Perpetual Controversy*, London School of Economics Law, Society and Economy Working Papers n. 29/2014; P. Nihoul, *The Ruling of the General Court in Intel: Towards the End of an Effect-based Approach in European Competition Law?*, in *Journal of European Competition Law & Practice*, 2014, 521; J.S. Venit, *Case T-286/09 Intel v Commission – The Judgment of the General Court: All Steps Backward and No Steps Forward*, in *European Competition Journal*, 2014, 203; W.P.J. Wils, *The judgment of the EU General Court in Intel and the so-called 'more economic approach' to abuse of dominance*, in *World Competition*, 2014, p. 405.

104 *I.e.*, «*rebates which were conditioned on* [the receiving computer manufacturers] *purchasing all or almost all of their x86 CPUs from Intel. Similarly, Intel awarded payments to MSH, which were conditioned on MSH selling exclusively computers containing Intel's x86 CPUs*» (cf. case T-286/09, *Intel*, cit., § 28).

naked restrictions[105]. The General Court held that both the practices represent a restriction by object of art. 102 TFEU[106].

From the general perspective, such assessment of the first conduct is by far the most interesting aspect of the judgement. Indeed, the treatment of exclusivity rebates has always been one of the most controversial topics in competition law. In a nutshell, by affirming that such conducts are *per se* prohibited under art. 102 TFEU, the General Court has basically confirmed the validity of the formalistic and non-welfarist approach to EU competition rules (and policy).

However, from the viewpoint of the extraterritorial application of artt. 101 and 102 TFEU, the second conduct is the one that matters most. Indeed, by implementing the so-called naked restrictions *vis-à-vis* some of its trading partners based outside the EU, Intel was essentially granting payments to foreign companies in order to incentivise them not to sell certain products (*i.e.*, those incorporating microprocessors built by Intel's competitor) within the EU. In other words, what was at stake was a foreign negative conduct (*i.e.*, a refusal to deal with EU consumers opposed by a foreign company), that only indirectly affected the internal market, since it was carried out by an "innocent" foreign company that did not commit any direct abusive behaviour, not even holding a dominant position. It was therefore doubtful whether Intel conduct could be considered as "implemented" in the internal market.

The General Court solved this question at its very roots, by saying that the effects doctrine was already fully recognized by the ECJ case law as a concept of EU competition law. As an alternative to the implementation doctrine, the Commission could therefore apply also the effects doctrine to assert its

105 *I.e.*, «*payments which were conditioned* on [the receiving computer manufacturers] *postponing or cancelling the launch of AMD CPU-based products and/ or putting restrictions on the distribution of those products*» (cf. case T-286/09, *Intel*, cit., § 32).

106 As far as exclusivity rebates are concerned, the General Court clarified that, when «*granted by an undertaking in a dominant position*», such rebates «*are by their very nature capable of restricting competition*» (cf. case T-286/09, *Intel*, cit., § 85). Similarly, the General Court affirmed that «*by applying naked restrictions* [Intel] *pursued an anti-competitive object*», because «[t]*he only interest that an undertaking in a dominant position may have in preventing in a targeted manner the marketing of products equipped with a product of a specific competitor is to harm that competitor*» (cf. case T-286/09, *Intel*, cit., § 204). Therefore, the Court found it «*permissible to conclude that the implementation of each of the so-called 'naked restrictions' amounted to an abuse of a dominant position within the meaning of Article 82 EC*» (cf. case T-286/09, *Intel*, cit., § 206).

extraterritorial jurisdiction over Intel's abuse[107]. Of course, it has still to be seen whether the ECJ will confirm such approach[108]. If this were the case, it would follow that, if jurisdiction can be established because the conduct was implemented in the EU, it is not necessary to examine whether the conduct had also any effects on the internal market[109]. However, if the conduct was not implemented in the EU, the Commission jurisdiction can be established (and justified under public international law) as far as "*the criteria of immediate, substantial and foreseeable effect in the European Union* [are] *satisfied*"[110].

9 The agreement between the EU and the Swiss Confederation concerning cooperation on the application of their competition laws: a preliminary introduction

December 1st, 2014, the agreement between the European Union and the Swiss Confederation concerning cooperation on the application of their competition laws came into force[111].

107 More specifically, according to the General Court, the ECJ case law points out that "*demonstrating the implementation of the practices at issue in the EEA or demonstrating qualified effects are alternative and not cumulative approaches for the purposes of establishing that the Commission's jurisdiction is justified under the rules of public international law*" (cf. case T-286/09, Intel, cit., § 236). On the one hand, in *Woodpulp* "*the Court of Justice relied solely on the implementation of the conduct at issue in the territory of the European Union*" (cf. case T-286/09, Intel, cit., § 237), while in Gencor "the Court [of First Instance] *confined itself to examining whether the criteria of immediate, substantial and foreseeable effect were satisfied*" (cf. case T-286/09, Intel, cit., § 242).

108 The judgment has been appealed by Intel and the case is still pending (cf. case C-413/14 P). Among many other and more substantial grounds of appeal, Intel contested also that the General Court has incorrectly established the Commission jurisdiction over its agreements with one of its foreign trading partners.

109 Cf. case T-286/09, Intel, cit., § 238.

110 Cf. case T-286/09, Intel, cit., § 243.

111 Agreement between the European Union and the Swiss Confederation concerning cooperation on the application of their competition laws, cit. Negotiations on the definition of the agreement started in November 2010 (and were carried on by the Commission, on behalf of the European Union, upon authorization by the Council). The negotiations were completed on December 7th, 2011, after ten rounds of consultations. On June 1st, 2012, the European Commission submitted two proposals for Council decisions on the signing and on the conclusion of the agreement, which occurred on May 17th, 2013 (cf. COM(2012) 244 final and COM(2012) 245 final). This was followed by the approval of both the European Parliament (20 June 2014) and the Council (21 October 2014). Finally, the Agreement entered into force on December 1st, 2014.

This agreement regulates the relationship between the European Union and the Swiss Confederation in the antitrust field, in the view of assuring the effective enforcement of the rules concerning competition in the case of cross-border anticompetitive conducts, in particular by regulating the exchange of information collected during investigations from the two authorities in charge for the protection of competition policy (the Commission for the European Union and the Swiss Competition Commission for the Swiss Confederation[112], named *breviter* COMCO).

As by art. 1, the purpose of the agreement is, in fact, «to contribute to the effective enforcement of the competition laws of each Party through cooperation and coordination, including the exchange of information, between the competition authorities of the Parties and to avoid or lessen the possibility of conflicts between the Parties in all matters concerning the application of the competition laws of each Party».

It is an international agreement – so it is suitable to bind the European Union and the Member States *ex* art. 216, § 2, TFEU – and not a plain administrative agreement between the two antitrust authorities[113]. It was in fact signed directly by the European Union[114] and by Switzerland, which are formally referred to as the "Parties".

The agreement in question is part of an articulated and extensive framework of bilateral agreements, between the European Union and Switzerland,

112 Established by the Federal Act on Cartels and other Restraints of Competition of 6 October 1995 (so-called Cartel Act or CartA). See in particular chapter IV, sez. I, articles from 18 to 25. Cf. also COMCO Internal Regulation, recently amended on 15 June 2015.

113 See *France v Commission* case (Court just., 9 August 1994, C-327/1991, *ECR* I-3641), as the Commission contended that the agreement signed on 23 September 1991 by itself and the USA Government regarding the application of their competition laws represented an administrative agreement which the Commission was competent to conclude. The Court did not accept that argument, as a consequence thereof the act whereby the Commission sought to conclude the agreement with USA was declared void, due to lack of power of the Commission to autonomously conclude international agreements in the competition field to be binding for the European Union (at that time European Community). For a keen analysis of the judgment, see C. Kaddous, *L'arrêt France c. Commission de 1994 (accord concurrence) et le contrôle de la "légalité" des accords externes en vertu de l'art. 173 CE: la difficile réconciliation de l'orthodoxie communautaire avec l'orthodoxie internationale*, in *Cahiers de droit européen*, 1996, p. 613 ss.; M. Mendez, *The Legal Effects of EU Agreements. Maximalist Treaty Enforcement and Judicial Avoidance Techniques*, Oxford University Press, Oxford, 2013, p. 78 ss.

114 Therefore the agreement shall not be construed as mixed agreement since, on the European side, it was signed only by the European Union and not jointly by this latter and the Member States.

which until have ensured the rapprochement of the two legal systems and the pursuit by the Swiss Confederation of an active European policy, despite lacking of accession to the European Union of this latter[115].

115 Switzerland, as known, is not an European Union Member State; however, it pursues a real "European policy" through agreements signed with the European Union in certain specific matters. The first agreement is the Free Trade Agreement of 1972, *OJ*, L 300, p. 189, which, in art. 32, provides a clause that allows the Union and Switzerland to extend their relations to other uncovered fields, in so far that this is considered useful for the economies of the two legal systems ("where a contracting party considers that it would be useful in the interests of the economies of both contracting parties to develop the relations established by the agreement by extending them to fields not covered thereby, it shall submit a reasoned request to the other contracting party"). The Free Trade Agreement gives ground to the expansion of the economic relations between the European Union and Switzerland, which are developed through a network of bilateral agreements based on the adoption, by Switzerland, of the European *acquis* or, more frequently, on the equivalence between the two legal systems. C. Sanna, *Gli accordi bilaterali tra la Svizzera e l'Unione europea*, in *Dir. comm. internaz.*, 2/2000, p. 547 ss. and particularly p. 550 points out that: "in tal modo è maggiormente preservata l'autonomia legislativa della Svizzera, anche se mantenere l'equivalenza, tenendo conto costantemente dell'evoluzione del diritto comunitario nei settori rientranti negli accordi settoriali, è, di fatto, nell'interesse della Confederazione". For a general overview on bilateral agreements signed between the European Union and the Swiss Confederation cf., *ex plurimis*, F. Emmert, *Switzerland and the EU: Partners, for Better or for Worse*, in *European Foreign Affairs Review*, 10/1998, p. 367 ss.; D. Felder, C. Kaddous (sous la direction de/herausg.), *Accords bilatéraux Suisse-UE: (commentaires), Bilaterale Abkommen Schweiz-Eu: (erste Analysen)*, Bruylant, Bruxelles, 2001; S. Breitenmoser, *Sectoral Agreements Between the EC and Switzerland: Contents and Context,* in *Com. Market Law Rev*, 2003, p. 1137 ss., who affirms that: "the system of the sectoral agreements might be called a new means of "differentiated integration", somewhere between cooperation and integration" (p. 1185); M. Maresceau, *Bilateral Agreements concluded by the European Community*, in *Collected Courses of the Hague Academy of International Law*, 2004, vol. 309, p. 412 ss.; A. Lang, C.Sanna (Eds.), *Federalismo e regionalismo. Esperienze italiana, svizzera e dell'Unione europea a confronto*, Giuffré, Milano, 2005; C. Kaddous, M. Jametti Greiner (sous la direction de/herausg.), *Accords bilatéraux II Suisse-UE et autres accords récents/Bilteral Abkommen II Schweiz-UE und andere neue Abkommen*, Helbing & Lichtenhahn, Bâle, 2006; E. Baroncini, *Il* treaty making power *della Commissione europea,* Libreria Bonomo, Bologna, 2008, p. 261 ss.; M. Condinanzi (Ed.), *Unione europea e Svizzera tra cooperazione e integrazione*, op. cit., whose *Presentazione* highlights that the "European policy" pursued by Switzerland since the Seventies led it to take on a "condizione giuridica marcatamente differenziata da quella degli altri stati terzi, pure legati all'Unione da accordi internazionali", so that "la prospettiva convenzionale bilaterale, che certo consegna le relazioni Svizzera – UE al modello della cooperazione, con

Nevertheless, the EU/Switzerland agreement in the antitrust field constitutes a new experience with significant traits of originality both *(i)* having regard to other bilateral international agreements today in force between the European Union and third Countries in this branch, and *(ii)* within the framework of bilateral relationships between the European Union and Switzerland, as it extends bilateral cooperation to a sector essentially remained apart from it.

As to the first point, the agreement aims to establish tighter and more efficient forms of cooperation between the competition authorities of both Parties than those currently possible on the basis of the other bilateral agreements concerning competition law to date in force between the European Union and third Countries (on these latter, see § 2 below). These agreements share the fact that they subordinate the exchange, between competition authorities, of confidential information relating to commercial activities of undertakings to the prior consent from these latter, to the extent that they are involved in the investigations; as known, this is the main limitation to the effective prosecution of cross-border anti-competitive conducts. The EU/Switzerland agreement tackles this issue, as it allows the exchange of information – to some extent – even in lack of the consent of the interested subject. It is of no surprise that, because of its innovative significance, the agreement in question was defined as the first agreement "of second generation" signed by the European Union with a third Country[116].

altrettanta sicurezza finisce con il presentare caratteri più 'intensi', evolutivi […] che spingono la relazione giuridica verso aspetti di integrazione", since "le norme convenzionali bilaterali ed uno spontaneo processo di 'adeguamento', sotto molti profili, al diritto dell'Unione europea, conferiscono all'ordinamento elvetico un elevato grado di "familiarità" con l'ambiente giuridico dell'Unione". See also: Swiss Federal Department of Foreign Affairs (FDFA), *Gli accordi bilaterali Svizzera-Unione europea*, 2014, available on line.

116 Cf. D. Mamane, S. Wittmer, *Competition Law Cooperation Agreement EU/ Switzerland*, 2012, available on line, who observe: "the Cooperation Agreement with Switzerland may be qualified ad a "second generation" cooperation agreement due to the fact that the scope of the information exchange is broader and information can be exchanged even against the will of the concerned companies, and in some cases outside of a formal investigation". See also: A.S. Papadopoulos, *The international dimension of EU competition law and policy*, in *The Cambridge Antitrust and Competition Law Series*, Cambridge, 2010, p. 83, where is pointed out that the second generation agreements feature more binding requirements than those found in first generation agreements, including the exchange of confidential information; P. Ducrey, *The agreement between Switzerland and the Eu concerning cooperation in the application of their competition laws*, in *Journal of European Competition law & practice*, 2013, p. 438 ss.

As to the second point, the agreement introduces, for the first time, a formal and official cooperation between the European Union and Switzerland in the field of antitrust law. It is therefore deepen the *ratio* behind such a recent choice[117]. Before this agreement came into force, in fact, the cooperation in the competition field between the two legal systems essentially was only informal and not legally binding[118], except for the air transportation sector, which is governed by an agreement providing – but only for the specific and limited sector of civil aviation – the enforcement of antitrust rules mainly descending from TFEU[119].

The present paper, after having put in context the EU/Switzerland agreement in light of the international and European experience in terms of cooperation in the competition field (§ 2), intends to analyse the contents thereof, in particular the innovative elements in respect of other agreements already signed by the EU with third Countries on the same subject (§ 3). In this view, a relevant part of the analysis will concentrate on the examination of the provisions that regulate the exchange of confidential information between the two competition authorities (§ 4). In more detail, the paper provides an analysis of the procedures and limits of transmission of information without the prior consent of the undertaking which provided the information and a survey of the consequences of this framework on the relationship between the European Commission and national competition authorities, which are expressly taken into account by art. 10 of the agreement in question for the exchange of confidential information.

Finally, the paper aims at presenting the effects of the innovative elements of the agreement (§ 5), with a view to verifying whether and to what extent the choice of formalising the antitrust cooperation with Switzerland, by over-

---

117 Together with several other States, Switzerland has long standing formalized and institutionalized its cooperation *(i)* within the European Free Trade Association (EFTA); *(ii)* through specific memorandum of understanding with foreign antitrust authorities; and *(iii)* through bilateral free trade agreements, which also provide a discipline of cooperation in competition field.

118 Based on the recommendations drawn up within the Organisation for Economic Co-operation and Development (OECD) and within the International Competition Network (ICN). For further analysis, see *infra*, § 10.

119 Agreement between the European Community and the Swiss Confederation on Air Transport, entered into force on June 1st, 2002, *OJ*, L 114, p. 73. For a support, see for example: A. Auer, U. Haldimann, S. Hirsbrunner, *Accord sur le transport aérien*, in C. Kaddous, M. Jametti Greiner (sous la direction de/herausg.), *Accords bilatéraux*, *op.* cit., p. 435 ss.; F. Rossi Dal Pozzo, *L'evoluzione delle relazioni tra l'Unione europea e la Svizzera in materia di trasporti*, in M. Condinanzi (Ed.), *Unione europea e Svizzera tra cooperazione e integrazione*, op. cit., p. 355 ss.

coming the principle of the prior consent to the exchange of information, reflects the "special" nature of the Swiss Confederation for the European Union, not only from a geographic standpoint – immediately perceivable – but also and increasingly from an economic and legal standpoint.

10 Bilateral agreements on competition issues in the international and the European framework: a short background

The EU/Switzerland agreement, as already pointed out, is part of the bilateral international agreements in the competition field. Such agreements aim at ensuring the coordination of antitrust policies of both the States Parties of the relevant agreement, with a view of reducing the (negative) incidence of the differences in the enforcement of the respective legislation and of prosecuting and effectively sanctioning cross-border competition infringements (thus determining or being capable to determine consequences in the territory of a State other than the one where they were enacted)[120].

Bilateral agreements emerged over time as an alternative to multilateral cooperation, which aimed to identify uniform antitrust rules at international level, both substantively and as for procedural rules. Nevertheless, the multilateral approach struck unsatisfactory solutions along the years, or in any case not effective ones, since they only relied upon non-binding procedures of cooperation through soft law instruments. In fact, in theory it would be preferable to coordinate different antitrust laws by means of a sole agreement so as to uniformly bind a plurality of legal systems[121]; but the experience reveals that a sole regime on competition law is not realistic and too ambitious[122], considered

120 Reference can be made, for example, to the international cartels, the mergers among multinational undertakings, the abuses of dominance by foreign undertakings. For comparisons between bilateral cooperation instruments in antitrust field and the unilateral extraterritorial application of competition law through the so-called "effects doctrine", see, *inter alia*, the references in note n. 145.

121 Cit. S. Bastianon, P. M. Ferrari, *Gli strumenti di cooperazione internazionale in materia antitrust e i rapporti intercorrenti tra l'Unione europea e la Svizzera*, in M. Condinanzi (Ed.), *Unione europea e Svizzera tra cooperazione e integrazione*, op. cit., p. 307 ss. e spec. p. 329 ss. Coordination through multilateral agreements may significantly reduce conflicts of jurisdiction and competence (and it would also prevent a possible cumulation of sanctions), as well as the time and costs for the compliance, and it would enhance the circulation and the penetration of foreign undertakings thanks to a common standard of protection.

122 D.P. Wood, *The Impossible Dream: Real International Antitrust*, in *University of Chicago Legal Forum*, 1992, p. 277, figuratively referred to an "impossible dream". In the world there are more than one hundred States that have an antitrust legislation and are also at quite different stages of economic development. These significant diversities make it particularly complex to achieve a *consensus*

that, at the current state, an international *consensus* may be achieved though soft law instruments only, the application of which however depends on each State's will, there lacking mechanisms for judicial control.

This is not the right place for listing up all multilateral experiences from the late 40's up to now[123]; still, it is worth mentioning the recommendations and guidelines developed by the Organisation for Economic Co-operation and Development (hereinafter, OECD) since 1967. In particular, the recommendations of the Council as of October 5, 1967[124], as of July 3, 1973[125], as of September 25, 1979[126], as of May 21, 1986[127], as of July 27, 1995[128], as of March 23, 2005[129] and the Best Practices for the formal exchange of information between competition authorities in hard core cartels investigations of October 2005.

---

on certain aspects of the antitrust field, characterized by wide indeterminacy and by a marked economic profile. See, on this last aspect, S. Bastianon, P. M. Ferrari, *op. cit.*, p. 319 and spec. the references made at note n. 25.

123 Among the most significant experiences at the international level, mention could be made to the Havana Charter for an International Trade Organisation in 1948, which provided a core of common standard for the prosecution of anticompetitive practices affecting international trade, and, however, never entered into force because of non-ratification by the United States; as well as the recommendations and the guidelines drafted since the Sixties within the Organisation for Economic Co-operation and Development (OECD) and from the twenty-first Century, within the International Competition Network (ICN), with a view to promoting inter-state cooperation on an informal and non-binding plan. The most significant example of the difficulty in drawing up a uniform regulatory and binding covenant in the antitrust field is the failed draft of an international antitrust code. It has been studied by the United Nations Conference on Trade and Development (UNCTAD), which, as early as December 1980, has adopted a non-binding Set of Multilaterally Agreed Equitable Principles and Rules for the Control of Restrictive Business Practices. The draft code was then developed within the World Trade Organisation (WTO): in 1993, during the Uruguay Round of trade Negotiations, the Draft International Antitrust Code was presented, but never came into force. The project was taken up within a few years, also on the impulse of the European Union, and in 1996 a new working group was established, in order to temporarily represent a new, resized and less ambitious draft than the previous one, focused only on some aspects (in particular, on cartels). This was in view of the opening of new negotiations to be launched in 2003. However, the draft code was, once again, suspended in 2004, due to lack of *consensus* within the WTO.

124 C(67) 53(Final).

125 C(73) 99(Final).

126 C(79) 154(Final).

127 C(86) 44(Final).

128 C(95) 130(Final).

129 C(2005) 34(Final).

These are soft law instruments[130] that became models of cooperation even for negotiations of bilateral agreements on competition, which contain, as described below, many of the elements already elaborated in OECD. A significant example in this sense is the aforementioned recommendation of July 1995 "concerning Co-operation between Member Countries on Anticompetitive Practices affecting International Trade", which calls upon all Member States to communicate, by means of a mutual notification mechanism, the opening of any investigative process in antitrust field that may affect important interests of other States. The recommendation also underlines the necessity for the States to coordinate their own enforcement activities, by way of exchange of information, cooperation and coordination, when they open investigations against anticompetitive practices affecting international trade. This act provides some legal instruments (notifications, coordination of enforcement activities, exchange of information) that are typically included in bilateral agreements too, these latter representing, as of today, the main forms of cooperation in competition field by using hard law.

As to the European experience, starting from the 90's European Union implemented bilateral agreements with third States in the competition field, in the view of formalising the enforcement activities of each antitrust system with binding effects and with more articulated terms compared to OECD recommendations. Particularly, the European Union concluded agreements

130 The soft law instruments can still entail a so-called lawfulness effect, as they legitimize towards the other States the behaviour of those Countries that choose to comply with them. For further analysis, see I. DETTER, *Law Making by International Organizations,* P.A. Norstedt & Söners, Stockholm, 1965; J.P. JACQUÉ, *Eléments pour une théorie de l'acte juridique en droit international public*, Librairie générale de droit et de jurisprudence, Paris, 1972; V.D. DEGAN, *Sources of international law*, Nijoff ed., The Hague-Boston, 1997; B. CONFORTI, *Diritto internazionale*, Ed. Scientifica, Napoli, 2014, 10 ed.

(still in force) with the USA[131], Canada[132], Japan[133] and South Korea[134]. The EU/Switzerland agreement is designed in a scheme very similar to the previous agreements and is included in an existing formal cooperation framework which has given rise to positive effects[135]. In fact, the agreement contains all the typical legal instruments already provided by the previous agreements and it has a structure comparable to those, such structure neither providing a regulation of substantive antitrust rules, nor a rigid and predetermined distribution of competences between the competition authorities of both contract-

---

131 Cf. Agreement between the Government of the United States of America and the Commission of the European Communities regarding the application of their competition laws, *OJ*, L 95, of 27 April 1995, p. 47. The treaty was concluded on September 23rd, 1991, but was declared void by the Court of Justice in the aforementioned judgment of August 9th, 1994, *France v Commission*. As a consequence thereof, the agreement was renewed upon an exchange of interpretative letters (*OJ*, L 131, of 15 June 1995, p. 38 f.), without prejudice to the legal effects produced in the meantime. See also the Agreement between the European Communities and the Government of the United States of America on the application of positive comity principles in the enforcement of their competition laws (*OJ*, L 173, of 18 June 1998, p. 26 ss.) and the Best Practices on Cooperation in Merger Investigations, of 14 October 2011, on the coordination between the American competition authorities (Federal Trade Commission and Department of Justice) and the European Commission.

132 Cf. Agreement between the European Communities and the Government of Canada regarding the application of their competition laws, *OJ*, L 175, of 10 July 1999, p. 50.

133 Cf. Agreement between the European Community and the Government of Japan concerning cooperation on anticompetitive activities, *OJ*, L 183, of 22 July 2003, p. 12 ss.

134 Cf. Agreement between the Government of the Republic of Korea and the European Community concerning cooperation on anti-competitive activities, *OJ*, L 202, of 24 August 2009, p. 36 ss.

135 This positive practice is confirmed in the annual Reports by the Commission to the Council and the European Parliament on the application of the agreements and also in the above captioned Commission proposal on the signing of the EU/Switzerland agreement (COM(2012) 244 final), which at pt. 1 states: "these agreements can be regarded as successful. Their main benefit is that they put case related cooperation and the policy dialogue into a structured framework and thereby contribute to a more efficient competition law enforcement". The most important results of this cooperation are overviewed by B. Nascimbene, *Aspetti internazionali della politica di concorrenza comunitaria*, in *Dir. comm. internaz.*, 2/2001, p. 309 ss. and spec. pp. 323-326. Cf. also D. Geradin, M. Reysen, D. Henry, *Extraterritoriality, Comity, and Cooperation in EC Competition Law*, in *Social Science Research Network*, 2008, available on line, p. 7 ss.

ing Parties, but instead it identifies new ways of coordination of enforcement activities by means of new procedural obligations[136].

The main feature of the EU/Switzerland, as seen more clearly below, is instead represented by a new and more advanced legislation on exchange of information. This aspect emerges even more clearly once considered that, at the international level, the experience of the so-called "second generation" agreements, among which we can include the one in question, is not particularly widespread, exactly on account of the reluctance of the States to bind themselves with new ways of cooperation entailing stricter rules and obligations[137].

11 Typical contents of the EU/Swiss Confederation agreement

With regards to the contents of the EU/Switzerland agreement in question, they are attributable to the following typical legal instruments: *(i)* notifications; *(ii)* coordination of enforcement activities; *(iii)* negative comity; *(iv)* positive comity; *(v)* exchange of information. These elements will be analysed hereinafter, highlighting – when relevant – the differences with other bilateral agreements concluded by the European Union in antitrust field (in particular, those with the USA, hereinafter named as "the EC/USA agreement of 1991" and "the EC/USA agreement of 1998") and leaving for last the analysis of the exchange of information, which is tackled by the next paragraph.

Notifications are set forth for by art. 3 and are largely inspired by the aforementioned OECD recommendation of 1995. Pursuant to this article, both Parties to the agreement shall notify in writing each other any enforcement activities that "may affect" the other Party's important interests. In this view, § 2 of art. 3 lists, by way of example, some (more frequent) cases when activities and investigative process implemented by the competition authority of one Party may affect important interests of the other Party. In particular, it refers to enforcement activities "*(a)* concerning anticompetitive activities other than concentrations against an undertaking incorporated or organised under the laws and regulations applicable in the territory of the other Party; *(b)* which involve conduct believed to have been encouraged, required or approved by the other Party; *(c)* which involve a concentration in which one or

---

136 Observation of C. Schepisi, *Le relazioni esterne in materia di concorrenza: gli accordi CE/USA e CE/Canada tra dimensione internazionale e dimensione comunitaria*, in L. Daniele (Ed.), *Le relazioni esterne dell'Unione europea nel nuovo millennio*, Giuffré, Milano, 2001, p. 311 ss. and spec. p. 324.

137 Cf. Agreement between the Government of the United States of America and the Government of Australia on mutual antitrust enforcement assistance, concluded on April 27th, 1999, which, despite entering in force way before the EU/Switzerland agreement, it appears to have had a rather limited practical application.

more parties to the transaction is an undertaking incorporated or organised under the laws and regulations applicable in the territory of the other Party; *(d)* which involve a concentration in which an undertaking controlling one or more of the parties to the transaction is incorporated or organised under the laws and regulations applicable in the territory of the other Party; *(e)* against anticompetitive activities other than concentrations which also take place or took place to a significant extent in the territory of the other Party; *(f)* which involve remedies that expressly require or prohibit conduct in the territory of the other Party or contain binding obligations for the undertakings in that territory". Finally, the last paragraph of art. 3, differently from the previous agreements on this matter, specifies the content of the notification, disposing that "notifications shall include in particular the names of the parties to the investigation, the activities under examination and the markets they relate to, the relevant legal provisions and the date of the enforcement activities".

For as it is set forth, notifications appear to be a tool for the effective pursuit of the agreement's goals, since they can prevent problems between the Parties in the exercise of their respective enforcement activities. It has to be noted that, for reasons of simplification and rapidity, this agreement provides, for the first time, that the notifications can be served by electronic means (art. 3, § 1) and, in order to facilitate communications, they shall be made in the English language (art. 12, § 1).

For what concerns the regulation on coordination of the enforcement activities enacted by the antitrust authorities of both Parties, art. 4 of the EU/Switzerland agreement provides that: "where the competition authorities of both Parties are pursuing enforcement activities with regard to related matters, they may coordinate their enforcement activities". Coordination may particularly regard "the timing of their inspections" and takes into account above all the following elements: "*(a)* the effect of such coordination on the ability of the competition authorities of the Parties to achieve the objectives of their enforcement activities;[138] *(b)* the relative abilities of the competition authorities of the Parties to obtain information necessary to conduct the enforcement activities; *(c)* the possibility of avoiding conflicting obligations

138 It has to be noted that the EU/Switzerland agreement is sided by an exchange of explanatory notes between the Swiss Federal Council and the European Commission, of May 17th, 2013 (at the same time of the conclusion of the agreement) regarding notification of acts of exercise of public Authority in the field of competition. This issue is dealt with outside of the agreement upon request of the Commission, since the notification of similar acts to undertakings established in the territory of the Union is a competence of the EU Member States and therefore mutual regulation would require the conclusion of a mixed agreement (also involving the EU Member States), such as to make more difficult and lengthen the negotiations and conclusion of the agreement.

and unnecessary burdens for the undertakings subject to the enforcement activities; *(d)* the opportunity to make more efficient use of their resources". In other words, coordination allows to avoid a duplication of the investigative process, throughout the allocation of specified tasks and the pooling of enforcement resources between competition authorities. This way, coordination not only ensures a better use of available funds, but also ensures more effective enforcement activities, such as foreclosing to an undertaking, which was alerted of the investigation from a competition authority of one Party, to have the time to alter or destroy the evidences localised in the territory of the other State Party to the agreement and related to the same antitrust infringement[139].

The importance of cooperation is evident even in the European Union secondary law. Reg. n. 1/2003[140] dedicates an entire chapter to the cooperation between the European Commission and national competition authorities (artt. 11-16), and contains clauses partially similar to those of the EU/Switzerland agreement examined above.

The major limitation consists in the fact that coordination of enforcement activities, as outlined in the EU/Switzerland agreement, remains – consistently with previous bilateral agreements concluded by the European Union – a purely voluntary instrument and the effectiveness of the provision can significantly be reduced if the Parties avail themselves of the safeguard clause in art. 4, § 3, which allows them to limit in any moment the coordination and to proceed independently on a specific enforcement activity.

Artt. 5 and 6 of the EU/Switzerland agreement provide the principles of comity, which confer specificity to the coordination of enforcement activities examined above.

The negative comity (or traditional comity) consists of mutual commitment of both antitrust authorities of the Parties to «give careful consideration to the important interests of the other Party throughout all phases of its enforcement activities» (art. 5, § 1), in order to strike the balance between the respective positions. As a consequence thereof, if the enforcement activity envisaged by the competition authority of a Party risks to affect important interests of the other Party, the former, while maintaining its full discretion, "shall use its best endeavours" to promptly inform the antitrust authority of the other Party about the significant developments relating to the interests of that Party. This authority has the opportunity to provide comments, which shall be taken into account by the proceeding authority, in full respect of the

139 S. Bastianon, P. M. Ferrari, *op. cit.*, p. 325 and particularly note n. 33.

140 Council Regulation (EC) n. 1/2003, of 16 December 2002, on the implementation of the rules on competition laid down in artt. 81 and 82 of the Treaty, *OJ*, L 1, p. 1 ss.

independence of both competition authorities in making their own decisions (art. 5, § 2). Moreover, in case the antitrust authority of a Party considers that its enforcement activities may "*adversely* [emphasis added]" affect important interests of the other Party, it shall use its best endeavours to find a solution that reconciles the respective interests (art. 5, comma 3)[141]. This might finally lead, *in extremis*, even to the decision of the proceeding authority of *non agere*, it meaning not to start an investigative process or not to adopt a specific measure, leaving it to the other Party's competition authority (for instance, when it is necessary to prevent a conflict of judgments).

As to the positive comity[142], it allows each competition authority, believing that anticompetitive activities carried out in the other Party's territory may adversely affect its own relevant interests, to request the competition authority of the other Party to intervene, according to this latter's competition law[143], for the repression of such behaviours, enacting or expanding ongoing enforcement activities. While submitting such request, it is necessary «taking into account the importance of avoiding conflicts regarding jurisdiction and

141 Art. 5, § 3, also states that: «in seeking such accommodation, the competition authority of the Party concerned should consider the following factors, in addition to any other factor that may be relevant in the circumstances: *(a)* the relative significance of the actual or potential effects of the anticompetitive activities on the enforcing Party's important interests as compared to the effects on the other Party's important interests; *(b)* the relative significance to the anticompetitive activities of conduct or transactions occurring within the territory of a Party as compared to conduct or transactions occurring within the territory of the other Party; *(c)* the extent to which enforcement activities by the other Party with respect to the same undertakings would be affected; and *(d)* the extent to which undertakings will be placed under conflicting requirements by both Parties».

142 The most significant and articulated regulation of positive comity principles is found in the EC/USA agreement of 1998, which was negotiated with the purpose to complete, clarify and strengthen the provisions on *comitas gentium* set out in the previous agreement of 1991. The agreement of 1998 specifically details the cases in which a request for investigation based on positive comity may be submitted; it also identifies the cases in which the requesting Party shall be entitled, and the cases in which the same shall be bound to suspend or postpone the enforcement of its measures if the authority of the requested Party has in place an ongoing investigative process (*e.g.*, when anticompetitive practices are carried out in the territory of the requested Party and are prevalently to be referred to it). For an analysis of the positive comity principle, with particular regard to the EC/USA agreements, see: S. Rigamonti, *I principi della* "comitas gentium" *negli Accordi tra Comunità europee e Stati Uniti in materia di concorrenza*, in *Dir. Un. Eur.*, 1997, p. 835 ss.; B. Nascimbene, *Aspetti internazionali della politica di concorrenza comunitaria*, op. cit., spec. p. 319 ss.

143 Obviously, the relevant conduct shall be considered as a prohibited conduct also in the light of the competition rules of the requested Party.

taking into account that the competition authority of the other Party may be in a position to conduct more effective enforcement activities with regard to such anticompetitive activities» (art. 6, § 1)[144]. The authority submitting the request shall accurately indicate the nature of the anticompetitive activities and their actual or potential effects on the relevant interests (art. 6, § 2). The requested competition authority shall attentively evaluate the request and "as soon as practically possible" inform the requesting authority of its evaluations and decisions, as well as the outcomes and the significant interim developments of the enforcement activities started or expanded (art. 6, § 3).

Also this provision, as for art. 4, § 3, is completed by a safeguard clause. In fact, the last paragraph of art. 6 provides that: «nothing in this Article limits the discretion of the requested competition authority under its competition laws and enforcement policies as to whether or not to undertake enforcement activities with respect to the anticompetitive activities identified in the request, or precludes the requesting competition authority from withdrawing its request». In essence, if, on the one hand, the requested competition authority does not have an obligation to take the required measures, but merely an option, on the other hand, the requesting competition authority is entitled to enact its own enforcement activities.

In conclusion, the principles of negative and, especially, of positive comity encourage the allocation of competence (to prosecute anticompetitive practices) in a flexible and more suitable manner for the specific features of the case at stake, as they allow certain conducts to be prosecuted by a single antitrust authority and, more specifically, by the one antitrust authority out of the two to be in the best position as for means, resources, powers and nation-

144 The scope of this provision can be evaluated on account of the practice. The first case, occurred back in the Nineties, of request based on positive comity for appropriate enforcement activities is the *Sabre v Amadeus* case. The US Department of Justice, following the complaint by Sabre Group of American Airlines, has called on the European Commission to investigate, according to EU competition rules, on a alleged anticompetitive conduct by Lufthansa, which favoured the electronic ticketing system called Amadeus, limiting the competitiveness in Europe of the American competitor Sabre system (for example, not communicating to this last all fares, especially those promotional). It has to be noted that the American antitrust authority made the request based on positive comity, considering that the European Commission would be best placed to investigate the anticompetitive conduct. This is because such conduct was put in place within the territory of European Union and specifically involved the European consumers. Cf. Commission Decision of 20 July 1999 on a procedure relating to the application of Council Regulation (EEC) n. 2299/89 (Electronic ticketing), notified under document n. C(1999) 2068) (1999/618/EC). For support, see. B. Zanettin, *Cooperation Between Antitrust Agencies at the International Level*, Hart Publishing, Oxford, 2002, p. 195 ss.

ality of the undertakings[145]. The EU/Switzerland agreement confirms again the choice already expressed in previous agreements, *i.e.* not to provide any stiff allocation criteria of competences between competition authorities of the two Parties to the agreement, but rather flexible ways, left to a case-by-case evaluation by the Parties, on the basis of appropriate procedural mechanisms for coordination and cooperation.

In respect of the last instrument – the exchange of information – it will be tackled in the following section. As for now, one shall bear in mind that the exchange of information has already been regulated in the agreements signed by the European Union with the United States, Canada, Japan and Korea, which recognise the opportunity for the competition authority of a Party to transmit to the other competition authority documents and information that it has become acquainted with, where relevant for the enforcement activities of the addressed authority. Even before the EU/Switzerland agreement, in fact, the commitment to mutually satisfy the request of relevant information for the enforcement activities has been recognised as crucial for the effective fight against anticompetitive practices affecting international trade. However, according to these previous agreements, no information obtained through the formal investigation may be shared with another competition authority without the specific, express consent (which constitutes a true exemption) by the undertaking which provided the information. For example, the EC/USA agreement of 1998 conditions the possibility of providing confidential infor-

145 Observation of C. Schepisi, *op. cit.*, spec. p. 341, where the Author states that the positive comity principle «indica, o in alcuni casi suggerisce, i criteri per regolare l'esercizio delle suddette competenze, prevedendo, ove si verifichino certe circostanze, l'opportunità o la necessità (ma tale valutazione è sempre rimessa alle Parti) che una Parte abdichi (temporaneamente) all'esercizio dei propri poteri, in favore dell'altra Parte ritenuta più idonea agli accertamenti del caso». Cf. also S. Bastianon, P. M. Ferrari, *op. cit.*, p. 327, according to whom, while the so-called "effects doctrine" "si risolve in un'affermazione unilaterale di competenza, il principio della "cortesia positiva" si orienta, invece, verso un declino concordato della stessa a favore di un'autorità straniera". For further analysis on this last aspect, see also U. Draetta, *Si estende la collaborazione internazionale in materia antitrust*, in *Dir. comm. internaz.*, 1/1997, p. 225 s., spec. p. 226, where the Author states: "appare chiaro lo sforzo di raggiungere l'effetto di una efficace repressione del comportamento anticoncorrenziale, senza ricorrere ad applicazioni extraterritoriali della normativa di ciascuna delle due parti"; S. Rigamonti, *op. cit.*, spec. p. 840, in which bilateral agreements are defined as "una "soluzione politica" all'applicazione extraterritoriale delle norme di concorrenza". See also P. Picone, *L'applicazione extraterritoriale delle regole sulla concorrenza e il diritto internazionale*, in F. Capotorti (Ed.), *Il fenomeno delle concentrazioni di imprese nel diritto interno e internazionale*, Cedam, Padova, 1989, p. 81 ss.

mation on that: "consent has been obtained from the source concerned"[146] and also provides that: "where pursuant to this Agreement the competition authorities of one Party provide information to the competition authorities of the other Party for the purpose of implementing this Agreement, that information shall be used by the latter competition authorities only for that purpose. However, the competition authorities that provided the information may consent to another use, on condition that where confidential information has been provided [...] on the basis of the consent of the source concerned, *that source also agrees to the other use* [emphasis added]"[147]. In other words, the prior consent of the concerned undertaking represents the unavoidable prerequisite for a legitimate exchange of information: lack thereof prevents the exchange and the transmission, and confidentiality requirements would prevail.

This is a notoriously weak point of these agreements, as highlighted on several occasions, especially with regard to the limits that it determines in the effective prosecution of international cartels[148]. The European Commis-

146 Art. 4, § 2, let. *c*), p. *iii*), EC/USA agreement of 1998.

147 Art. 5 of the EC/USA agreement of 1998, which refers in its turn to art. 8 of the EC/USA agreement of 1991. See also art. 3 of the same agreement of 1991. It has to be noted that even the administrative agreements concluded between the USA competition authorities, on the one hand, and the European Commission, on the other, while allowing the participation of their officers in meetings and hearings with the undertakings under investigation, subordinate this possibility to prior consent by the undertakings. With reference to the other agreements concluded by the European Union, seg.: art. 7 of the EC/Canada agreement, which provides: «in the case of concurrent action by the competition authorities of both Parties with a view to the application of their competition law, the competition authority of each Party shall, on request by the competition authority of the other Party, ascertain whether the natural or legal persons concerned will consent to the sharing of confidential information related thereto between the Parties competition authorities»; art. 9 of the EU/Japan agreement and art. 7, § 6, let. a), of the EC/Republic of Korea agreement.

148 Cf. Best Practices for the formal exchange of information between competition authorities in hard core cartel investigations of October 2005; Cooperation between Competition Agencies in Cartel Investigations, Report to the ICN Annual Conference, Moscow, May 2007, p. 5; B. Nascimbene, *Aspetti internazionali della politica di concorrenza comunitaria*, cit., p. 325 ss., having regard to the *Microsoft* case, notes that the successful cooperation between the United States and the European Union is decisively attributable to the consent by the undertaking so as to let the two authorities exchange information which – otherwise – would have remained covered by confidentiality. Cf. also C. Cocuzza, M. Montini, *International Antitrust Co-operation in a Global Economy*, in *Eur. Comm. Law Rev.*, 1998, p. 156; J. Parisi, *Enforcement Co-operation Among Antitrust Authorities*, in *Eur. Comm. Law Rev.*, 1999, p. 133.

sion itself had been stating for a long time that it was necessary to execute "second generation" agreements, which would provide for the exchange of confidential information as a general principle[149]. Even in the proposal on the signing of the EU/Switzerland agreement, the Commission reaffirmed: «the Swiss Competition Commission and the Commission have already cooperated in a certain number of cases outside the framework of a formal agreement. As in the case of "first generation" agreements, this cooperation is significantly limited by the fact that they cannot exchange confidential information. This agreement between the EU and the Swiss Confederation concerning cooperation on the application of their competition laws addresses this limitation by allowing the Commission and the Swiss Competition Commission to exchange confidential information. [...] By including the possibility to exchange, subject to specific conditions, confidential information between the competition agencies of both Parties, the Agreement will also enable the Commission to benefit from the results of information gathered by the Swiss Competition Commission»[150].

Thus, the EU/Switzerland agreement addresses exactly this specific profile, with the aim to overcome the above captioned limitations in relation to the previous agreements, and to allow the exchange of confidential information (also) in the lack of consent of the undertaking concerned and even expanding to national competition authorities of European Union Member States – subject to specific conditions – the opportunity to benefit from the transmission of such information, with significant consequences to be examined below.

In doing so, the Union's *external* cooperation in the competition field aligns itself more to the *internal* cooperation model in the same sector, based on the European Competition Network (ECN). Here, in fact, the exchange of confidential information has already been successfully used, as an integral

149 «That effective cooperation in combatting cartels is seriously hampered by the agencies' inability to exchange confidential information. A so-called "second generation" agreement allowing such communications would greatly improve the situation in this regard. However, domestic legal constraints on the exchange of confidential information complicate the prospect of concluding such a further agreement»: XXIXth Report on Competition Policy, p. 332, COM(2000) 618 final. See also the Report from the Commission to the Council and the European Parliament on the application of the agreement between the European Communities and the Government of the United States of America regarding the application of their competition laws – 1 January 1998 to 31 December 1998, p. 4, that indicates the opportunity of implementing a new bilateral agreement allowing the exchange of confidential information.

150 See COM(2012) 244 final, cit., pt. 3 and 4.

part of the forms of cooperation between the Commission and national antitrust authorities[151].

12 Innovations introduced for the exchange of information: the overcoming of the principle of prior consent by the undertaking and the exchange of information to the national competition authorities of EU Member States

In the light of the above, it is no coincidence that the provisions on the exchange of information constitute the most complex and significant part of all the EU/Switzerland agreement (articles from 7 to 10).

Preliminarily, the information that can be exchanged are all those concerning the enforcement of competition laws of the two Parties, necessary for implementing the cooperation, including – in particular – the ones obtained by investigative process. These latter are defined as the information «obtained by a Party using its formal investigative rights or submitted to a Party pursuant to a legal obligation» (art. 2, pt. 6)[152]. On account that that the powers of investigation of each antitrust authority of the two Parties are largely similar, it appears that the type and extent of information they may collect and share is substantially equivalent. These are, more in detail, the information that can be obtained through requests, interviews and inspections of undertakings (entering any premises of undertakings, examining and/or

---

151 See artt. 11 and 12 of Reg. n. 1/2003 and the *Commission Notice on cooperation within the Network of Competition Authorities*, OJ, C 101, of 27 April 2004, p. 43, pt. 26-28.

152 The EU/Switzerland agreement, under art. 2, pt. 6, let. a) and b), states that, for the European Union, such information are those "obtained through requests for information according to Article 18 [...], oral statements according to Article 19 and inspections conducted by the European Commission or on behalf of the European Commission according to artt. 20, 21 or 22 of Regulation (EC) n. 1/2003 or information acquired as a result of the application of Regulation (EC) n. 139/2004"; while for Switzerland, «this means information obtained through requests for information according to Article 40 Acart, oral statements according to § 1 of Article 42 Acart and inspections conducted by the competition authority according to § 2 of Article 42 Acart, or information acquired as a result of the application of the Ordinance on the Control of Concentrations of Undertakings of 17 June 1996». In literature, it has been observed, in a critical sense, that: «with regards to the Swiss procedure, an information exchange is possible even if the competition authorities have not opened a formal investigation (Art. 27 Cartel Act) but merely a preliminary investigation (Art. 26 Cartel Act), in which case even the Swiss Administrative Procedure Act does not fully apply. At this stage of the procedure, the parties have no access to the file and cannot even judge what kind of information could be transmitted abroad»: D. MAMANE, S. WITTMER, *op. cit.*

copying of the books and other records related to the business, asking for explanations on facts or documents relating to the subject-matter and purpose of the inspection, enforcing coercive measures).

Under the rules provided for in artt. 7 to 10 of the EU/Switzerland agreement, it seems possible to distinguish five different forms of information exchange: *(i)* discussion; *(ii)* written transmission; *(iii)* use; *(iv)* protection; *(v)* sharing with the competition authorities of Member States.

Discussion is governed in § 2 of art. 7, which provides: «the competition authorities of the Parties may discuss any information, including information obtained by investigative process, as necessary to carry out the cooperation and coordination provided for under this Agreement». In other words, any information necessary for cooperation between the two competition authorities may be subject to debate between them.

Written transmission is instead subject to stricter conditions. It emerges, in fact, an increase in the level of guarantees required for sharing information than the level in the case of (mere) discussion. Transmission may occur upon consent of the undertaking providing the information (art. 7, § 3) or in the absence of the same (art. 7, § 4).

When transmitting upon consent of the undertaking (for example, when an undertaking notifies a merger to the competition authority, waives confidentiality and authorises the authority to share information with one or more foreign competition authorities), this information must already be in possession[153] of one of the two competition authorities and consent to the exchange must have been acquired in advance in writing. In addition, in the specific cases of information containing personal data, the transmission of the latter is only possible if the two authorities are investigating "the same or related conduct or transaction".

Partially different is the case of transmission of information obtained by investigative process in the absence of consent that, as mentioned, constitutes the innovation introduced by the EU/Switzerland agreement. In such case, the sharing of information is enhanced with even greater caution, so as to avoid the risk of a generalised and indiscriminate search for information. The exchange in the absence of consent may in fact only take place upon express written request of the competition authority of a Party to the other, only for the purpose of using the information as evidence and only if the informa-

153 Such limitation, to be applied also in case of exchange of information without prior consent, according to D. Mamane, S. Wittmer, *op. cit.*, "underlines that the Cooperation Agreement is not a basis for the collection of information solely on behalf of the other foreign authority. Rather, the information qualifying for being shared with the foreign authority must have been collected within the framework and for purposes of domestic proceedings".

tion is already in the possession of the competition authority of a Party and both competition authorities are investigating the same or related conduct or transaction[154]. art. 7, § 4, also deals with the content of the request, stating that it «shall include a general description of the subject matter and the nature of the investigation or proceedings to which the request relates and the specific legal provisions involved». The request should also identify the undertakings involved in the investigative process, whose identity is available at the time of the request. The requested authority determines, in consultation with the requesting authority, what information in its possession are relevant and may be transmitted.

The provision above, despite its innovative nature as it allows the exchange of confidential information without the consent of the involved undertaking, is however expected to be mitigated by the ensuing §§ 5, 6 and 7 of art. 7.

§ 5 entails, as already marked in respect of other instruments of the agreement (in particular, coordination of enforcement activities and positive comity), a safeguard clause according to which: «neither competition authority is required to discuss or transmit information obtained by investigative process to the other competition authority, in particular if it would be incompatible with its important interests or unduly burdensome». In other words, the decision on the opportunity to proceed to the exchange of information is still left to the – particularly wide – discretion of the Parties.

§§ 6 and 7 contain two exceptions to the exchange of information: *(a)* if the information was obtained under the Parties' leniency or settlement procedures: in this case, exchange is conditioned to the express consent in writing of the involved undertaking; and *(b)* if the use of information obtained during investigative process is «prohibited under the procedural rights and privileges guaranteed under the respective laws of the Parties and applicable to their enforcement activities, including the right against self-incrimination and the legal professional privilege[155]».

---

154 «Un caso in cui i mercati interessati da un cartello non sono esattamente identici tra la Svizzera e l'UE costituisce un esempio di comportamento correlato. Lo stesso dicasi del caso in cui le imprese che partecipano a un cartello non sono esattamente le stesse in Svizzera e nell'UE» as stated in the Message concerning approval of the EU/Switzerland agreement, of 22 May 2013, p. 13.

155 As for the European Union, one should bear in mind that, according to the Court of Justice, the correspondence exchanged between the undertaking and its lawyer should be considered subject to confidentiality "provided that, on the one hand, such communications are made for the purposes and in the interests of the client's rights of defence and, on the other hand, they emanate from independent lawyers, that is to say, lawyers who are not bound to the client by a relationship of employment": Court just., 18 May 1982, 155/79, *AM & S v Commission*, *ECR* 1575, pt. 18-28. It emerges that the principle of "secret professionnel" is

Such exceptions are also present in previous bilateral agreements signed by the Union in the field of competition, which preclude the possibility of exchanging information in the event that this would be contrary to national laws or would be incompatible with important interests of the Parties (which can occur, for example, in the case of different procedural rights provided for in the laws of the two Parties to the agreement[156]). For example, art. 8, § 1, of the EC/USA agreement of 1991 provides that: «notwithstanding any other provisions of this Agreement, neither Party is required to provide information to the other Party if disclosure of that information to the requesting Party *(a)* is prohibited by the law of the Party possessing the information, or *(b)* would be incompatible with important interests of the Party possessing the information»[157]. The provision of art. 7, § 5, of the EU/Switzerland agreement, rather than contributing to a more precise wording, which would enable to circumscribe the possible application of the safeguard clause[158], seems to expand the scope thereof, adding to the case where the exchange

---

interpreted rather narrowly, given that with in-house lawyers communications are not covered by legal privilege. In this respect, there may be problems arising from the different level of protection accorded to the abovementioned principle in the two European and Swiss legal systems.

156 Cf. General Court, 27 September 2006, T-59/02, *Archer Daniels Midland v Commission*, *ECR* II-3627, pt. 262 ss., which argues that, where the Commission, in assessing the evidence in its possession, relies on a statement made in a context different from that of the procedure initiated before it, it is required to guarantee to the undertaking concerned procedural rights equivalent to those conferred directly by the Commission in proceedings before it. In § 265 of the judgment it is stated that: "compliance with those procedural safeguards entails, in a context such as this one, the need for the Commission to carry out an examination automatically if, prima facie, there is serious doubt as to whether the procedural rights of the parties concerned were complied with in the procedure during which they provided such statements. If there is no such serious doubt, the procedural rights of the parties concerned must be deemed to have been adequately safeguarded if, in the statement of objections, the Commission clearly indicates, if necessary by annexing the relevant documents to it, that it intends to rely on the statement in question. In this way, the Commission makes it possible for the parties concerned to comment not only the content of those statements, but also on any irregularities or special circumstances concerning their composition or submission to the Commission". Cf. S. Bastianon, P. M. Ferrari, *op. cit.*, p. 323 and spec. note n. 32.

157 Cf., in similar terms, art. 10, § 1, EC/Canada agreement.

158 It should be noted that need for greater clarity had already led, with regard to the EC/USA agreement of 1991, to an exchange of interpretative letters annexed to the agreement itself and to a communication of the Commission (COM(98) 510 final), such as to specify to what kind of information prohibition pursuant to art. 20 Reg. 17/1962 (later replaced by Reg. n. 1/2003) was to apply and, instead, to what kind transmission was permitted.

of information would compromise "relevant interest" of the Parties, also the case that this would appear "unduly burdensome". It is clear that the vagueness of the clause results, essentially, in a wide discretionary power left to the Parties to the agreement which may undermine its effectiveness, as it threatens to significantly affect, on a practical level, the importance of innovation introduced by the agreement.

Need for greater clarity also emerges with reference to the exception relating to leniency or settlement procedures. For these latter, the provision does not clarify whether the exception already applies from the start of negotiations or just from signature of the settlement[159]. With regard to the leniency programs, the question is whether the exception extends to the sole report or also to the side correspondence.

With regard, finally, to the exception for the protection of the procedural rights and privileges of the undertakings involved in the investigation, provided for in § 7 of art. 7, this should apply in the event of regulatory discrepancies between the two legal systems, ensuring the highest level of protection offered by each legislation. The rule, in fact, establishes the principle of the so-called "double fence", according to which an authority can only transmit information that itself could use in its own procedures and shall apply the guarantees provided for by its legal system when using the information received from the other authority. The exception may have, however, a reduced practical relevance, if we consider that "both systems recognise similar procedural rights of the parties and the rights of legal privilege and non-self-incrimination"[160].

Art. 7 contains no rule that legitimate undertakings to appeal against the decision of transmitting information which may be unlawful or, likewise, against the inadmissibility of evidence obtained on the basis of an exchange of information operated in violation of the procedural rights and privileges guaranteed to the undertakings. This possibility to appeal would therefore

---

159 D. Mamane, S. Wittmer, *op. cit.*: «firstly, a settlement can occur at many stages of a procedure and there seem to be no rules in the Cooperation Agreement on what should happen to information that has been discussed and/or exchanged prior to the settlement. Secondly, it is unclear whether the initiation of settlement talks itself blocks the discussion or transmission of information, or whether only the signature of the settlement agreement, which may occur much later in the process, will block the information exchange. Thirdly, it also remains unclear whether the information already discussed or transmitted may be used by the competition authorities if at a later stage of the procedure the parties conclude a settlement agreement and refuse to consent to an information exchange between the authorities».

160 See COM(2012) 244 final, cit., pt. 5.

seem permitted only in conjunction to appeals against final decisions that ascertain the competition infringement[161].

The point is of great relevance, as it sees the conflict between different interests of public nature: on one side, the (temporary) limitation on the right of defence of the undertakings involved in an investigative process (limitation all the more significant if we consider that the exchange of information can take place in the absence of their consent) and, on the other side, the need not to compromise the objectives of the enforcement activities and to ensure the effectiveness of the latter. The introduction of the possibility to appeal against the decision to exchange information, per se a guarantee of the right to be heard and of the right of defence of the undertakings, could at the same time undermine the effectiveness of the investigations by the antitrust authorities and lend itself to abuse and to delaying tactics by the undertakings themselves. This kind of appeal against intermediate decision would require indeed to promptly notify the undertakings about the intention of the two antitrust authorities to exchange information concerning them and, above all, would require the introduction of a right of access to the case file, aimed at enhancing the effective protection of the rights of defence of the undertakings in relation to the content of the information that the Parties to the agreement would share.

The problem was also highlighted by the European Parliament, which stated that: «a *coherent approach* to appeals against final decisions in both jurisdictions would be desirable and calls on the European Commission and the Swiss Competition Commission to examine this potential area of further cooperation; notes, however, that *allowing* the parties to appeal against intermediate decisions, such as those on the exchange of information, *would block investigations* and could *compromise the effectiveness* of this agreement [emphasis added]»[162].

161 For a critical comment on lack of a right to appeal against the decision of transmitting information, see D. Mamane, S. Wittmer, *op. cit.*: «given the far-reaching scope of the information that may be exchanged and in light of the criminal nature of competition law fines, it is surprising that the Cooperation Agreement does not foresee any right to appeal a decision to exchange information if there is no consent by the party. While this would be standard in procedures subject to the Swiss Act on International Mutual Assistance in Criminal Matters, the Cooperation Agreement leaves the parties unprotected». *Contra* P. Ducrey, *op. cit.*, p. 442, according to which the absence of such a provision is «due to the comprehensive protection provided when obtaining information in both legal systems and the corresponding prohibitions of transmissions in § 7 as well as the adequate legal protection provided in relation to using transmitted information».

162 European Parliament Resolution, as of 5 February 2014, on EU cooperation agreements on competition policy enforcement – the way forward (2013/2921(RSP)).

The draft of the provision and the considerations about the possible negative consequence to the effectiveness of the investigations would lead to prefer an interpretation which excludes the possibility for undertakings to severally appeal against the intermediate decision authorizing the exchange of information.

Such a solution would seem, at first sight, more consistent with the European Competition Network, in which there is not a system of notifications *ex ante* to undertakings, and also with the provisions of art. 9 of the EU/Switzerland agreement, which enshrines the general principle of protection and confidentiality of information (see below). In fact, appeals by the undertakings against the intermediate decision of exchange of information – and thus the right of access of these latter to the case file held by the antitrust authorities – would imply that the confidentiality provision *ex* art. 9 does not apply to them (it remaining in force only for third parties). However, the same art. 9, § 1, letter *d*) also gives rise to an opposite interpretation, which enhances the possibility of an intermediate appeal of undertakings. The provision, in fact, when listing the situations in which the disclosure of information is exceptionally permitted, refers precisely to the case in which "it is indispensable for the exercise of the right of access to documents *under the laws of a Party* [emphasis added]". As a matter of fact, the EU/Switzerland agreement does not exclude or limit the possibility of evaluating the decision on the exchange of information on account of the criteria on judicial control according to the *national* law – either European or Swiss – with the result that such decision could be challengeable in accordance with the provisions of the European Union or the Swiss legal system, depending on which one between the Commission and the COMCO has given rise to the decision[163].

The practical application of the agreement will offer further clarification on this aspect, taking into account also the fact that the Swiss Cartel Act,

163 In this sense, see also the aforementioned Message concerning approval of the EU/Switzerland agreement, where it is highlighted, at p. 14 s., that: "la trasmissione da parte della COMCO di informazioni già in possesso della Commissione europea o viceversa non costituisce una decisione e non è dunque impugnabile mediante ricorso […]. In un ambito come il diritto dei cartelli, l'efficacia delle misure di applicazione richiede uno scambio rapido ed efficace, mentre una procedura di ricorso che può durare diversi mesi toglierebbe senso all'esistenza stessa dell'Accordo. L'Accordo non limita invece le possibilità del *diritto interno* delle Parti *di ricorrere contro una decisione* finale o *incidentale* della COMCO invocando la violazione dei propri diritti qualora ravvisassero una violazione degli stessi durante la raccolta di informazioni. Inoltre, se la trasmissione dovesse violare le rigide condizioni del diritto di audizione o una delle numerose salvaguardie previste dall'Accordo, l'impresa coinvolta potrebbe far valere questo fatto per contestare la decisione dell'autorità che ha ricevuto le informazioni [emphasis added]".

art. 42 b[164], which was specifically set to implement the agreement with the European Union, provides conditions for the exchange of information not wholly consistent with those of the agreement. In particular, the last paragraph of that art. 42 b states that «the competition authorities shall notify the undertaking concerned and invite it to state its views before transmitting the data to the foreign competition authority». The need for prior consultation with undertakings inevitably seems to have an impact on the possibility of severally appealing against the decision of exchanging information without previous consent of the undertaking.

As to the use of the information, it is regulated by art. 8 of the EU/Switzerland agreement. The rule limits the use of information exchanged by the antitrust authorities to a specific goal: «only for the purpose of enforcing that Party's competition laws by its competition authority» (§ 1). This limitation would thus seem to exclude not only the possibility that the information exchanged are transmitted to other competition authorities, other than the recipient (e.g. criminal or tax authorities), but also the possibility that the same information are used in the private enforcement[165].

Information obtained by investigative process and exchanged with the antitrust authority of the other Party to the agreement may be used by the latter only «for the enforcement of its competition laws with regard to the same or related conduct or transaction» (§ 2).

A specific provision is reserved to information exchanged in the absence of the undertaking consent: in this case, the information may be used by the receiving antitrust authority only for the purpose defined in its request (§ 3). Essentially, the provision prevents the information, once received by the requesting authority, from being diverted out of the legal context of the request and used for a reason other than what specified therein.

Therefore, the combined provisions of artt. 7 and 8 of the agreement determines that, when the undertaking has given its consent to the exchange of information, these latter may be used in order to apply the competition law of the receiving antitrust authority; if the undertaking has denied its consent, the information exchanged may only be used for the application of

---

164 Swiss Cartel Act, article 42b, inserted by the Annex to the Federal Decree of 20 June 2014 on the Approval of the Agreement between Switzerland and the EU concerning Cooperation on the Application and Implementation of their Competition Laws, in force since 1 December 2014.

165 See. *infra*, in note n. 177, for further considerations on account of the new rules set out by the directive n. 2014/104/EU of the European Parliament and of the Council, of 26 November 2014, on certain rules governing actions for damages under national law for infringements of the competition law provisions of the Member States and of the European Union, *OJ*, L 349, of 5 December 2014, p. 1 ss.

the competition law of the receiving antitrust authority exclusively in relation to the same or related conduct and within the limits of the purpose defined in the request[166].

In any case, no information exchanged "shall be used to impose sanctions on natural persons" (§ 4)[167].

Finally, the last paragraph of art. 8 provides that each antitrust authority may request to the other that the information exchanged are used "subject to the terms and conditions it specifies". Therefore, also this rule is suitable to criticism for the use of broad and undefined concepts ("such terms and conditions"), leaving in practice a considerable margin of discretion with the antitrust authorities, such as to affect the effectiveness of the agreement.

The regulation provided for in art. 9 requires, as a general rule, the protection and the confidentiality of information exchanged between the competition authorities. In particular, it is set out that: "the competition authorities of the Parties shall treat the fact that a request has been made or received as confidential. Information obtained pursuant to this Agreement shall be kept confidential by the receiving competition authority according to its respective legislation. Both competition authorities shall in particular oppose any application of a third party or another authority for disclosure of information received" (§ 1).

Disclosure is thus prohibited, except for certain mandatory cases expressly listed in § 1: «*a)* obtaining a court order in relation to the public enforcement of the competition laws of a Party[168]; *b)* disclosure to undertakings which are subject to an investigation or a procedure under the competition laws of the Parties and against whom the information may be used, if such disclosure is required by the law of the Party receiving the information; *c)* disclosure to courts in appeal procedures; *d)* disclosure if and in so far as it is indispensable for the exercise of the right of access to documents under the laws of a Party».

---

166 As pointed out by D. Mamane, S. Wittmer, *op. cit.*

167 Such exclusion avoids any coordination problems in relation to the provision of art. 12, § 3, Reg. n. 1/2003, which states: «information exchanged pursuant to § 1 can only be used in evidence to impose sanctions on natural persons where: *(i)* the law of the transmitting authority foresees sanctions of a similar kind in relation to an infringement of Article 81 or Article 82 of the Treaty or, in the absence thereof *(ii)* the information has been collected in a way which respects the same level of protection of the rights of defence of natural persons as provided for under the national rules of the receiving authority. However, in this case, the information exchanged cannot be used by the receiving authority to impose custodial sanctions».

168 Also in this case, therefore, the scope of private enforcement is excluded.

In the exceptional cases of disclosure, protection of business secrets[169] and of personal data, in accordance with the respective legislation of the Parties, shall be fully guaranteed (§ 1 and § 3 of art. 9).

In this respect, it is interesting to note that the European Union has expressly recognized, since 2000[170], the presumption of equivalence between the European and the Swiss data protection laws. This is also expressed in the Commission proposal on the signing of the EU/Switzerland agreement, in which the Commission is «satisfied that the Swiss rules on confidentiality are comparable to the EU ones and therefore that business secrets and other confidential information that it may transmit to the Swiss Competition Commission will enjoy an adequate level of protection. When implementing this agreement, both authorities shall also ensure the protection of personal data, under their respective laws on personal data. The Swiss rules can be considered to be equivalent. The Commission has taken a decision concluding that Switzerland generally provides an adequate level of protection for personal data transferred from the EU»[171].

It remains to examine art. 10, which allows the Commission to inform the national competition authorities (and the EFTA Surveillance Authority[172]). This can occur when important interests of a Member State are involved and it is therefore necessary, before adopting the final decision, that the Member State itself examines the documents exchanged by the Commission with the

169 For a clear distinction between trade secrets and confidential information see A. Saggio, C. Iannone, *Le informazioni riservate e i segreti commerciali nel diritto comunitario della concorrenza*, in *Riv. Dir. eur.*, 1997, p. 547 ss., spec. p. 550 and 574, where it is highlighted that: «sono coperte dal segreto commerciale le informazioni relative ad aspetti strategici dell'attività di impresa, tali cioè che la loro divulgazione compromette in modo sensibile gli interessi dell'impresa e, in definitiva, il buon funzionamento del mercato che costituisce la primaria finalità delle regole di concorrenza. Costituiscono invece informazioni riservate, le (residue) informazioni sull'attività commerciale delle imprese, informazioni di importanza minore, la cui divulgazione non pregiudica in modo determinante le imprese stesse ma potrebbe comunque compromettere il buon andamento delle inchieste amministrative» and, therefore, «la differenza tra le due categorie di informazioni [...] è correlata tanto al contenuto delle informazioni quanto agli interessi che la segretezza è in concreto destinata a proteggere».

170 Commission Decision of 26 July 2000, on the adequate protection of personal data provided in Switzerland, *OJ*, L 215, p. 1, which stresses that Switzerland generally offers an adequate protection of personal data transmitted by the European Union and sets out a presumption of equivalence between the protection standards provided by the two legal systems.

171 See COM(2012) 244 final, cit., pt. 10.

172 See *infra* for the issues concerning the exchange of information from the European Commission to the national competition authorities of the Member States.

COMCO, or when the Commission meets its obligations of information arising from Reg. n. 1/2003 within the European Competition Network. More precisely, the disclosure to the national antitrust authorities may be made by the Commission to: «*(a)* inform the competent authorities of a Member State whose important interests are affected of the notifications sent to it by the competition authority of Switzerland [...]; *(b)* inform the competent authorities of a Member State of the existence of any cooperation and coordination of enforcement activities; *(c)* only disclose information transmitted by the competition authority of Switzerland pursuant to art. 7 of this Agreement to the competent authorities of the Member States in order to fulfil its obligation of information under artt. 11 and 14 of Regulation (EC) No 1/2003 and art. 19 of Regulation (EC) No 139/2004».

The provision is worth mentioning, as it introduces an innovative element and determines some significant effects in the relationship between the Commission and national authorities. In previous agreements – particularly in the EC/USA – no mention is made of the national authorities, which are referred to, with regard to the agreement signed with the United States, only in the interpretative letters and in the Declaration of the Commission on transparency annexed to the agreement[173]. In these latter it is agreed that the Commission may forward a copy of the notifications by US antitrust authorities to the Member States whose interests are involved, after notifying it to the said US authorities. Similarly, when the Commission serves notifications with the US authorities, it shall send a copy to the Member State whose interests are involved. As noted by relevant literature, "quanto espresso nei citati documenti non implica, tuttavia, che le autorità nazionali siano costantemente informate di tutti i procedimenti pendenti dinanzi alle autorità statunitensi che rivestano rilevanza (anche) comunitaria, né, soprattutto, è previsto quali effetti la notifica sia atta a produrre nei loro confronti. Ne deriva, in apparenza, l'estraneità al funzionamento degli Accordi dell'operato delle autorità nazionali e dei loro rapporti con la Commissione"[174].

The EU/Switzerland agreement, however, expressly mentions the national antitrust authorities, making them as "indirect" Parties of the agreement. One reason for this difference lies in the fact that the EU/Switzerland agreement was negotiated as the Reg. n. 1/2003 had already entered into force and is therefore influenced by its rationale, unlike the EC/USA agreement, which entered into force when the domestic antitrust legislation to the European

173 See interpretative letters (*OJ*, L 131, of 15 June 1995, p. 38 f.) and Declaration of the Commission on transparency annexed to the agreement (COM (98) 510 final).

174 As observed by C. Schepisi, *op. cit.*, pp. 334-335.

Union was still constituted by the Reg. n. 17/62[175], replaced by the aforementioned Reg. n. 1/2003 only on 1 January 2004. It appears that art. 10 of the EU/Switzerland agreement considers the European action in antitrust field as a whole, in accordance with the new competition policy that decentralises the application of antitrust rules and, simultaneously, strengthens the coordination between the authorities (central: the Commission; decentralised: the national competition authorities)[176].

The last paragraph of art. 10 creates a coordination rule, specifying that: "information, other than publicly available information, communicated to the competent authorities of a Member State [...] shall not be used for any purpose other than enforcement of the Union's competition laws by the European Commission, and shall not be disclosed". Thus it seems possible to infer that national authorities may not rely on any information provided to them by the Commission, pursuant to art. 10, when proceeding under the national competition laws and that they are still bound to respect the protection and confidentiality obligations already binding the Commission.

The involvement of the national authorities, if, on the one hand, it is significant to the extent that it is more consistent with the *ratio* of Reg. n. 1/2003, on the other hand it could give rise to some uncertainty[177]. In fact, the shared competence of the national authorities, outlined in Reg. n. 1/2003,

---

175 Council Regulation n. 17 (EEC), of 6 February 1962, First Regulation implementing artt. 85 and 86 of the Treaty, *OJ*, L 13, p. 87.

176 This feature had long been expected by attentive literature, stressing that "tanto più si "decentra", tanto più occorre rafforzare il coordinamento con e tra le Autorità nazionali della concorrenza, al fine di assicurare la continuità delle procedure che interessano più paesi e l'efficacia dei relativi provvedimenti": A. Tizzano, *L'applicazione «decentrata» degli art. 85 e 86 Ce in Italia*, in *Foro it.*, 1997, vol. 120, n. 1, c. 33 ss.

177 Especially in light of the new rules on the disclosure of evidence included in the file of a competition authority outlined in chapter II, art. 5-8, of the abovementioned Directive n. 2014/104/EU in the private enforcement. In particular, art. 6, § 5, provides for the possibility for national courts to order the disclosure of the following categories of evidence, after a competition authority has closed its proceedings: «*a)* information that was prepared by a natural or legal person specifically for the proceedings of a competition authority; *b)* information that the competition authority has drawn up and sent to the parties in the course of its proceedings; and *c)* settlement submissions that have been withdrawn". § 6 of art. 6 states that: "national courts cannot at any time order a party or a third party to disclose any of the following categories of evidence: *a)* leniency statements; and *b)* settlements submissions". Finally, art. 6, § 9 bears a closing rule, according to which: "the disclosure of evidence in the file of a competition authority that does not fall into any of the categories listed in this Article may be ordered in actions for damages at any time, without prejudice to this Article».

persists also in cases where anticompetitive practices produce effects in the national territory (and therefore in the EU) and, at the same time, in Switzerland. However, national authorities are not the "substantial Parties" of the agreement, which imposes obligations solely for the Commission and the COMCO, except for, as mentioned, the last paragraph of art. 10. In order to dispel any possible doubt about the extent of the obligations for national authorities from their (indirect) involvement in the EU/Switzerland agreement, in the absence of more specific provisions, the primary law and the general principles come to aid. More specifically, art. 216, § 2, TFEU, which enshrines the primacy of the international agreement on the secondary law, and the principles of sincere cooperation and of conforming interpretation. This latter, according to solid case law[178], even extends to international agreements concluded by the European Union. As to the duty of sincere cooperation, it can be construed as a supplementary key to understanding the behaviour of national authorities, since it leads to believe that they are required to assist the Commission in the execution of the agreement and they shall refrain from any activities that could jeopardise its effectiveness[179].

13 Concluding remarks

In conclusion, the EU/Switzerland agreement is of significant importance, at least theoretically, as it represents an unprecedented innovation[180]. It aims to ensure effective cooperation in the prosecution of transnational antitrust infringements, dealing with a specific and quite detailed regulation on one aspect – *i.e.* the exchange of confidential information in the lack of the undertaking's consent – which, until now, was considered like a taboo. In fact, despite the fact that many underlined the need and the importance of overcoming the principle of *consensus*, no bilateral agreement signed by the European Union had gone thus far. In this respect, therefore, the novelty introduced by the EU/Switzerland agreement certainly appears of great im-

---

178 About the interpretation of the European Union law – as far as possible – in light of international law (particularly when the Union acts are aimed at performing an international agreement concluded by this latter), see Court just., 10 September 1996, C-61/94, *Commission v Germany*, *ECR* I-3989, pt. 52; 14 July 1998, C-284/95, *Safety Hi-Tech v S. & T.*, *ECR* I-4301, pt. 22.

179 See C. Schepisi, *op. cit.*, p. 333 ss., also for the significant analysis related to the effects of the application of comity principles, under the EC/USA and EC/Canada agreements, on the European Union rules on antitrust. Cf. also P. Eeckhout, *External Relations of the European Union. Legal and Constitutional Foundations*, Oxford University Press, Oxford, 2004.

180 Former European Commissioner for Competition, J. Almunia, described the agreement in question as "unprecedented".

portance and also of a strong "symbolic" meaning, since it can be included within a framework of agreements concluded by the European Union with Switzerland which attempt at ensuring a more stringent form of cooperation, also in sectors other than competition but equally significant (for example, reference is made to the agreement signed on May 27, 2015, on the automatic exchange of tax information).

This confirms that relations with Switzerland increasingly reflect a special importance for the Union, both from an economic and political point of view[181], leading to more binding forms of cooperation. These are enabled also thanks to the existing regulatory convergence between the two legal systems, which is the result of the process whereby Switzerland, despite no accession to the Union, in order to facilitate its relations with it constantly takes into account the development of European law and examines its legislative proposals in the terms of compatibility with the European Union law (in the areas covered by the agreements, but with inevitable effects also upon other sectors)[182]. Such new features are also to be found in the agreement in question, which entails a purely procedural content, whose prerequisite

---

181 From a political standpoint, the relationship between the two legal systems is well articulated, it being subject to more than a hundred bilateral agreements concluded between the European Union and Switzerland, starting from the 1972 Free Trade Agreement mentioned at the beginning of this work. From an economic standpoint, Switzerland is the European Union's second largest trading partner, following the United States, while the European Union and its Member States are the main partners of Switzerland. The two economies are deeply integrated. See B. Nascimbene, *I rapporti tra la Svizzera e l'Unione europea. Gli accordi bilaterali e la politica europea della Svizzera*, in M. Condinanzi (Ed.), *op.* cit., p. 3 ss.

182 C. Sanna, *Gli accordi bilaterali tra la Svizzera e l'Unione europea*, cit., p. 550, who argues that: «sin dal 1988, i progetti di disposizioni giuridiche che hanno una dimensione transfrontaliera sono sistematicamente esaminati in termini di compatibilità con il diritto comunitario (e di altre organizzazioni o conferenze europee). In pratica, Consiglio federale e Parlamento tentano di evitare l'elaborazione del diritto svizzero prescindendo dal diritto comunitario e di creare nuove divergenze giuridiche, non motivate, che ostacolerebbero le relazioni tra la Svizzera e la CE. E' per tale motivo che le autorità federali cercano di negoziare con l'UE strumenti che consentano loro di partecipare al progetto decisionale comunitario. In tal senso, nonostante il carattere settoriale e non globale degli accordi negoziati e il fatto che essi non incorporino il patrimonio normativo comunitario, va rilevato che la Svizzera ha ottenuto che i suoi rappresentanti possano partecipare in qualità di osservatori attivi (diritto di parola ma non di voto) alle riunioni dei comitati comunitari nei settori della ricerca, del trasporto aereo, della sicurezza sociale e del riconoscimento dei diplomi. Inoltre, nelle materie in cui la legislazione svizzera è equivalente al patrimonio normativo comunitario, la Commissione, nel preparare le proposte di atti normativi, consulterà gli esperti svizzeri allo stesso titolo degli esperti degli Stati membri».

(and not its point of arrival) is the convergence between the two systems of enforcement of competition rules[183]. The objective pursued by the agreement may therefore be even stretched further, touching delicate profiles such as the exchange of confidential information and the disclosure thereof within the European Competition Network.

The success, at least theoretically, of this agreement is confirmed by the fact that the Commission seems to be inclined to apply a similar approach for other agreements and, as of today, negotiations are currently underway for a similar agreement – of "second generation" – with Canada[184]. Therefore, the EU/Switzerland agreement could even become the first of a new generation of bilateral relationship between the European Union and third Countries[185].

From a different perspective, however, several weak points of the agreement are to be pointed out, as result of the analysis above. Reference is made to those clauses drafted in flexible terms, non-binding and of rather uncertain content (for example: art. 4, § 1, art. 5, § 2, art. 8, § 5), and to the safeguard clauses (art. 4, § 3, art. 6, § 4, art. 7 § 5), which can also heavily impair the effectiveness of the agreement, relying upon a broad (and sometime excessive) discretion of the Parties for the proper implementation of the agreement. Even the final clause provided for in art. 13 applies the same logic, providing that: «nothing in this Agreement shall be construed to prejudice the formulation or enforcement of the competition laws of either Party». A similar provision can also be found in the previous agreements signed by the European Union[186], even though in the agreement under examination it appears at least counterbalanced by the provisions of art. 11, which allows Parties, through

183 Cf. preamble to the Agreement, which stated that: «considering the close relations between the Union and Switzerland and recognising that cooperation in addressing anticompetitive activities will contribute to improving and strengthening their relationship; […] bearing in mind that the competition enforcement systems of the Union and of Switzerland are based on the same principles and provide for similar rules».

184 Report on Competition Policy 2013 from the Commission to the European Parliament, the Council, the European Economic and Social Committee and the Committee of the Regions, of 6 May 2014, COM(2014) 249 final.

185 For their relevance, see the observations of A. Tizzano, *Note in tema di relazioni esterne dell'Unione europea*, in *Dir. Un Eur.*, 1999, p. 465 ss., who argues: «chi volga oggi lo sguardo al panorama delle relazioni internazionali dell'Unione europea (U.E.) non può non restare colpito dalla straordinaria affermazione di questa sulla scena mondiale, dal dinamismo della sua azione, dalla sua crescente autorità e dal rilevante ruolo che essa gioca, in una misura che non ha uguale per alcun'altra entità non statuale».

186 Cf., for example, art. 9 of the EC/USA agreement of 1991, which provides: "nothing in this Agreement shall be interpreted in a manner inconsistent with the existing laws, or as requiring any change in the laws, of the United States of

special *ad hoc* consultations, to «examine the possibility of further developing their cooperation». In this respect, it is interesting to observe that the EU/Switzerland agreement does not establish common and permanent organs such as joint committees (governing the management of the agreements and the resolution of disputes in most bilateral agreements concluded between the European Union and Switzerland), opting instead for a consultation system to be activated upon the request of the Parties or of the antitrust authorities.

The agreement also often recurs to unclear and hardly interpretable definitions, so as to limit the exchange of information (when it is incompatible with "important interests" of a Party or "unduly burdensome") and the use of the information discussed or transmitted (which can be conditioned to "such terms and conditions"), and to numerous precautions that surround and limit the possibility of exchanging information without the consent of the undertaking concerned (art. 7, §§ 5, 6, 7).

It should be noted, in this regard, that the presence of flexible clauses and of several derogations does not impair only the full implementation of the agreement, but it may also negatively affect the possibility of attributing direct effect to the provisions of the agreement and, therefore, the possibility of enforce them before the national Courts[187].

It will be essentially the practical application that will tell the effective consistency of these elements of weakness, in relation to the overall functioning of the agreement and to the ambitious goals thereof; practice will also respond to some open questions (such as the problem arising from the lack of provision for a right of appeal against the decision to exchange of information) and clarify[188] the effects of the agreement on investigative processes initiated before its entry into force, but still pending.

America or the European Communities or of their respective States or Member States". In similar terms see art. 7 of the EC/USA agreement of 1998.

187 The direct effect of the agreements concluded by the European Union is recognized to the extent that they entail clear, precise and unconditional obligations. Such characteristics, as known, were deemed not to be fulfilled in the case of the General Agreement on Tariffs and Trade (so-called, GATT), because of the forecast of numerous flexible clauses and exceptions in it: cf. Court just., 12 December 1972, joined cases 21/72, 22/72, 23/72, 24/72, *International Fruit Company e and Others v Produktschap voor Groenten en Fruit*, ECR 1219; 24 October 1973, 9/73, *Schlüter v Hauptzollamt Lörrach*, ECR 1135; 5 October 1994, C-280/93, *Germany v Council*, ECR I-4973; 12 December 1995, C-469/93, *Amministrazione delle finanze dello Stato v Chiquita Italia*, ECR I-4533.

188 As neither the agreement, nor Art. 14 thereof, which governs its entry in force, provide any indication to this end.

Alice Pisapia*

The Judicial Cooperation between the European Union and the Swiss Confederation: Half Way between International law and European law

Abstract: The paper illustrates the evolution of judicial cooperation between Switzerland and the European Union both in the civil and commercial matter and, more recently, in criminal matters. The analysis is conducted following the research question whether it is possible to design a conceptual framework, which reflects one of the two classic methods (intergovernmental or 'communautaire'), for the relationship between Switzerland and the European Union or if there is a third perspective to be taken.

1 Preliminary remarks

The scope of this paper is to analyse the different legal instruments, currently into force, for designing a consistent picture of the existing legal framework for what concerns the judicial cooperation between the European Union and Switzerland. It will be highlighted the main judicial instrument adopted in relation with the political crucial moments for the creation of the current scenario, firstly for what concern the civil matters and, secondly, for what concern the judicial cooperation in criminal matters. The analysis suggested will be mainly based on the distinction for the adoption of supranational judicial instrument between inter-governmental method and "*méthode communautaire*"[1]. Indeed, as known the EU method, created by Jean Monnet

---

* Professore a contratto in European Law and EU Competition Law (Università degli Studi dell'Insubria, Varese), PhD in European and International Law (Università degli Studi di Udine), LL.M in European Law (College of Europe, Bruges).

1 See between all P. de Schoutheete, *La coopération politique européenne*, Labor, Bruxelles, 1986; V. Giscard d'Estaing, *Le Pouvoir et la Vie*, Compagnie 12, Paris, 1988, T. I, p. 119; M. Barnier, A. Vitorino, *La méthode communautaire*, Secrétariat de la Convention européenne, Document CONV 231/02, 3 September 2002; P. de Schoutheete, H. Wallace, *Le Conseil européen*, Études et Recherches n. 19, Notre Europe, September 2002; J. Delors, *Mémoires*, Plon, Paris, 2004, p. 227; Y. Bertoncini, V. Kreilinger, *Séminaire sur la Méthode communautaire. Éléments de synthèse*, seminar of 28 February 2012 in Bruxelles,

and initially applied in the CECA, was characterised by a dialogue between the European Commission – independent institution charged by the legislative initiative – and the Council representing the Member States. Following the modifications of the founding Treaties, nowadays the mechanism illustrated is completed by the crucial role of the European Parliament[2]. This method represents the highest form of integration developed by an international organisation and it could be considered as one of the strongest element of progression for Europe[3].

Although Switzerland is one of very few countries in Europe that has chosen to remain outside the EU, it is closely integrated with the Union. The present contribution wonder if the strong collaboration with EU could really be considered as integration. Switzerland is not represented in the EU's institutions – Commission, Council and Parliament, consequently has no right to participate in the legislative adoption of the *aquis* formulated by the EU's

Préface de Jacques Delors, Synthèse, Notre Europe, May 2012 ; J. PETERSON & M. SHACKLETON (Eds.), *The Institutions of the European Union*, 3 ed., Oxford University Press, Oxford, 2012.

2 T. BALLARINO, *Manuale di diritto dell'Unione europea*, Cedam, Padova, 2011; G. BISCOTTINI, *La natura giuridica delle Comunità Europee*, in *Tavole rotonde di diritto comunitario*, Giuffré, Milano, 1980; B. CONFORTI, *La dottrina di diritto comunitario: questa sconosciuta*, in *Dir. Un. Eur.*, 1-2004, p. 2; A. LA PERGOLA, *Unione europea tra il mercato comune e un moderno tipo di confederazione. Osservazioni di un costituzionalista*, in *Riv. trim. dir. e proc. civ.*, 1993, p. 1 ss; F. PALERMO, *La forma di Stato dell'Unione europea. Per una teoria costituzionale dell'integrazione sovranazionale*, Cedam, Padova, 2005; M. PANEBIANCO, *Quale* leadership *democratica nel nuovo Trattato di Roma?*, in *Dir. com e degli scambi int.*, Vol. 3/2005, pp. 421-435; M. PATRONO, *Il governo della prima Europa*, Cedam, Padova, 2003; C. PINELLI, *Ipotesi sulla forma di governo dell'Unione europea*, in *Riv. trim. dir. pubbl.*, 1989, p. 315 ss; G. TESAURO, *Diritto dell'Unione Europea*, 7 Ed., Cedam, Padova, 2012; A. VALVO, *Futuri assetti decisionali ed istituzionali dell'Unione europea*, in *Riv. cooperaz. giur. int.*, 2003, 13, p. 111 ss.; C. ZANGHÌ, *Istituzioni di diritto dell'Unione europea; verso una costituzione europea*, 4 Ed., Giappichelli, Torino, 2005.

3 R. BIEBER, *On lacunae of legitimacy and the contradictions of financial crisis management in the European Union*, in *EUI Law Working Papers*, n. 16, 2011, http://cadmus.eui.eu/bitstream/handle/1814/19696/LAW_2011_16_Bieber.pdf; J.-P. JACQUÉ, *Droit institutionel de l'Union Européenne*, Cours, 2015; P. PONZANO, *Un nuovo metodo dell'Unione*, in G. AMATO, R. GUALTIERI (Ed.), *Prove di Europa unita. Le istituzioni europee di fronte alla crisi*, Astrid, Firenze, 2013; F. SORRENTINO, *Profili costituzionali dell'integrazione comunitaria*, Giappichelli, Torino, 1996, p. 55.

governmental bodies[4]. So, it could be wondered why Switzerland is willing to implement the EU norms? If those relationship attribute to a form of mere pragmatism for cooperation with the EU only in areas of mutual interest[5], why Switzerland adopted the *aquis communautaire*, especially with reference to the jurisprudence of the Court of Justice of the European Union, as an internal standard to comply with?

The analysis of this paper will be conducted following the research question whether it is possible to design a conceptual framework, which belong to one of the two method, for the relationship between Switzerland and the European Union or if there is a third perspective to be taken[6]. Considering that the Switzerland case has been defined by distinguished doctrine as an "integration without membership"[7] or a "limited integration"[8] it is needed to

---

4 S. Lavenex, *Switzerland's Flexible Integration in the EU: A Conceptual Framework*, in *Swiss Political Science Review*, 15(4), pp. 547-575.

5 This pragmatic step-by-step approach has made it possible to devise tailor-made contractual solutions to a wide range of economic and political questions. The agreements not only provide both parties with extensive market access, they are also a basis for close cooperation in key policy areas.

6 New models of policy making without legislating have become an integral part of EU governance in various sectors, especially from the mid-1990s onwards. Usually referred as "network governance" are characterised by the process-oriented forms of policy making in individual sectors. Normally in contrast with the traditional Community method. See A. Héritier, *Common goods: reinventing European and international governance*, Rowman&Littlefield, Boulder, CO, 2002, pp. 185-206; A. Héritier, D. Lehmkuhl (Eds.), *The Shadow of Hierarchy and New Models of Governance*. Special issue *Journal of Public Policy* 28(1)/2008. Distinguished doctrine analysed the evolution of the civil judicial cooperation, without aiming to completeness see S. Bariatti, *La cooperazione giudiziaria in materia civile del terzo pilastro dell'Unione europea al titolo V del Trattato CE*, in *Diritto dell'Unione europea*, 2001, p. 261 ss.; S.M. Carbone, M. Frigo, L. Fumagalli, *Diritto processuale civile e commerciale comunitario*, Giuffré, Milano, 2004; F. Picone (Ed.), *Diritto internazionale privato e diritto comunitario*, Cedam, Padova, 2004; F. Pocar, *La comunitarizzazzione del diritto internazionale private: una "European Conflict of Law Revolution"?*, in *Riv. Dir. Inter. Priv.*, 2000, p. 873 ss.

7 M. Vahl, N. Grolimund, *Integration Without Membership: Switzerland's Bilateral Agreements with the European Union*, Centre for European Policies Studies, 2006; C. Church (Ed.), *Switzerland and the European Union*, Routledge, London, 2007.

8 S. Kux, Ul. Sverdrup, *Fuzzy borders and adaptive outsiders, Norway, Switzerland and the EU*, in *Journal of European Integration*, Vol. 22/2001, pp. 237-270 G. Edwards, *The Construction of Ambiguity and the Limits of Attraction: Europe and its Neighbourhood Policy*, in *Journal of European Integration*, Vol. 30(1)/2008, pp. 45-62.

research how the notion of integration has been implemented in the judicial cooperation and to which extent the flexible integration could be successfully in the judicial cooperation matters[9].

2 Switzerland as a part of the European Free Trade Area

Since the Free Trade Agreement signed in 1972, an increasingly numbers of agreements have been developed in several steps[10]. This bilateral approach enables Switzerland to adopt a policy based on full openness and cooperation with its European neighbours, and it has been endorsed by the Swiss electorate in various referendums[11]. However, in view of its geographic proximity and, particularly, owing to its political and economic relevance, the EU is by far Switzerland's most important commercial partner. The economic relationship is especially important: Switzerland earns one in every three francs through trade with the EU. In 2014, 55% of Switzerland's exports went to the EU and 73% of its imports originated from there[12]. The value of the commercial exchange between Switzerland and the EU it is estimated to be one billion of Swiss francs per day[13].

Thanks to the signature of this first international Treaty, adopted obviously to start dealing as a special commercial partner in the relationship between Swiss and EU, industrial goods originating in one of the States Parties

---

9 R. Ginsberg, *Conceptualizing the European Union as an International Actor: Narrowing the Theoretical Capability-Expectations Gap*, in *Journal of Common Market Studies*, Vol. 37(3)/1999, pp. 429-454; M. Jachtenfuchs, *The Governance Approach to European Integration*, in *Journal of Common Market Studies*, Vol. 39(2)/2001, pp. 245-264; A. Tovias, *Exploring the "Pros" and "Cons" of Swiss and Norwegian Models of Relations with the European Union: What Can Israel Learn from the Experiences of These Two Countries?*, in *Cooperation and Conflict*, Vol. 41(2)/2006, pp. 203-222.

10 C. Amalfitano, *Conflitti di giurisdizione e riconoscimento delle decisioni penali nell'Unione europea*, Giuffré, Milano, 2006; S. Bariatti, *Cases and materials on EU Private International Law*, Hart Publishing, Oxford-Portland, 2011; P. Bertoli, *Corte di giustizia, integrazione comunitaria e diritto internazionale privato e processuale*, Giuffré, Milano, 2005; A. Malatesta, S. Bariatti, F. Pocar (Ed.), *The external dimension of EC private International law in family and succession matters*, Cedam, Padova, 2008.

11 C. Dupon, P. Sciarini, *Back to the Future: The First Round of Bilateral Negotiations with Europe*, in C. Church (Ed.), *Switzerland and the European Union*, Routledge, London, 2006.

12 https://www.eda.admin.ch/eda/en/fdfa/foreign-policy/european-politics.html.

13 From the statistics of the European Union Delegation in Switzerland. Available at http://eeas.europa.eu/delegations/switzerland/eu_switzerland/political_relations/index_fr.htm.

to the agreement are not subject to customs duties[14]. Similar to artt. 28 and 29 of the Treaty on Functioning of the European Union (hereinafter TFEU), limitations on quantity – quotas – and any similar measures such as tariffs or duties are prohibited. In the case of processed agricultural products, dealt with in Protocol 2 of the EFTA, no customs duties apply to the industrial component of such products. As for the agricultural component, Switzerland has reduced its duties and export subsidies, and the EU has eliminated all duties and export supports.

Following the classic intergovernmental method in 1989 another international agreement was adopted: the Insurance Agreement[15]. Insurance companies operating in the field of direct damage insurance in Switzerland and the EU are guaranteed the freedom to choose their domicile. Agencies and branches are granted equal access and operating conditions on the territories of the States Parties. The agreement is not applicable to life insurance companies, reinsurance companies or statutory social insurance schemes, and it makes no provision for cross-border services.

3 The Lugano Convention

The Convention done in Lugano (hereinafter LugC) on the 16th September 1988 on jurisdiction and the enforcement of judgments in civil and commercial matters, signed by the Member States of the EU and Switzerland to strengthen in their territories the legal protection of persons, is a parallel convention to the Brussels Convention of 1968 which extends the application of those rules to Switzerland in its quality of States members of the European Free Trade Association[16]. Another important tool, adopted under the intergovernmental method, arise from the awareness of the links between Switzerland and EU, which was regulated in the economic field by the European Free Trade Association. Consequently, considering the need to determine the international jurisdiction of the courts, to facilitate recognition, and to intro-

14 A. Bonomi (Ed.), *Diritto internazionale privato e cooperazione giudiziaria in materia civile*, Giappichelli, Torino, 2009; S.M. Carbone, *Lo spazio giudiziario in materia civile e commerciale*, Giappichelli Torino, 2009; A. Tizzano, *Relazione sui protocolli relativi all'interpretazione da parte della Corte di giustizia della Convenzione di Roma del 19 giugno 1980 sulla legge applicabile alle obbligazioni contrattuali*, in GUEU C 219, 3 September 1990; T. Treves (Ed.), *Verso una disciplina comunitaria della legge applicabile ai contratti*, Cedam, Padova, 1983.

15 W.M. Hauschild, *L'importance des conventions communautaires pour la création d'un droit communautaire*, in *Rev. trim. droit eur.*, 1975, p. 6.

16 *Convention on Jurisdiction and the Enforcement of Judgments in Civil and Commercial Matters*, Sep. 16, 1998 O.J. (L319) 9, available at http://curia.europa.eu/common/recdoc/convention/en/c-textes/lug-idx.htm.

duce an expeditious procedure for securing the enforcement of judgments, authentic instruments and court settlements, this new act of international legislation enter into force[17]. As it will be highlighted in this paper, the EU norms adopted with the *méthode communautaire* and which created the area of freedom security and justice find its first legal basis in those convention adopted as international instruments[18].

Few years after, due to the enlargement of 1995, the Member States of the EU increased and not all the EU Member States were also parties to the LugC. Consequently the rules for determining the jurisdiction, recognition and enforcement of judgments diverged. A new revised version of the LugC was needed and a group of experts worked in this direction, however the EU Member States abstained from ratifying the revised version of the LugC adopting instead the Brussels regulation (Brussels I)[19]. However from the Swiss point of view another international convention was needed for apply-

17 A. Bonomi, E. Cashin Ritaine, G. Romano (Ed.), *La Convention de Lugano. Passé, présent et dèvenir*, Schulthess, Génevre-Zurich-Basel, 2007; A. Bucher (Ed.), *Loi sur le droit international privé, Convention de Lugano*, Helbing, Basel, 2011; E. Cannizzaro, *Le relazioni esterne della Comunità: verso un nuovo paradigma unitario?*, in *Diritto dell'Unione Europea*, 2007, p. 223 ss.; Y. Donzallaz, *La Convention de Lugano du 16 septembre 1998 concernant la competence judiciaire et l'exécution des décisions en matière civile et commerciale*, 1998, Berna; H. Gaudemet, Tallon, *Competénce et exécution des jugements en Europe*, LGDJ, Paris, 2010; N. Lavranos, *Opinion 1/03, Lugano Convention*, in *Common Market Law Review*, 2006, p. 1087 ss; L.S. Rossi, *Conclusione di accordi internazionali e coerenza del sistema: l'esclusività della competenza comunitaria*, in *Riv. Dir. Intern.*, 2007, p. 1008 ss.

18 I. Anrò, *La cooperazione giudiziaria e amministrativa*, p. 187, in M. Condinanzi (ed.), *Unione europea e Svizzera tra cooperazione e integrazione*, Giuffré, Milano, 2012; Ch. Kohler, *Interrogations sur les sources du droit international privé européen après le traité d'Amsterdam*, in *Revue critique de droit international privé*, 1999, p. 1 ss.; D. Vidal, *Rapport introductif*, in *Rev. Aff. Eur.*, n. 2/2005, p. 139.

19 Council Regulation (EC) No 44/2001 of 22 December 2000 on jurisdiction and the recognition and enforcement of judgments in civil and commercial matters. See R. Clerici, *Art. 65*, in F. Pocar (Ed.), *Commentario breve ai Trattati della Comunità e dell'Unione europea*, Cedam, Padova, 2001, p. 308 ss.; E. Gualco, *L'opposizione al decreto di* exequatur *nel regolamento 44/2001: la natura atecnica della nozione di "ricorso" secondo la giurisprudenza della Corte di Cassazione italiana*, in *Dir. mar.*, 2012, p. 1072 ss.; L. Mari, *Il diritto processuale civile della Convenzione di Bruxelles, I. Il sistema della competenza*, Cedam, Padova, 1999; G.P. Romano, *Litispendenza e connessione di cause nel regolamento n. 44*, in *Diritto internazionale privato e cooperazione giudiziaria in materia civile*, A. Bonomi (Ed.), Giappichelli, Torino, 2009, p. 103 ss.; L.S. Rossi, *L'incidenza dei principi comunitari sul diritto internazionale privato: dalla «comunitarizzazione» alla «costituzionalizzazione»*, in *Riv. dir. int. priv. proc.*, 2004, p. 63 ss.

ing the norms of Brussels I. On 30th October 2007 the revised version of the LugC was signed in Lugano[20]. The working group while writing the revised version considered to eliminate every form of *exequatur* to establish a common judicial area, however the solution was too premature for the state of reality of the integration achieved[21]. Consequently, even if the LugC is defined as "*part of Community rules and that therefore the Court of Justice of the European Communities has jurisdiction to give rulings on the interpretation of the provisions of this Convention as regards the application by the courts of the Member States of the European Community*"[22], however the current provision still provide Member States the power to invoke the public order to refuse the recognition of judgement as for example in case of limitation of the right of defence[23].

---

20 See A. Markus, "*Espace Lugano*": *aspects choisis de la coopération civile entre l'Union européenne et l'AELE*, in M. Dony, C. Kaddous (Ed.), *D'Amsterdam à Lisbonne: dix ans d'espace de liberté, de sécurité et de justice*, Bruylant, Bale-Bruxelles-Paris, 2010; L. Muller, *The Revised Lugano Convention from the Swiss Perspective*, available at http://www.cjel.net/online/18_1-muller/.

21 F. Pocar, *Relazione esplicativa alla Convezione concernente la competenza giurisdizionale, il riconoscimento e l'esecuzione delle decisioni in materia civile e commerciale conclusa a Lugano il 30 settembre 2007*, in OJEU C 319 of 23 December 2009. Art. 34 establish "*A judgment shall not be recognised: 1. if such recognition is manifestly contrary to public policy in the State in which recognition is sought; 2. where it was given in default of appearance, if the defendant was not served with the document which instituted the proceedings or with an equivalent document in sufficient time and in such a way as to enable him to arrange for his defence, unless the defendant failed to commence proceedings to challenge the judgment when it was possible for him to do so; 3. if it is irreconcilable with a judgment given in a dispute between the same parties in the State in which recognition is sought; L 339/12 EN Official Journal of the European Union 21.12.2007 4. if it is irreconcilable with an earlier judgment given in another State bound by this Convention or in a third State involving the same cause of action and between the same parties, provided that the earlier judgment fulfils the conditions necessary for its recognition in the State addressed*".

22 Third paragraph in the preamble of Protocol n. 2 of the LugC.

23 G. Biagioni, *L'art. 6 della Convenzione europea dei diritti dell'uomo e l'ordine pubblico processuale nel sistema della Convenzione di Bruxelles*, in *Riv. Dir. Intern.*, 2001, p. 723 ss.; N. Boschiero, *L'ordine pubblico processuale comunitario ed "europeo"*, in P. De Cesari, M. Frigessi di Rattalma (Ed.), *La tutela transnazionale del credito*, Giappichelli, Torino, 2007, p. 163 ss.; P. Chevalier, *L'execution des decisiones jurisdictionelles etrangres hors espace judiciare europeen: etat de lieu de la jurisprudence*, in *Rev. gén. dr. int. public*, 2013, p. 503 ss.; G. Cuniberti, *The recognition of foreign judgments lacking reasons in Europe: access to justice, foreign court avoidance and efficiency*, in *International and Comparative Law Quaterly*, 2008, p. 25 ss.; E. D'Alessandro, *Il riconoscimento delle senten-*

As mention, one of the most relevant innovation introduced by the revised version is the possibility for the European Court of Justice to be referred for the interpretation of the convention[24]. Thanks to this provision European judge had the opportunity, within the opinion 1/03 to clarify that the competence for the negotiations and signature of the revised LugC belonged to the Union[25]. Indeed, the legal base of art. 81 TFEU allows the Union to develop judicial cooperation in civil matters having cross-border implications[26].

---

ze straniere, Giappichelli, Torino, 2007; M. De Cristofaro, *Ordine pubblico "processuale" ed enucleazione dei principi fondamentali del diritto processuale "europeo"*, in V. Colesanti, C. Consolo, G. Gaja (Ed.), *Il diritto processuale civile nell'avvicinamento giuridico internazionale. Omaggio ad Aldo Attardi*, Cedam, Padova, 2009, p. 893 ss.; M. Farina, *Titoli esecutivi europei ed esecuzione forzata in Italia*, Aracne, Roma, 2012; O. Feraci, *L'abolizione dell'*exequatur *nella proposta di revisione del regolamento n. 44/2001: quale destino per i motivi di rifiuto del riconoscimento e dell'esecuzione delle decisioni?*, in *Riv. dir. int.*, 2011, p. 833; O. Feraci, *L'ordine pubblico nel diritto dell'Unione europea*, Giuffré, Milano, 2012; O. Lopes Pegna, *I procedimenti relativi all'efficacia delle decisioni straniere in materia civile*, Cedam, Padova, 2009; P. Lotti, *L'ordine pubblico internazionale*, Giuffré, Milano, 2005; B. Nascimbene, *Riconoscimento di sentenze straniere e ordine pubblico comunitario*, in *Riv. dir. intern. priv. e proc.*, 2002, p. 658 ss.; S. Othenin-Girard, *La réserve d'ordre public en droit International privé suisse*, Schulthess, Zurich, 1999; C.E. Tuo, *La rivalutazione della sentenza straniera nel regolamento di bruxelles I: tra divieti e reciproca fiducia*, Giuffré, Milano, 2012; F. Seatzu, *Diritto alla difesa, ordine pubblico dello Stato richiesto dell'exequatur e Convenzione di Bruxelles del 1968*, Litotipografia operai Cagliari, 2001.

24 Protocol 2 of the Lugano Convention.

25 F. Mosconi, *Un confronto tra la disciplina del riconoscimento e dell'esecuzione delle decisioni straniere nei recenti regolamenti comunitari*, in *Riv. dir. int. priv. proc.*, 2001, p. 545 ss.

26 "*The Union shall develop judicial cooperation in civil matters having cross-border implications, based on the principle of mutual recognition of judgments and of decisions in extrajudicial cases. Such cooperation may include the adoption of measures for the approximation of the laws and regulations of the Member States. 2. For the purposes of paragraph 1, the European Parliament and the Council, acting in accordance with the ordinary legislative procedure, shall adopt measures, particularly when necessary for the proper functioning of the internal market, aimed at ensuring: (a) the mutual recognition and enforcement between Member States of judgments and of decisions in extrajudicial cases;(b) the cross-border service of judicial and extrajudicial documents; (c) the compatibility of the rules applicable in the Member States concerning conflict of laws and of jurisdiction;(d) cooperation in the taking of evidence; (e) effective access to justice; (f) the elimination of obstacles to the proper functioning of civil proceedings, if necessary by promoting the compatibility of the rules on civil procedure applicable in the Member States; (g) the development of alternative methods of dispute settlement;(h) support for the training of the judiciary and judicial staff. 3. Notwithstanding paragraph 2,*

Choosing the European Court of Justice as a competent judge for interpreting the convention it could be considered as the key moment for the transferring from the intergovernmental method to the EU method creating a needed parallelism between the regulation n. 44/2001 applicable inside the EU and the LugC applicable with Swiss. Moreover this provision ensures the consistency of the entire system thanks to the consistency of its jurisprudence[27]. However, it could be wondered if it is appropriate this minimal solution of integration which devolves to the judicial activism all the future progress of the Brussels-Lugano system or if it is a way to still remain, for what concern the content, in the international law mechanism.

4 Switzerland as a part of the bilateral agreement

Currently Iceland, Liechtenstein and Norway even if they are not EU members, however they are part of the European Economic Area (EEA). The EEA

---

measures concerning family law with cross-border implications shall be established by the Council, acting in accordance with a special legislative procedure. The Council shall act unanimously after consulting the European Parliament. The Council, on a proposal from the Commission, may adopt a decision determining those aspects of family law with cross-border implications which may be the subject of acts adopted by the ordinary legislative procedure. The Council shall act unanimously after consulting the European Parliament. The proposal referred to in the second subparagraph shall be notified to the national Parliaments. If a national Parliament makes known its opposition within six months of the date of such notification, the decision shall not be adopted. In the absence of opposition, the Council may adopt the decision".

27 G. Biagioni, *L'abolizione dei motivi ostativi al riconoscimento e all'esecuzione nella Proposta di revisione del Regolamento di Brussels I*, in *Riv. dir. int. priv. e proc.*, 2011, p. 971 ss.; P. Franzina, *Le condizioni di applicabilità del regolamento (CE) 44/2001 alla luce del parere 1/03 della Corte di giustizia*, in *Riv. dir. intern.*, 2006, p. 948 ss.; A. Dickinson, *Free Movement of Judgments in the EU: Knock Down the Walls but Mind the Ceiling*, in E. Lein (Ed.), *The Brussels I Review Proposal Uncovered*, 2012, London, British Institute of International and Comparative Law, p. 140; B. Hess, *The Brussels I Regulation: recent Case Law of the Court of Justice and the Commission's proposed recast*, in *Comm. Mar. Law Rev.*, 2012, p. 1101; E.X. Kramer, *Cross Border Enforcement and the Brussels I-bis Regulation: Towards a New Balance between Mutual Trust and National Control over Fundamental Rights*, in *Netherlands Int. Law Rev.*, 2013, p. 343 ss.; P.A. Nielsen, *The new Brussels I Regulation*, in *Comm. Mar. Law Rev.*, 2013, p. 524; A. Nuyts, *La reforme du règlement Bruxelles I* bis, in *Rev. crit. DIP*, 2013, p. 22; F. Pocar, *Con la nuova proposta di abolizione dell'*exequatur *lo spazio giuridico europeo cerca il rafforzamento*, in *Giuda al diritto*, 2011, p. 9; L.S. Rossi, *Conclusione di accordi internazionali e coerenza del sistema: l'esclusività della competenza comunitaria*, in *Riv. dir. intern.*, 2007, p. 1008 ss.

was formed in 1994 in order to extend the European Union's provisions on its internal market to countries in the EFTA. EU legislation relating to the internal market becomes part of the legislation of the EEA countries once they have agreed to incorporate it. Switzerland is neither an EU nor EEA member, but is part of the single market. Following rejection of the EEA, it has been decided to come back to intergovernmental method and to launch negotiations on a sector-by-sector basis to ensure market access for Swiss companies without discrimination in key economic sectors[28]. The EU and Switzerland have signed more than 120 bilateral agreements, including a free trade agreement in 1972 already analysed I the first paragraph of this paper and two major series of sectorial bilateral agreements. The scope of all those agreements is to ensure an alignment of a large portion of Swiss law with the EU norms[29]. However, the international instrument can only ensure that alignment at the time of the signature. Indeed, the international conventions does not have the characteristics to up to date with the development of the EU law.

In 1993 the EU started the negotiations in seven sectors on condition that the negotiations be conducted in parallel and that they be signed and take effect together. This condition of parallelism was requested because the interest of both partners was only to achieve a single package adoption for all the different dossiers. The agreements were therefore linked in legal terms by a so-called "guillotine clause", stipulating that they can only take effect together: if one of the agreements were not to be prolonged or terminated, the other could also cease to have effect. The first block of sectorial agreements - Bilateral I - was signed in 1999 and entered into force in 2002[30]. Due

28 M. Egeberg, J. Trondal, *Differentiated Integration in Europe: The Case of EEA Country*, in *Journal of Common Market Studies*, 37, n. 1/1999, pp. 133-142.

29 S. Breitenmoser, *Sectoral Agreements between the EC and Switzerland: contents and context*, in *CMLR*, 2003, pp. 1137-1186; C. Dupont, P. Sciarini, C. Egli, *Entre coherence et efficacité: la Suisse dans les négotiations bilatérales avec l'Union Européenne*, in *Rev. Suisse de Science Politique*, 7, n. 4/2001, pp. 5-37; D. Felder, C. Kaddous (Ed.), *Accords bilatéraux Suisse – UE (Commentaires)*, Basel-Geneva-Munich-Bruxelles- Paris, 2006; C. Sanna, *Gli accordi bilaterali tra la Svizzera e l'Unione europea*, in *Dir. comm. int.*, 1999, p. 547; R. Schwok, *Les accords sectoriels Union europèenne-Suisse: une nouvelle forme de flexibilité dans la dimension extérieure de l'UE,* in *RMCUE*, 1999, p. 613 ss.

30 C. Dupont, P. Sciarini, *Back to Future: the First Round of Bilateral Negotiations with Europe*, in C. Church (Ed.), *Switzerland and the European Union*, Routledge, London, 2006; N. Grolimund, M. Vahl, *Integration without Membership: Switzerland's Bilateral Agreements with the European Union*, Centre for European Policy Studies, Brussels, 2006; N. Levrat, *Switzerland's Relation with the EU after the adoption of Seven Bilateral Agreements*, in *EFA Rev.*, 2001, p. 335 ss.; G.H. Samaden, *Les septs accords bilatéraux entre la Suisse et l'Union européenne*, in *Revue du Marché commun de l'Union européenne*, n. 433/1999, pp. 696-699.

to the Swiss constitutional provisions the bilateral in order to enter in the Swiss system had to be object of referendum[31]. The Bilateral I are composed by seven agreements: free movement of persons, air transport, land transport, trade in agricultural products, technical trade barriers, public procurement and research cooperation.

Despite mutual declarations of intent, the European Commission was sceptical about further negotiations of this kind. In order to proceed with the negotiations it should have been included areas of special interest to Switzerland, including cooperation in the areas of security and asylum, with Swiss participation in the Schengen/Dublin arrangements (cooperation in police and justice, asylum and migration matters). Switzerland also wanted negotiations in areas mentioned in the joint declaration of intent to Bilateral Agreements I: processed agricultural products, statistics, the environment, MEDIA, education, pensions and services. Furthermore Switzerland wanted to protect the interests of its financial centre, beginning with banking secrecy. A further set of sectorial agreements – Bilateral II – was signed in 2004 and entered into force in 2005. They are basically related to strengthening economic cooperation and extending cooperation on asylum and free travel within the Schengen borders[32]. While the agreements intensified economic relations, they also created a complex and sometimes incoherent network of obligations, which are not easy to sustain. As mentioned, the nature of the bilateral agreements – instruments of international law – is static given that there are no mechanisms to adapt the agreements to evolving EU legislation.

More than 120 sectorial bilateral treaties are currently linking the EU with Switzerland however, the issue of immigration and asylum seekers has been a sensitive one and the bilateral relations since the anti-immigration initiative of February 2014 are facing difficulties, especially after the latest parliamentary elections on 18 October 2015[33]. The political position of the Swiss parliament is likely to take a hard line with the EU for the anti-immigration vote. Consequently, nowadays it does not seems to be achievable the implemented

31 The Bilateral I have been approved by 67.2% of the Swiss electorate on 21 May 2000 and came into force on 1 June 2002. Together with the Free Trade Agreement, they make it possible for the Swiss private sector to have extensive access to the Single European Market of more than 505 million potential consumers.

32 C. Kaddous, M. Jametti-Greiner (Ed.), *Accords Bilateraux II Suisse-UE et autres Accoords récents*, in *Dossier de droit européen*, N. 16/2006, Bruylant, Bruxelles.

33 The anti-immigration initiative in February 2014 was promoted by the populist right-wing anti-immigrant Swiss People's Party (SVP). The SVP won the biggest share of the vote in the elections (29.4%), increasing its number of seats as the largest party in Switzerland's lower house of parliament from 54 to 65.

integration with the EU method. It should be wondered if any further negotiations with the intergovernmental method will still be possible.

5 The judicial cooperation in criminal matters

For what concerns the judicial cooperation in criminal matters it will appear, even more clearly, that the instrument for adopting norms still belong to the classical international method. In 1967 Switzerland signed the European Convention on Extradition[34] and the one for the Judicial Assistance in Criminal Law[35]. Moreover, Swiss is also part to the Convention of the Council of Europe on the international validity of repressive judgements and the one on the transferring of persons during criminal proceedings[36]. Switzerland signed with some EU Member States international convention based on geographical

---

34 The European Convention on Extradition ha been signed by Switzerland on the 29th November 1965 and has been ratified on the 20th December 1966. Switzerland is also part of the first and second protocol to the Convention, however does not signed the third protocol. Between all see G. Catelani, *I rapporti internazionali in materia penale*, Giuffré, Milano, 1995; E. Calvanese, *Art. 723*, in G. Tranchina (Ed.), *Codice di procedura penale*, Giuffré, Milano, 2008; G. Di Chiara, voce *Rapporti giurisdizionali con autorità straniere*, in *Enc. dir.*, II, 1998, p. 890 ss; G. Diotallevi, *Rapporti giurisdizionali con autorità straniere*, in G. Lattanzi, E. Lupo, *Esecuzione e rapporti giurisdizionali con autorità straniere*, in *Cod. proc. pen.*, VIII, 2008, Milano, Giuffré, p. 507 ss.; A.C. Kiss, La Convention européenne d'extradition, in *Annuaire francais de droit international*, n. 1, Vol. 4/1958, pp. 493-495; M.R. Marchetti, *La Convenzione europea di estradizione*, Giuffrè, Milano, 1990; M. Pisani, *La convenzione di estradizione*, in *Ind. P.*, 1980, p. 11 ss.; A. Tizzano, *La convenzione europea di estradizione*, in *Annuario di diritto internazionale*, 1965, p. 204 ss.

35 G. Gaja, *Trattati internazionali*, in *Dig. disc. pubb.*, XV, Giappichelli, Torino, 2000, p. 344 ss.; M. Cartabia, *La Cedu e l'ordinamento italiano: rapporti tra fonti, rapporti tra giurisdizioni*, in *All'incrocio fra Costituzione e Cedu. Il rango delle norme della Convenzione e l'efficacia interna delle sentenze di Strasburgo*; M. Pisani, *La Convenzione europea di assistenza giudiziaria in materia penale e l'ordinamento italiano (spunti riepilogativi)*, in *Studi in onore di G. Vassalli, Evoluzione e riforma del diritto e della procedura penale*, Giuffré, Milano, 1991, p. 505 ss.; D. Vigoni, *Rogatoria penale internazionale e strumenti alternativi*, in *Ind. P.*, 1986, p. 484 ss.

36 F. Capotorti, *Cours général de droit international public*, in *RCADI*, tome 248 (1994-IV), p. 209; R. De Lange, *The European Public Order, Constitutional Principles and Fundamental Rights*, in *Erasmus Law Review*, 2007, p. 12; J. Frowein, *The European Convention on Human Rights as the Public Order of Europe*, in *Collected Courses of the Academy of European Law*, Vol. I, Book 2, p. 267 ss.; F. Sudre, *Existe t-il un ordre public européen?*, in B. Tavernier (Ed.), *Quelle Europe pour les droits de l'homme?*, Bruylant, Bruxelles, 1999, p. 39.

need of proximity. Indeed, it is clear that the participation of Switzerland to the mentioned international convention belongs to a form of primary cooperation which does not imply a strong trust in the criminal system of others countries neither a transferring of the power of the State[37].

The evidence that the cooperation with Switzerland is genetically different from any cooperation in criminal matters developed in the Union is also given by the application of the *ne bis in idem* principle. The Swiss national judge is supposed to ensure the consistent application and interpretation of EU law which includes also the so called *aquis Schengen*. Exactly for this reason Switzerland has to present on yearly basis an annual relation illustrating how the *aquis* has been interpreted and applied by the national authorities. The Convention for the application of Schengen also provide Switzerland with the right to present observations in the preliminary reference in front the Court of Justice of the European Union while the pending question is about the *aquis* Schengen. However, the Switzerland does not have the obligation to apply the Chart of Fundamental Rights that is legally binding only for the EU members[38]. Until now the EU accepted, with a classical intergovernmental method, that Switzerland was making a selection "à la carte" of the EU norms which would have accepted as legally binding and applicable in its judicial system. The opportunity above illustrated of being part of a judicial proceedings in front of the EU Court without being part of the Union illustrates clearly the half way road in which are now the relationship between Switzerland and EU.

After the signature by Switzerland of the Schengen Treaty, in accordance with Art. 216, para. 1 TFEU, individual Member States does not enjoy anymore the competence to stipulate directly with Swizerland any convention for the judicial cooperation in criminal matters, since it belong to an exclusive competence of the Union[39]. However, the Member States can implement and

---

37 C. Kaddous, *Role and Position of the High Representative of the Union for Foreign Affairs and Security Policy under the Lisbon Treaty*, in *The Lisbon Treaty, EU Constitutionalism without a Constitutional Treaty?*, 2008, Vienna, Springer Verlag, pp. 205-221; E. Lopez, *Les accords des Schengen*, in L. Moreillon (Ed.), *Aspects pénaux des Accords bilateraux Suisse/Union européenne. Accords de Schenge, Dublin et autres engagements bilatéraux*, 2008, Basel, p. 113 ss.

38 C. Amalfitano, *La cooperazione giudiziaria in materia penale tra Unione europea e Svizzera. In particolare, l'operatività del principio del* ne bis in idem, in M. Condinanzi (Ed.), *op. cit.*, Giuffré, Milano, 2012, pp. 225-257.

39 S. Peers, *Mission accomplished: EU Justice and Home Affairs Law after the Treaty of Lisbon*, in *Common Market Law Rev.*, 2001, p. 661 ss.; R. Roth, B. Amirdiviani, *L'entraide judiciaire Suisse en matière pénale à un tournant? Etat de la question à la veille d'une adhèsion à Schengen*, in G. De Kerchove, A. Weyembergh (Ed.), *Sécurité et justice: enjeu de la politique extérieure de*

strengthen the cooperation by adopting agreements which simplify what already prescribe by the EU law[40].

6 Concluding remarks

In this paper it has been illustrated how the notion of integration has been implemented in the judicial cooperation first in the civil and commercial sector and, only recently, in criminal matters. All the agreements analysed are based on a classic form of cooperation between governments without transferring of any legal or decision making authority to a supranational body, except for what concern the Court of Justice of European Union. Each of the parties is responsible for implementing the agreements on its own sovereign territory. The Bilateral Agreements are based either on the equivalence of legislation, as in the case of the dismantling of technical barriers to trade and the Agreement on public procurement markets, or on the adoption of the *acquis communautaire* as in the case of Schengen. The agreements and their further development are administered by joint committees where both parties to the contract are represented with equal rights for exchanging information and for mutual consultations. In the joint committees the two parties must reach a unanimous decision. The Bilateral Agreements can only be amended with the joint agreement of the parties and are not subject to automatic amendment. It is generally necessary to adopt developments of relevant EU law in order to maintain the existing condition. The conclusion of new agreements it will be possible only if EU and Switzerland will tackle the issue related to the free movement of persons. The positive economic impact of the Agreements is recognised. Swiss companies now find new business opportunities in markets that were formerly closed to them. Also foreign suppliers gain free access to the Swiss market. Indeed, the biggest economic impact is that resulting from liberalisation of the movement of persons, which makes it easier to transfer Swiss staff to positions in the EU states, and also to recruit workers for the

---

l'Union européenne, Ed. Université de Bruxelles, Bruxelles, 2003, p. 247 ss.; L.S. Rossi, *From EU Pillar to Area: The Impact of the Lisbon Treaty on the External Dimension of Freedom Security and Justice*, in *Dir. Un. Eur.*, 2011, p. 999 ss.; R. Vincente, *L'espace deliberate, de sécurité et de justice après le traité de Lisbonne*, in *Annuaire Suisse de droit européen*, 2010, p. 37 ss.

40 R. Balzaretti, *L'importanza della cooperazione Schengen – Dublino per la Svizzera: situazione attuale e prospettive*, in AA.VV., *Accordi bilaterali Svizzera-Unione europea. Atti della giornata di studio del 4 giugno 2007*, 2008, Lugano, p. 21 ss.; E. Lopez, *Les accords des Schengen*, in L. Moreillon (Ed.), *Aspects pénaux des Accords bilateraux Suisse/Union européenne. Accords de Schenge, Dublin et autres engagements bilatéraux*, Helbing Lichtenhahn, Basel, 2008, p. 793.

Swiss labour market. Thanks to the Agreement on the free movement of persons the Swiss labour market effectively includes the entire area of the EU.

It seems quite obvious that the European Union, considering the economic importance of the agreement with Switzerland accepted the selection of EU norms characterised by the intergovernmental method. Consequently, I do believe that in the relationship between Switzerland and EU we can only talk about a reduced integration, needed from commercial and economical point of view, defined in a positive way as a flexible integration, however not successfully nor satisfactory in the judicial cooperation matter, especially not at all in the criminal matters.

Chiara Giussani*

The impact of the Common Reporting Standards of the OECD and of the Agreement Concerning Tax on Savings Incomes between the European Union and the Swiss Confederation Regarding Bank Secrecy

Abstract: After an introduction on the notion of bank secrecy, the author recalls the main regulatory initiatives adopted both at international and at Swiss level to combat money laundering and terrorist financing. The relationship between Switzerland and the European Union are then analysed, taking into account double taxation agreements, the II packages bilateral agreements and the agreement on tax of savings incomes.

1 Introduction: the notion of banking secrecy

The Swiss banking system, one of the most important in the world, probably owes part of its development and of its success to its banking secrecy, introduced in 1934, and governed by art. 47 of the Federal Law on Banks and Savings Banks (hereinafter also the "Banking Act"), as a professional obligation to the bankers, the violation of which can also be pursued in criminal proceedings[1].

As defined by the Swiss Federal Department of Finance, bank secrecy is the "*protection of the privacy of bank customers from unjustified interventions by the State*", and it is based on art. 13 of the Federal Constitution,

---

* PhD candidate in European Union Law at the University of Milan.

1 According to art. 47, §§ 1 and 1a of the Banking Act, in fact: «*Shall be punished by imprisonment up to three years or a monetary penalty anyone who intentionally: a. reveals a secret that is confided or of which is news in his capacity as a member of an organ, employee, trustee or liquidator of a bank, a member of an organ or employee of an audit company, or; b. attempts to induce such a violation of professional secrecy; c. divulges a secret that was revealed in accordance with subparagraph a, or exploits it for themselves or others. Shall be punished by imprisonment of up to five years or a monetary penalty anyone who, by committing an act referred to in paragraph 1 letter a or c, obtains for himself or for another a patrimonial advantage*».

rule that states that everyone has "*the right to the respect of his private and family life*". Among the fields protected by this provision falls, in fact, even the financial reports relating the assets and income, except in cases where they constitute an abuse of a criminal nature.

If such is the reconstruction of the concerned professional obligation, it is easy to understand how the banking secrecy expression, usually and commonly used, does not precisely express its own function: the bank customer protection, rather than the protection of the bank itself.

Specifically it is a duty of confidentiality comparable to that of doctors or lawyers, aimed at protecting the privacy of citizens by prohibiting bank employees to provide third parties with information about the relationship entertained by the bank with the customer[2]. The most correct term for, therefore, is that of "*secrecy related to bank customers*".

Banking secrecy, however encounters limitations. Several provisions of civil and criminal law, of the legislation on debt collection and bankruptcy, of the administrative criminal law and judicial assistance in criminal matters in fact provide for derogations tooth's confidentiality. For example, whenever an order from a supervisory authority or a judicial authority is issued, the aforesaid duty of secrecy will be revoked against the wishes of the customer. As is well understandable, there is in fact an obligation for lenders to cooperate and hand over all the documentation requested by the courts in case of criminal activities, criminal proceedings, forced execution and tax fraud. In addition to that, whenever it is to be ascertained, or is established, the fulfilment of criminal illegal activities, the right to access to bank information is also given, regardless of whether the offense was committed in Switzerland, to the foreign judicial authorities by virtue of specific international treaties (v. *infra*, § 2).

---

2 In Switzerland, the protection of financial privacy is a right of the citizens. The banks are bound by the obligation of discretion with respect to the financial affairs of their clients or third parties. The holder of the secret is the customer and not the bank, and for this reason the bank can not unilaterally decide to failing in secret. The customer may, however, release the bank from the obligation of discretion and allow, or even require it to disclose information covered by banking secrecy. In addition, the competent authorities may force the bank, in the cases provided by law, to publish information about their customers, especially when there is suspicion of a crime.
In addition to the rule of the Federal Constitution mentioned in the text, banking secrecy is primarily governed by civil law, as a contractual obligation of the banker to maintain secrecy about the balance of their client's situation. The customer privacy is also protected by the general provisions of the Swiss Civil Code concerning the protection of privacy (art. 27 ss. of the Commercial Code) and by legislation on data protection.

Swiss banking secrecy has been, over the years, the object of many perplexity, when not of outspoken criticism[3], because of recognition of its questionable consistency with a higher ethics in business matters, increasingly invoked and implemented at a global level, and which found new impetus in efforts to fight against international terrorism after the events of September 2001 ending up to be closely connected with the tendency of States to strengthen their territorial sovereignty and thus fiscal and financial. The climate of suspicion on the international image of Swiss banks, generated by the global mentioned phenomenon, has prompted for some response in the Swiss legal order and in its "national sample", succinctly described as banking secrecy.

Since the late nineties, and more specifically from April 1, 1998, the new Federal Law relating to the fight against money laundering in the financial sector (hereinafter also the "MLA")[4] provides for duties of care for credit institutes, inspired by the Convention on to the obligation of diligence for banks institutes (hereinafter also the "CDB"), the latter consisting of a self-regulatory code that the same Swiss banks have adopted, in order to combat money laundering[5]. Over the years, in the field the regulatory, the importance of the impulses contained in the Circular and the Notices of the former Federal Commission on Money Laundering of the Banks, replaced, starting in 2009, by the Swiss Financial Market Supervisory Authority (hereinafter also the "FINMA") increased[6].

3 Among which we remember the stock, naturally secreted at Swiss banks by assets deposited by Jewish citizens in the historical period from the rise of Nazism and the outbreak of World War II.

4 Federal Law of 10 October 1997 on the fight against money laundering in the financial sector. The legislative text is available at the following address: https://www.admin.ch/opc/it/classified-compilation/19970427/index.html.

5 The Convention on the duty of care for the banks (CDB) has been in existence since 1977 and represents a source of self-discipline of banks in the fight against money laundering, adopted long before the provisions on money laundering entered into force and even before in Swiss penal Code punitive provisions of this offense were introduced. The CDB has been revised every five years, the last time in April 2008. Its focus is the identification of the policyholder and the determination of the beneficial owner. It describes in detail the procedures to be followed for carrying out the necessary checks and verification of documents. For the purpose at issue here, among many provisions, the CDB prohibits to the banks to put in place any type of active assistance that might facilitate the transfer to Switzerland of capital from countries whose legislation restricts the placement abroad; it also prohibits any activity to pre-ordained tax evasion and similar practices by issuing incomplete certifications.

6 Namely the Federal Supervisory Authority for Financial Markets that, as of 1 January 2009, took over the business of the Federal Banking Commission ("SFBC"), the Federal Office of Private Insurance (BPV) and the supervisory authorities control

Among the measures incorporated into the AMLA it is included the identification of the contracting and actual holder of the economic relationship, as well as the contextualization of a banking transaction, to assess if the same appears unusual or if there are indications of money laundering operations in progress. Based on these evaluations banks are obliged to inform the competent authorities in those cases that they consider as suspicious. Basically, with the entry into force of the new MLA, given the strong international pressure, the Swiss banking system first had to transpose the provisions of European and world anti-money laundering legislation[7] (v. *infra* § 2), abolishing the bearer savings books, introducing identification checks, providing controls and acceptance criteria in the bank for politically exposed clients (which carry a higher risk of money laundering/corruption).

On the basis of the above, to date, it is therefore no longer possible to open an anonymous account in Switzerland, since the law itself imposes the so-called *principle of identification of the account holder*. Alternatively, however, the banks allow the opening of numbered accounts (identified by numbers/invented names) permitted, according to official statements, the sole purpose of limiting the spread of the data of the person owning the account and certainly not in order to circumvent and avoid intervention of judicial authorities. Despite this declaration of intent, however, in practice it appears that whenever it is necessary to investigate the numbered account, the investigating magistrate is required to prior acknowledge all the data relating

---

for the fight against money laundering ("AdC LRD"). FINMA was established as a public corporation of the federal government with its own legal personality. The entity brings together into a single authority the duties and functions of supervising banks, stock exchanges and insurance companies, as well as the fight against money laundering. It shall also deal with the reorganization and winding-up procedures, the supervision of the disclosure of holdings and takeover bids for listed companies. At the international level, FINMA is working with the Basel Committee on Banking Supervision ("BCBS"), with the International Organisation of Securities Commissions ("IOSCO"), the Financial Action Task Force (GAFI/FATF) and the international authorities for the fight against money laundering. The aim of these forms of cooperation is the exchange of information and joint efforts to influence the evolution of the discipline internationally.

7 Just think about, in this regard, the Code of Conduct on the Prevention of Money Laundering of the Basel Committee, the 40 recommendations of the FATF as well as the EU Directive 2015/849 of the European Parliament and of the Council on the prevention of the financial system money laundering or terrorist financing, in OJEU L 141, 5 June 2015, p. 73 ss., also better known as "anti-money laundering Directive IV" (as after three previous directives governing the matter in question, namely Directive 91/308/EEC, "The anti-money laundering Directive", Directive 2001/97/EC, "the anti-money laundering Directive", Directive 2005/60/EC, "III Anti-Money Laundering Directive).

to this account, with the result that any investigation (and in specific case is strongest for cross-border investigations), refers to this type of accounts, ends up to be much longer and more complex.

In addition to the aforementioned principle, the MLA has also introduced, for the financial intermediaries, the obligation to report in case of suspicion of money laundering, and has set up the office deputy to receive such communications, namely the Office of Communication on money laundering (from now on, "MROS"). Once received, the MROS analyzes suspicious warnings and, if it consider so, it shall forward the warnings to the relevant judicial authorities. In addition, it has the task to exchange information with foreign counterparts' authorities, namely the Financial Intelligence Unit (hereinafter, also the "FIU" acronym)[8].

On this point, it is interesting to note that, according to the provisions of the Swiss legislation in force until 2012, whenever the MROS exchanged the information requested by the competent foreign authorities, it was not authorized to provide from time to time relevant financial data (i.e.: numbers bank accounts, elements of money transactions, information on account balances). According to Swiss law, in fact, such information is protected by bank secrecy and professional secrecy. This "bottleneck" has always been a strong limit to the efforts to combat money laundering in place at international level, considered the application by the various FIU of the so-called *principle of reciprocity*, with the result, very significant in practical terms, that they refrained from sending to MROS relevant financial information concerning Swiss taxpayers also operating in foreign markets.

2 The first openings in the field of combating money laundering and terrorist financing

As known, a result of the G7 Summit held in Paris in 1989, the *Groupe d'action financiere* – Financial Action Task Force (hereinafter also "FATF") was founded. Even Switzerland is a member of this intergovernmental body that develops international standards for combating money laundering and terrorist financing and make recommendations "only" politically binding for the acceding countries[9].

8 FIUs around the world gathered in the Egmont Group, which since 1998, being the date of entry into force of the MLA, also adheres the MROS. The Group has, among other objectives, also that to promote the efficient and secure exchange of information between FIU members and has identified, for this purpose, the basic principles for international cooperation.

9 Are constituent members of the FATF the G7 countries, the European Commission and eight other states. Today, 34 countries are members of the FATF, the European Commission and the Gulf Cooperation Council. The FATF is an independent

In fact, despite the non binding character of FATF Recommendations, they have however become dominant even on a legal level, providing definition of the practical steps that an acceding country is required to adopt to effectively combat money laundering and terrorist financing. As evidence of this, it is relevant that the World Bank, the International Monetary Fund and the Security Council of the United Nations officially recognized the FATF recommendations as the international standards, and also that about one hundred and fifty countries around the world as well, as we shall see, the European Union itself, have pledged to respect them.

Some FATF recommendations were revised in 2011 and 2012. These include in particular the FATF Recommendations concerning the competence of the national FIU on the communication of information on money laundering[10]. Changes made to these texts have basically introduced the requirement for the FIU of countries adhering to the FATF to exchange all information that they have available, not being therefore no longer permissible to interpose limits to the exchange of information and data by appealing to national rules protecting certain obligations of secrecy.

As a result, the Swiss MROS has seen the introduction of profound changes in its rules and operating procedures, now leading to the obligation

---

inter-governmental body that develops and promotes policies to protect the global financial system against money laundering, terrorist financing and the financing of proliferation of weapons of mass destruction. Based on its mandate, the FATF deals with defining international standards and promote effective legislative measures, regulations and operational procedures to combat money laundering, financing of terrorism and the financing of proliferation of weapons of mass destruction, as well as other threats currently faced on the integrity of the international financial system. In collaboration with other international organizations, the FATF analyzes existing vulnerabilities at national level to protect the international financial system against illegal usage.

10 Namely the *International Standard for combating money laundering and the financing of terrorism and proliferation of weapons of mass destruction*. The revised text, in force since February 2012, is available in Italian language at the following address: http://www.dt.tesoro.it/export/sites/sitodt/modules/documenti_it/prevenzione_reati_finanziari/prevenzione_reati_finanziari/RACCOMANDAZIONI_GAFI_2012_ITALIANO.pdf following the adoption of the new recommendations of the FATF in 2012, the EU launched a comprehensive review of its legislation and proceeded, at the beginning of 2013, to the drafting of the proposal of the IV anti-money laundering Directive, Council Directive (EU) 2015/849 the European Parliament and of the Council of 20 May 2015 concerning the use of the financial system for money laundering or terrorist financing, amending Regulation (EU) No. 648/2012 of the European Parliament and of the Council and repealing Council Directive 2005/60/EC of the European Parliament and of the Council and Directive 2006/70/EC, in OJEU L 141, 6 May 2015, p. 73 ss.

to exchange information without being able to "repair anymore behind the wall of bank secrecy".

The strength of the Swiss Confederation with regulatory changes that have occurred between 2011 and 2012 at the level of the international community was, however, significant, to the point that there were strong pressures from the European Union, FATF and G20, for Switzerland to be included in the list some so-called *non-cooperative countries*, drawn up by the Organisation for Cooperation and Economic Development (hereinafter also the "OECD") – which, if the inclusion in the list had to occur, would end up putting Switzerland to the margin of the international community (not just the financial one) – in the case that had continued to adopt a too bland attitude against international money laundering.

The federal government has finally taken steps to adapt its internal legislation, in particular by introducing further changes to the MLA, adapting to the international practice on the exchange of information. In mid-January 2012, in fact, the Federal Council of the Swiss Confederation approved a draft revision of the law on banking secrecy, submitted for consultation in the month of April 2012, in the light of which it was introduced the obligation for MROS to transmit all relevant financial information for the purpose of cooperation, and the competencies for the same office were expanded for what concerns the actual information retrieval subject of request for cooperation[11]. The amendment bill, approved in June 2013 by the Federal Assembly, has resulted in a partial modification to the provisions of the Money Laundering Act, which came into force with effect from November 2013, involving a first and important "erosion of the principle of banking secrecy" and the consequent opening of the Swiss Confederation to reciprocity on anti-money laundering information exchange with other countries, aimed at allowing the identification of suspects by the number of bank account[12].

---

11 In other words, the MROS now has responsibility to collect information also from financial institutions that are not among the persons obliged to send in advance the reporting of suspicious transactions to the MROS.

12 See in particular the new provisions of §§ 1 and 2 of art. 30 of the MLA, which states that: «the *MROS can pass on to overseas communication offices personal data and other information in its possession or that it is authorized to collect in accordance with this law, if the overseas communication office: a. ensures that it will use the information exclusively for the purpose of analysis in the context of the fight against money laundering, its predicate offenses, organized crime or terrorism financing; b. guarantees that will accept the similar claims from Switzerland; c. ensures that it will respect confidentiality or professional secrecy; d. guarantees that will transmit to third parties the information furnished exclusively with the explicit consent of the reporting office; e. It complies with the conditions and restrictions on use of the Communication Office.*

3 Exchange of information on tax matters: international and European regulatory environment

In addition to national and international anti-money laundering legislation, the legal framework is completed by the legislation affecting the automatic exchange of information between competent authorities, which, in a nutshell, overwhelms the bank secrecy of the of the so-called tax havens. Even on this front, and in order to ensure complete fiscal transparency, in fact, instruments have been introduced to combat the phenomenon of tax evasion and, consequently, declare the end of the international banking secret.

Fundamental in this respect was the intervention conducted by leading international and supranational organizations such as the European Union and the OECD, aimed at ensuring an efficient exchange of information between the tax authorities of the Member States. This administrative procedure requires that the signatories of the agreements and international treaties, from time to time relevant, shared among them the information related to resident taxpayers, without necessitating an intervention of the courts.

In the attempt to provide a clear overview of the main sources of law on this point, it should first be recalled that the exchange of information in tax matters finds its main international source of discipline in art. 26 of the OECD Model Convention Against Double Taxation (OECD model/Common Reporting Standards Convention, henceforth also "OECD Model" or "CRS"), and in its Commentary[13].

The latest version of the OECD's CRS was adopted on October 29, 2014 by fifty-one states, the so-called *early adopters*, through the signature of a specific agreement for its implementation starting from 2017, known as the Multilateral Agreement on implementation principles of the automatic exchange of information (*Multilateral Competent Authority Agreement,* hereinafter also "MCAA"), which is nothing but the implementing instrument of the standard for the automatic exchange of information created by the OECD[14].

The Communications Office is authorized to transmit in particular the following information:
a. the name of the financial intermediary, provided that the anonymity of the author of the communication or of the person who has fulfilled the obligation to notify laid down by this law is guaranteed; b. the name of the account holder, the account number and the account balance; c. the beneficial owner; d. information on transactions».

13 Both available at the following address: http://www.oecd.org/tax/automatic-exchange/common-reporting-standard/.

14 The Agreement is based on the idea that the OECD standard on the automatic exchange of information is applied uniformly. It is based on art. 6 of the Convention on administrative assistance, also placed in consultation. The Agreement provides

However, it is expected that, from 2018, additional thirty-four countries will join the *early adopters*[15].

In order to better understand the practical consequences of the regulation set under the rule in comment with respect to bank secrecy, the following example can be worth: under the latest version of the Standards at issue, whenever a bank entertain current accounts relations with a non-resident on its national territory, it will be required to automatically communicate the information regarding this relations to the tax authorities of the foreign country of residence of the the account holder.

The amplitude of the automatic exchange of information provided for by the CRS, should be assessed, moreover, in three aspects. *In primis* the objective scope of application: the information exchanged relates to all types of income, included interest, dividends and other financial income, among which also periodic account balances as well as income arising from the divestment of financial assets. Secondly the subjective scope: the acquired information is

---

for the exchange of information obtained in accordance with the standards developed by the OECD with the Member of the G20 for the automatic exchange of information (Common standard declaration). The common standard declaration specifies who has to collect the type of information on such accounts.
With regard to the evolution which over the years has undergone the Art. 26, now under consideration, are worth mentioning, the amendments made about two years ago, on 18 July 2012, date on which the OECD published the document Update to the Arti. 26 of the OECD Model Tax Convention and its Commentary, which amended Art. 26 of the OECD Model then in force, as well as the related Commentary. The underlying purpose of those amendments was to give greater effectiveness to the provisions of agreements on the exchange of information. In particular, it was added to § 2 of art. 26 the following provision: «*Notwithstanding the foregoing, information received by a Contracting State may be used for other purposes when such information may be used for such other purposes under the laws of both States and the competent authority of the supplying State authorizes such use*». This modification allowed – and allows even today, not having been removed or changed in the text of the last and most recent version of the CRS – the competent authorities of the Contracting States to use the information received also for purposes other than those indicated in that § 2, whenever certain conditions are cumulatively fulfilled, namely that such use is permitted by the laws of both Contracting States, and is authorized by the requested State.

15 Italy has been one of the main actors for the implementation of this new agreement. The new model of automatic exchange of information was, in fact, proposed for the first time in a letter sent on 10 April 2013 by France, Germany, Italy, Spain and the United Kingdom to the European Commission with the aim to ensure bank transparency as a key measure to combat tax evasion. The multilateral agreement model is inspired by the international information exchange promoted by the United States as part of US law, contained in the *Foreign Account Tax Compliance* ("FATCA"), on which *infra*, § 2.

not only that relating to the physical persons, but also information on companies and institutions, included trusts and foundations. Third, the scope of its application to financial intermediaries: in fact, it provides for the acquisition of information not only from banks and depositaries of financial assets, but also by brokers, collective investment entities, as well as certain insurance companies.

As to the substance of the discipline in comment, it should be noted that the basic rule concerning the exchange of information is included in the first sentence of § 1, art. 26 CRS, according to which the competent authorities of the Contracting States shall *exchange information*, which are foreseeable relevant to ensure the correct application of the rules of the Convention or of the domestic laws of the Contracting States concerning taxes of any kind and description applied in those States. On this point, in the commentary of the OECD Model, is clarified that an application should not be refused on the grounds that an accurate assessment of the relevance of the information on an ongoing investigation appears possible only after receiving all information[16]. If this is the "*recommended reading*" of art. 26, we can appreciate how the importance of predictable standard allows the maximum extent possible for the exchange of information on tax matters, however, it make it clear, at the same time, that States Parties are not free to take the so-called fishing expeditions that is to say requests for all information related generally to a taxpayer and that, in their generic character, may hardly prove to be relevant in relation to its tax profiles.

To provide further clarification of what foreseen in section 1, the rule set forth in § 9, ensure that information is exchanged in three different ways: on request, for a given case, taking into account that, before a State submits a request for information to another, it should be in the first place used the normal sources of information available under the internal taxation proce-

16 Cf. S. Vorpe, G. Macchi, G. Molo, *Il nuovo standard OCSE in materia di assistenza amministrativa ammette le domande raggruppate*, in *Rivista Ticinese di diritto*, vol. II, 2012, p. 727 ss. and, in particular, p. 733, where the authors underline how, as a consequence of the modifications introduced at art. 26 already since 2012, the Commentary today «*in order to clarify the meaning of the relevance of the information, it therefore requires a greater communication effort between tax authorities involved*». The authors also stress that the Commentary, § 5.2 recognizes that the likely relevance «*can be met both in cases involving an individual taxpayer (referred to by its name or by other means), both in cases involving groups of taxpayers (identified by their name and other means)*" and that, therefore, "*the ban on fishing expeditions, that the new commentary defines how the requests for information in respect of which it is unlikely that there is a connection with an investigation or an investigation under way, also applies to applications for groups of taxpayers*».

dure; automatically, as it happens whenever the information concerning one or more categories of income, which originate in a Contracting State and are perceived in the other Contracting State, are systematically forwarded to another State; spontaneously, for example in cases where a State acquires, during some controls, information it deems to be relevant for the other State. However, in hindsight, the art. 26 of the OECD Model does not limit the possibilities to exchange information to the above three forms: the Contracting States may, in fact, use other techniques to obtain information, such as simultaneous checks, tax audits abroad and the exchange of information about an industrial field[17].

Finally, the most relevant for the purposes of this paper, is the rule provided for in § 5 of art. 26, which prevents a Contracting State from refusing to provide information to another Contracting State on the basis of the mere fact that the subject of the request information is guarded by a bank or other financial institution, by a person acting as agent or trustee, or because it constitutes an information related to the entitlement of proprietary rights.

Ultimately, therefore, anticipating our conclusions, the automatic exchange of information resulting from the last version of the CRS must be seen as the ultimate goal of a long path leading to the progressive "crumbling" of bank secrecy, which had already started by time as well, as will be seen below, at European level.

Again with reference to international regulations to contrast tax evasion practices, shall also deserves attention the role played by *Tax Information Exchange Agreement* (hereinafter, also "TIEA") and by *Foreign Account Tax Compliance Act* (hereinafter, also "FATCA").

The TIEA, which was also developed by the OECD, is clearly inspired by the CRS, although the obligations and arrangements for cooperation provided for therein are "lighter". This agreement has a subjective scope which could be defined as residual, as it is aimed at the regulation of information exchange practices in tax matters and administrative channels for those countries, among which were not stipulated Conventions against double taxation (now also the "CDI", better known also as Rubik agreements, on which in the following § 3), whenever there is no need to regulate the taxation of cross-

17 Moreover, given this background, the exchange of specific information on request can be completed by one of the Contracting States against another Contracting State, only after unsuccessful application by the Requesting State, of all the means provided for by its national law to obtain the information. Also, it is provided that the request, as a rule be made in writing, must be the most detailed and circumstantial as possible, thus enabling the requested State to proceed to the collection and subsequent transmission of information within the shortest time possible.

border income, but at least one of the Contracting parties desire to receive information to avoid an internal tax shortfall[18].

FATCA is, instead, a US law, brought to approval on March 18, 2010[19], addressed to the *Foreign Financial Institutions* (hereinafter, also "FFI") and other financial intermediaries[20], aimed at countering tax evasion by US citizens and US residents through the use of offshore accounts. Therefore, it represents a clear example of anti-avoidance legislation that affects the subject, whose bond with the American territory is deemed significant, who uses foreign vehicles (such as foreign company forms) in an attempt to hide incomes to the US fiscal administration, the International Revenue Service (hereinafter also the "IRS").

The provisions of FATCA, as anticipated, is not only directed to the taxpayer, but also – and above all – to foreign financial institutions that manage banking relationships.

Specifically, it is provided for: the effective implementation of FATCA rules through the exchange of information; the reduction of compliance costs for financial institutions; reciprocal treatment; finally, in case of failure to meet the burden declarative, the application of a withholding tax of 30% on all financial payments of US source[21]. FFI who does not comply with FATCA

---

18 Until now, the Swiss Federation is a signatory of six TIEA, entered into respectively with San Marino, Andorra, Greenland, Jersey, Guernsey and Isle of Man. More insights and information are available at the website https://www.news.admin.ch/message/index.html?lang=it&msg-id=52984.

19 The provisions of FATCA were enacted in the *Hiring Incentives to Restore Employment* ("HIRE") *Act*, converted into US law on 18 March 2010. The FATCA is completed by the orientation issued by the *Treasury Department of the United States* (commonly called the FATCA Regulations).

20 Under FATCA Regulations, an FFI is defined as a foreign financial institution if it meets the following requirements: accepts deposits within the ordinary course of a banking or similar; hold financial assets on behalf of others as considerable part of its activities; is an operational entity in investing activities (as defined by the regulations issued by the US Treasury); It is an insurance company or a holding company belonging to a larger group of related companies which includes an insurance company, or is a parent company or a treasury centre. In general terms, foreign entities such as banks, brokers/broker-dealers, insurance companies, hedge funds, securitization vehicles, parent company, certain trusts and private equity funds will be deemed FFI. Among the entities exempted from this legislation include the listed corporations, foreign governments and agencies wholly owned by organizations or foreign central banks.

21 According to FATCA Regulations, the FFI is required to register with the IRS and to conclude with this one "FFI Agreement" that will give them the status of "participating FFI". The FFI agreement mainly oblige a participating FFI to: declare their intention to comply with FATCA; conduct a due diligence process for existing

regulations will be excluded from the American capital market and will not be able to maintain relations with financial institutions FATCA-compliant.

Under those provisions, from the date of the approval of FATCA, many governments have concluded or will conclude intergovernmental agreements (so-called "IGA") with the United States, which have allowed a large automatic exchange of information as a way to fight fraud and tax evasion[22].

Currently, there are two different types of IGA. Very briefly and without pretending to be exhaustive, the FATCA-1 model, chosen by leading EU countries[23], provides for an automatic exchange of information between tax authorities[24],without any prior consent from the customers.

FATCA-2 model, instead, is the model adopted by Switzerland with effect from 1 July 2014[25], provides for forms of collaboration and administrative assistance to be implemented, by the financial institutions involved, through the direct notification to the US tax authorities of information on US citizens or residents customers, also including identification data of these customers and their bank accounts, subject to the consent of the same to the transmission. In other words, this second model of collaboration, provides for no automatic

---

and new accounts of individuals and legal entities to identify the account holders or investors as a US or non-US on the basis of the so called "American clues"; apply a withholding tax of 30% whenever individuals do not provide the appropriate documentation or whenever there is fastened a business relationship with legal entities fail to conform; report information on accounts to the IRS directly or indirectly via their national government that has signed an intergovernmental agreement. If an FFI does not enter into such an agreement, the FDAP payments (payments that are fixed, determinable, annual or periodic) related to relations of US origin, as dividends and interest paid by US corporations, will be subject to a fixed withholding tax of 30%.

22 An intergovernmental agreement is a bilateral agreement between a given country (so-called jurisdiction partner) and the US government that facilitates the implementation of the FATCA compliance and at the same, also reducing the burden on the FFI for certain procedures. It is mandatory for FFI, located in partner jurisdictions to comply with FATCA. For this purpose, the model agreements enable FFI in designated jurisdictions partner to comply with FATCA, particularly where there are laws relating to privacy.

23 Among which, we remember, United Kingdom, France, Germany, Spain, Italy, the Netherlands, Hungary.

24 Thus FFI communicate the relevant information to their national tax authority which, in turn, provides for the transmission of the same information to the IRS.

25 Cf. The cooperation agreement between Switzerland and the United States of America for the application facilitated of the FATCA legislation came into force on 2 June 2014. By decision of 6 June 2014, the Federal Council put into force, with effect from next June 30, 2014, the relevant law on implementation. Among the other countries that have acceded to that second model of cooperation are also included Japan and the Bermuda Islands.

exchange of information. On the contrary, with regard to US customers that have not expressed their consent to the transmission, the FFI can and must communicate to the IRS, the only information about the number of accounts involved and the total assets. It is understandable that, through the signing of a GIGA on FATCA-2 model the Swiss Confederation wanted to preserve and protect, even within the possible extent, the "privileges" provided for by its legal framework, descending from bank secrecy rules.

Moving on to analyze the legislation "of a strictly European-style", deserves first mention and analysis the provisions laid down in Directive 2011/16/EU[26] on administrative cooperation in the field of taxation (so-called *Cooperative Directive*), which provide for meaningful obligations regarding the automatic exchange of information, which, as easily understandable, can certainly not be easily reconciled with banking secrecy.

According to the rule contained therein, in fact, and more precisely by the combined provisions of art. 8 and art. 29, as of 1 January 2015, the competent authorities in each Member State is required to automatically notify the competent authority of any other Member State with the information available in the relevant tax years and regarding certain categories of income of the residents of those other States.

In practical terms, the previous Directive 77/799 /EEC[27], no longer considered adequate to account for the contrast to the elusive phenomena[28], is

26 In the OJEU, L 64, dell'11 March 2011, p. 1. Under art. 30 came into force on the same day of its publication in the OJEU.

27 Directive 77/799/EEC concerning mutual assistance by the competent authorities of the Member States in the field of direct taxation and those on insurance premiums, the practical application of which denoted strong operating limits as detected by the Tax Fraud Group, created by the EU Council in 1999 with No Report. 8668/00 of 22 May 2000; in the Commission Communication of 27 September 2004 (so-called "*Parmalat Communication*") COM(2004) 11 final and the Commission Communication on the fight against tax fraud of 31 May 2006 COM(2006) 254 final. For a detailed analysis of the above law and, more generally, on the automatic exchange of information, please refer toF. Persano, *La cooperazione internazionale nello scambio di informazioni*, Giappichelli, Torino, 2006.

28 See *consideranda* 4, 5 and 6 according to which: «*(4) […] the existing Council Directive 77/799/EEC of 19 December 1977 concerning mutual assistance by the competent authorities of the Member States in the field of direct taxation and taxation of insurance premiums (3) no longer provides for appropriate measures. Its deep weaknesses have been looked into by the Ad hoc Council Working Party on Tax Fraud in its report of 22 May 2000 and more recently by the Commission Communication on Preventing and Combating Corporate and Financial Malpractice of 27 September 2004 and the Commission Communication concerning the need to develop a coordinated strategy to improve the fight against fiscal fraud of 31 May 2006. (5) Directive 77/799/EEC, even with its later amendments, was*

replaced by the directive under consideration, which extend both the substantive scope (to include natural and legal persons, trusts, foundations, funds investment), both the objective scope (extending it to taxes of every kind).

For these reasons, it can be stated that Directive 2011/16/EU first of all regulates the "ideal" model of *disclosure*, which is implemented precisely through the automatic exchange of information. This implies, however, in terms of infrastructure, the creation of a database in each Member State, which should be made available, for example, to the tax authorities of the country of domicile of the various tax entities that hold assets or gain incomes in this last country, which is a third country with respect to the State in which they have their fiscal residence.

In the attempt to provide a specific, even though incomplete, analysis of the discipline in question here, with regard to the scope of application, it is to be preliminarily pointed out that the Cooperative Directive, pursuant to art. 2, must be observed not only with regard to the relationships between the Member States, but also with respect to the third Countries for what concern all taxes of any kind levied by, or on behalf of, a Member State or the Member State's territorial or administrative subdivisions, including the local authorities[29]. It is so, in the obvious purpose of protecting the competition in within

---

designed in a different context to current internal market requirements and is no longer able to meet the new requirements of administrative cooperation. (6) Due to the number and the importance of adaptations to be made to Directive 77/799/EEC, a mere amendment thereof would not be sufficient to fulfil the objectives described above. Directive 77/799/EEC should therefore be repealed and replaced by a new legal instrument. That instrument should apply to direct taxes and indirect taxes that are not yet covered by other Union legislation. To this end, this new Directive is considered to be the proper instrument in terms of effective administrative cooperation».

29 See. art. 24, according to which: «*1. Where the competent authority of a Member State receives from a third country information that is foreseeably relevant to the administration and enforcement of the domestic laws of that Member State concerning the taxes referred to in Article 2, that authority may, in so far as this is allowed pursuant to an agreement with that third country, provide that information to the competent authorities of Member States for which that information might be useful and to any requesting authorities. 2. Competent authorities may communicate, in accordance with their domestic provisions on the communication of personal data to third countries, information obtained in accordance with this Directive to a third country, provided that all of the following conditions are met: (a) the competent authority of the Member State from which the information originates have consented to that communication; (b) the third country concerned has given an undertaking to provide the cooperation required to gather evidence of the irregular or illegal nature of transactions which appear to contravene or constitute an abuse of tax legislation.*».

the single market against the fiscal policies of third Countries, policies that may prove to be capable of affecting the European trade policy on taxation.

Pursuant to art. 8, starting from 1 January 2015 – therefore, on a date delayed from that of entry into force of the Directive – the requirement of automatic exchange of information is also operative for the following categories of income: income from employment, director's fees, life insurance products not covered by other Union legal instruments on exchange of information and other similar measures, pensions and ownership of and income from immovable property. On the contrary, such a model of cooperation does not apply to value added tax and customs duties, or to excise duties covered by other Union legislation on administrative cooperation between Member States, as well as for compulsory social security contributions due to the Member State.

The automatic exchange is not, however, the only form of cooperation governed by the legislation at issue, since the directive also provides for the exchange of information on request (art. 5, according to which, the tax authority of a State is entitled to ask information to another State with respect to one or more taxpayers); the spontaneous exchange (art. 9, according to which whenever the authorities of a State takes over a "domestic" news concerning a taxpayer of another country and considering that the information relates evasive transactions, proceeds to the communication, if required, of such information to the member State concerned); as well as other forms of administrative cooperation[30].

Since, quite understandably, the Directive is based on the OECD Cooperative Model, the information exchanged is «*information probably relevant for the administration and enforcement of the national laws of the Member States*»[31]. It remains, therefore, fixed and stable the ban on fishing expeditions, or the prohibition for Member States to require non foreseeably relevant information with tax issues the taxpayer for the administration.

---

30 In particular, the provisions of Chapter III of Directive 2011/16 which provide for other forms of cooperation between the administrative authorities such as: the possibility, subject to an agreement between the requesting authority and the requested authority, to officials appointed by the requesting authority to be present in administrative offices and to participate in administrative enquiries in the requested Country (art. 11); simultaneous controls of people who have a common or complementary interest between two or more EU countries in the view of exchanging information obtained (art. 12); after receiving an application from a Member State, a duty on the part of the competent authority of another Member State to notify the addressee, with all acts and decisions of the administrative authorities of the requesting Member State, concerning the application in its territory of legislation on taxes covered by this Directive (art. 13); sharing best practices and experiences to improve cooperation (art. 15).

31 Cf. art. 1, § 1.

Under this present work, it is important to point out, in the end, as the exchange of information, in the manner described above, in accordance with art. 18, § 2 – under condition of literal recall of the standards referred to in CRS –, can not find obstacles in the refusal by the requested State to provide information only by opposing that "*this information is held by a bank, other financial institution, nominee or person acting in an agency or fiduciary or because it relates to property interests of a person*".

The action of the European legislator in the field of administrative cooperation, however, was nit limited to the adoption of the *Cooperative Directive* of 2011. In fact, given the increasingly strong need to adapt European regulations to the new global single standard of automatic exchange of information pursuant to art. 26 of the OECD Model, in June 2013 a new proposal for a directive was presented[32], then placed under discussion in the EU Council in October 2014[33], in order to expand the objective scope of application of Directive 2011/16/EU to dividends, capital gains, any income generated by assets held by a financial statement and any amount in respect of which the financial institution might both be the obligor or the debtor, including any redemption payments and account balances. With the result of including in cooperation also the sums that constitute funding derived from unremunerated banking relationships.

At its meeting of December 9, 2014, the Ecofin Council finally approved the amendments to Directive 2011/16/EU, which will come into force between 2016 and 2018. These changes have led to the adoption of Directive 2014/107/EU (also, "DAC 2"), which expands the scope of the existing directive in order to make more effective the fight against tax evasion and avoidance[34].

The main changes are the following. First, the elimination of the reference to the "minimum amount" at art. 8, § 3 of the Cooperative Directive of 2011, under which the competent authority of a Member State may indicate to the competent authority of any other Member State that it "*does not wish*

32 COM(2013) 348 final, available at the following address: http://ec.europa.eu/taxation_customs/resources/documents/taxation/tax_cooperation/mutual_assistance/direct_tax_directive/com_2013_348_it.pdf.

33 Cf. declarations of Minister Pier Carlo Padoan in October 2014, available on http://italia2014.eu/en/news/post/ottobre/combating-tax-evasion/, according to which: «*We decided to implement within the EU the new global standard on automatic exchange of information developed by the OECD and endorsed by the G20. This shows the EU is still at the forefront of the fight against cross-border tax fraud and evasion, for the benefit of all citizen*».

34 In OJ L 359, 16 December 2014, p. 1 ss. The deadline for transposition of the directive into domestic law of the Member States shall be 31 December 2015. transposed rules will have to be applied from 1 January 2016.

to receive information on income or capital referred to in paragraph 1" (*i.e.* income work, director's fees, life insurance products, pensions, property and rental income), regardless the amount of the same. Secondly, the introduction at art. 8 of the Directive 2011/16/EU, § 3 bis, which provides for the possibility for the competent authority of a Member State to inform the competent authority of any other Member State information, naturally held by banking institutions, with reference to the following categories of income: dividends, capital gains, other financial income and current account balances. Moreover, the introduction of amendment in the art. 8, § 5 of the Directive 2011/16/EU[35], according to which any proposals from the European Commission may concern not only the categories of income already indicated in art. 8, but also new categories of income identified by the new directive. Finally, after modification of art. 8, § 5 (a) action was taken to strengthen and expand the methods of operation and the object of the automatic exchange of information the competent authority of each Member State shall, by automatic exchange, communicate to the competent authority of any other Member State, information regarding taxable periods as from 1 January 2017 «concerning residents in that other Member State on all categories of income and capital listed in para. 1» [36].

In addition to the mechanisms related to the automatic exchange of information provided for by the provisions under exam[37], it is also provided the mechanisms of automatic information exchange, concerning the payment of interest, by Directive on cross-border savings n. 2003/48/EC, pending since 2009, better known as the *Saving Directive*[38], since it emerged from the need to prevent tax competition and ensure that the interest payments made in the European Union, in favor of natural persons, having their tax residence in a Member State other than that in which the interest is paid, are subject to effective taxation in accordance with the national legislation of their member

35 Which provides that, before 1 July 2017, the European Commission should present a report concerning an assessment on the operation of the instrument of administrative cooperation between Member States through an analysis of the costs, the benefits from the automatic exchange of information and the operational aspects related to it.

36 The original text of art. 8, § 5(a) of the *Cooperative Directive* limited, instead, the information subject to automatic exchange on «*at least three of the specific categories of income and capital listed in paragraph 1, as they are to be understood under the national legislation of the Member State communicating the information*».

37 Cf. considering n. 10: «*It is recognised that the mandatory automatic exchange of information without preconditions is the most effective means of enhancing the correct assessment of taxes in cross-border situations and of fighting fraud. […]*».

38 GU L 157 of 26 June 2003, p. 38 ss.

State of residence[39]. To meet these purposes, the provisions of the directive in question drew a system based on the so-called *coexistence model*, which is the combination of an automatic obligation to exchange information between competent authorities, and the application of taxation clearances at source.

In order to avoid distortions related to the movement of capital between Member States, inconsistent with the internal market, the Directive has introduced and regulated a nominative information exchange system between the tax authorities of the States of the European Union – certainly related also to banking relationships. On a transitional basis only, some of these States (such as, for example, Austria, and Luxembourg), characterized by strict national provisions on banking secrecy, in lieu of exchange of information, opted for a withholding tax to be applied to payments of interest made directly to individuals resident in another member State[40].

The spatial efficacy of the discipline under consideration is increased by the fact that equivalent measures have been and are still being applied also

---

39 Cf. art. 1, § 1 of directive 2003/48/CE.

40 Cf. in particular, art. 11, §§ 1 and 2 of the directive under examination, which, in its present version, provides that: «*during the transitional period referred to in Article 10, where the beneficial owner is resident in a Member State other than that in which the paying agent is established, Belgium, Luxembourg and Austria shall levy a withholding tax at a rate of 15 % during the first three years of the transitional period, 15 % for the subsequent three years and 35 % thereafter. 2. The paying agent shall levy withholding tax as follows: a) in the case of an interest payment within the meaning of Article 6(1)(a): on the amount of interest paid or credited; in the case of an interest payment within the meaning of point (b) of the first subparagraph of Article 6(1): on the amount of any income paid, realised or credited; (c) in the case of an interest payment within the meaning of point (c) or (e) of the first subparagraph of Article 6(1): either on the amount of interest or income referred to in those points or by a levy of equivalent effect to be borne by the beneficial owner on the full amount of the proceeds from the sale, redemption or refund; (d) in the case of an interest payment within the meaning of point (d) of the first subparagraph of Article 6(1): on the amount of income referred to in that point; (e) in the case of an interest payment within the meaning of Article 6(4): on the amount of interest attributable to each of the beneficial owners who fall within the scope of Article 1(1). The total amount on which tax is levied shall not exceed the amount of the interest payment received or secured by the entity or legal arrangement; (f)where a Member State exercises the option under Article 6(5): on the amount of annualised interest or other relevant income;(g)in the case of an interest payment within the meaning of point (f) of the first subparagraph of Article 6(1): on the benefit calculated in accordance with that provision. Member States may allow paying agents to levy withholding tax only on the benefits about which the competent authority of the Member State of residence of the beneficial owner has not yet been informed, by the paying agent or its fiscal representatives pursuant to any legislative provision different from those necessary to implement this Directive.*»

by non-EU countries (such as Andorra, Liechtenstein, Monaco, San Marino and, referring for further details on this point to § 3, also by Switzerland[41]), as well as by the dependent or associated territories of the Member States (the Channel Islands, Isle of Man, dependent or associated territories in the Caribbean), that is to say any country by definition not included in the territorial scope of the Directive, with but on which the European institutions have collaborated in order to prevent that taxpayers of the Member States may circumvent the actual provisions of the Directive through investments in financial centres outside the EU.

Basically, the *Saving Directive* introduced the rule of the automatic report to tax authorities of the Country of the recipient, who can so control the exact fulfilment at the place of taxation of the interested person. In lack of any coordination of national tax systems relating to the aforementioned income tax, and in particular with regard to the treatment of interest received by residents of a Member State, the latter can often avoid any form of taxation in their member State of residence on interest they perceive in another member State.

Following to numerous suggestions for changing over the years, in the recent times, in partial modification of the directive, it was also adopted Directive 2014/48/EU[42], which disposes on the one hand for the introduction of new articles[43] in the text of Directive 2003, and on the other hand for the modification of certain existing rules[44], in order to expand and modernize: the definition of "savings income" that should also include the income equivalent to interest on invested savings (question, for example, of investment funds established inside and outside the European Union, as well as all those financial instruments not classified as producers of interests such as shares, mainly common equity nature funds, alternative investments, capitalization and life policies and others characterized instruments, structured in a manner such that there is no interest); the definition of "beneficial owner", so that it can not be limited to the physical persons, but gets to encompass also interposed

41 Cf. the Memorandum of Understanding OJ L 385, 29 December 2004, p. 30 ss. and the Agreement in the form of an exchange of letters between the European Community and the Swiss Confederation providing for measures equivalent to those laid down in Directive. 2003/48/EC of 3 June 2003 on taxation of savings income in the form of interest payments in OJEU L 385, 29 December 2004, p. 51 ss. Available at the following address: https://www.admin.ch/opc/it/classified-compilation/20042402/index.html.

42 Council Directive 2014/48/EU amending Directive 2003/48/EC on taxation of savings income in the form of interest payments, in OJEU L 111, 15 April 2004, p. 50 ff, that MS are required to transpose into their national law by 1 January 2016.

43 In particular, artt. 1 bis, 18 bis and 18 ter.

44 In particular, artt. 2, 3, 4, 6, 8, 9, 11, 14.

legal entities; of "interests"; 'paying agent', with the express specification of intermediate structures established in one of the Member States and obliged to act as "paying agent" upon receipt; finally, the identification of "beneficial owners", by recording of date and place of birth of the beneficiary and, where available, of the tax code of the latter.

Modifications have not brought changes in terms, however, of exchange of information regime which, even today, remains governed by the provisions of 2003, according to which, if the beneficial owner is resident in a Member State other than that in which it is established by the paying agent, is held by the latter to notify the competent authority of the member State of the minimum information, namely: the identity and residence of the beneficial owner, the name or designation and address of the paying agent, the account number of the beneficial owner or, in the absence of such a reference, the identification of the credit that produces interest, and information concerning the interest payment. Likewise, the minimum information which the paying agent is required to disclose concerning interest payment must differentiate the interests according to the specific categories listed in the Directive.

4 Relations between Switzerland, European Union and other States in the international community: the CDI and Bilateral agreements II, in particular the Agreement on tax of savings income

Moving on to the attempt to determine the impact of the aforementioned international and European legislation on the Swiss organization, we should start by saying that «*regulation on exchange of information in taxation represents one of the most sensitive issues among those who have been at the centre of negotiations between Switzerland and the European Union*»[45]. The dispute that have opposed, for years, Switzerland and the European Union alleges on the fact that Swiss authorities persisted, until recent times, in their refusal to comply with international rogatories for tax evasion, since the same is not considered a crime by the Swiss law but it is only subject to administrative

45 Cf. A. Pedroli, *Lo scambio di informazioni fiscali*, in *Accordi bilaterali Svizzera-Unione europea, Atti della giornata di studio del 4 giugno 2007*, State Chancellery of the Canton of Ticino and Helbing Lichtenhahn, Basel, 2009, p. 58 and in particular where the author specifies: «*Traditional Swiss closure, against requests for assistance, judicial and administrative, concerning tax investigations abroad is obviously explained by the concern to protect the banking secrecy. The contrast between the European Union instances, interested in affecting as much as possible this last secret, and the defensive attitude of the Swiss negotiators, determined to limit the damage as much as possible, explains the importance that has been attached to the question of exchange of information relating to taxes*».

penalties. Anticipating what will be deepened in this same paragraph, now we can safely say, that the administrative assistance conditions defined with Bilateral Agreements II have been largely superseded by subsequent events. In fact, if the negotiations with the European Union, culminating in the signing of the Agreements of 2004, were based on this historical distinction in Swiss law, in the field of direct taxation, between tax evasion and tax fraud[46], the Federal Council on 13 March 2009, did succumb to the pressures of the EU, the OECD and the United States, giving up this distinction, in the grant of the cooperation with foreign tax authorities.

As for almost all the national legal systems, even for the Helvetic system, the exchange of tax information can be incorporated in administrative or legal assistance. Among the various criteria of delimitation of the two forms of cooperation, the most convincing – and certainly easier – is based on the nature of the authority that gives assistance: if it is an administrative authority it comes to administrative assistance, but if is a judicial it comes to legal assistance.

Focusing on forms of administrative assistance in tax matters – the only one to be analyzed in this paper[47] –, these are primarily governed by bilateral treaties concerning double taxation (DTA), the so-called Rubik agreements

46 We recall that the Swiss legislation on tax investigations and banking secrecy has always been characterized by a certain degree of complexity, being based on the aforementioned distinction between fiscal violations and tax offenses, and, among the latter, on the distinction between "simple tax evasion" and "qualified tax evasion" and "tax fraud". In the first case, i.e. in the presence of behaviours qualifying the crime of simple tax evasion, bank secrecy is enforceable against tax authority, which, therefore, can not acquire compulsorily the bank records either by the taxpayer or by the bank. In the different and second case of "tax fraud", however, the initiation of criminal investigations enables a court to also access information routinely covered by banking secrecy and, later, to the documentation may also have access the tax authority with reference to specific suspects of a tax offense, no longer being opposable the already overcome bank secrecy in the criminal proceedings. In applying these rules, to a procedure of international administrative assistance pursuant to art. 26 of the OECD Model, in order to assess the legality of overcoming the limitations imposed by banking secrecy, the Swiss AFC is therefore called upon to assess whether from the request for assistance arise solid evidence of of tax fraud or sufficient grounds for suspicion.

47 With regard to the forms of legal assistance, Cf. for all I. Anrò, *La cooperazione giudiziaria civile tra Unione europea e Svizzera. In particolare, il rilievo dell'ordine pubblico nella circolazione delle decisioni in material civile e commerciale*, nonché C. Amalfitano, *La cooperazione giudiziaria in materia penale tra Unione europea e Svizzera. In particolare l'operatività del principio del* ne bis in idem, both in M. Condinanzi (Ed.), *Unione europea e Svizzera tra cooperazione e intergrazione*, Giuffré, Milano, 2012, p. 185 ss.

concluded from time to time between the Swiss Confederation and the individual countries, inspired by the model of collaboration governed by art. 26 of the OECD Model, progressively updated, as well as aiming to meet a very specific purpose: to prevent that the same tax asset can undergo the fiscal sovereignty of two or more States. To sum, these agreements provide for the regularization, through the introduction of an anonymous withholding tax, capable of liberating the non declared assets held in Switzerland by the citizens of those States with which a CDI was signed.

From this historical perspective, before 2004, Switzerland always concluded CDI in the light of the reserve by the same worded in relation to the application of art. 26, §§ 1 and 5 of the OECD Model[48]. In other words, because of the adoption of such a restrictive position, the Swiss Confederation has succeeded in limiting the application of art. 26 of the OECD Model – and consequently also its scope of support – in the first place to cases of tax fraud and, secondly, to the only "information that is necessary in order for the provisions of the Convention (the "little assistance"), without getting to encompass all the "foreseeably relevant" information to the application of domestic law of the State requesting for support (so-called "great assistance")[49]. Therefore, the CDI entered into over the years by Switzerland, have provided, as a rule, the sole exchange of information needed to apply the provisions of the CDI from time to time relevant to "*prevent fraud or similar offenses*" concerning taxes falling within the scope of that CDI, with no reference to cases of request for cooperation aimed at implementing the national legislation of the requesting State. Understandably, on the basis of these premises, the CDI concluded by the Confederation also excluded a paragraph, compli-

48 Basically finalized, as we have seen, to neutralize any possible obstacles to full cooperation. They provide for, in brief, i) that the exchange of information relates to any information, predictably relevant to the implementation of the Convention's provisions and the implementation of domestic laws concerning taxes of every kind imposed on behalf of each Contracting State; ii) that States Parties shall not decline to act in the light of the sole ground that the information requested is held by a bank or other financial institution. The latter provision should also prevail upon the law or internal administrative provisions which prohibit the Administrations acquiring bank records for the purposes of tax assessment.

49 Most CDI currently in force have been adopted when Switzerland could still deal with according to the reserve foreign States that had formulated in relation to art. 26, in order to restrict the application of the article to the «*information that is necessary to make the disposition of the Convention operational*». An updated overview of all CDI with/without provision for the exchange of information in accordance with the OECD standard and all the automatic exchange of information is available on the website of the State Secretariat for International Financial Matters (SIF): www.sif.admin.ch > Temi > Politica fiscale internazionale > Doppia imposizione e assistenza amministrativa.

ant with the rules set forth at art. 26, § 5, of the OECD Model, which might render ineffective the privilege of banking secrecy. On the contrary, in order to strengthen the effectiveness of this latest "Swiss privilege", the agreements in question provided for «*a sanatorium "anonymized" mechanism, which also [provided] only very limited possibilities, in terms of both quantity and quality, of presentation of requests for information by the tax authorities of the Member State of residence*»[50].

In 2004, however, after the adoption by the Fiscal Affairs Committee of the OECD of a new version of art. 26, for the further extension of the scope of the exchange of information, the Swiss reserves was amended, with the clarification that the same would not apply to cases involving «*acts of fraud punishable by imprisonment under the law of both Contracting States law*». But it is only from 2009 that the most important development on this point occur (on which, *Infra*, in this same paragraph).

For a long time, and before 2009, the only exception to the aforementioned "Swiss rule" exclusion of all forms of "great care" was represented by the Agreement with the US, dated 24 May 1951, to avoid double taxation in the context of income taxes. In fact, this convention provides at art. 16 for an exchange not only of all the information necessary and instrumental for implementation of the Convention, but also of the information relating to tax fraud and similar crimes[51].

---

50 In this sense C. PAOLINI, *Profili fiscali svizzeri e diritto dell'Unione europea*, in M. CONDINANZI (ED.), *Unione europea e Svizzera tra cooperazione e integrazione*, Giuffrè, Milano, 2012, p. 409.

51 More recently, a similar exception has been implemented on these new agreements with South African Republic (Convention of 8 May 2007 for the avoidance of double taxation with respect to income tax); with Colombia (Convention of 26 October 2007, aimed at preventing double taxation with respect to taxes on income and capital); with Chile (Convention of 2 April 2008 to prevent the double taxation with respect to taxes on income and capital); with Turkey (Convention of 22 May 2008 to avoid double taxation with respect to taxes on income); in an additional agreement to the agreement with France in 12 January 2009; Finally, in the protocols that have increased the agreements with Germany (Revision Protocol of 12 March 2002 to the Convention of 11 August 1971 between the Swiss Confederation and the Federal Republic of Germany for the avoidance of double taxation with respect to taxes on income and wealth in the version of the Protocol of 21 December 1992), Norway (Protocol of 12 April 2005 between the Swiss Confederation and the Kingdom of Norway amending the Convention for the avoidance of double taxation with respect to taxes on income and on capital and its Protocol, signed Berne September 7, 1987), Finland (Protocol of 19 April 2006 between the Swiss Confederation and the Republic of Finland amending the Convention for the avoidance of double taxation with respect to taxes on income and on capital and its Protocol, signed in Helsinki 16 December 1991), Austria

To grasp the scale of the different scope of application of the information exchange permitted by the Convention with the United States, it is essential to make a fleeting reference to the case that the Federal Administrative Court has been recently busy on, in relation to a requests for administrative assistance submitted by US tax authorities with regard to alleged conduct of tax evasion realized by UBS American clients[52]. In that specific case, in 2008 the American IRS forwarded to the Swiss tax authorities, the Federal Tax Administration ("AFC"), a request to exchange information according to the CDI between the two countries, and in particular under Art. 26 of the OECD Model, concerning their bank details of American clients of the UBS Credit Institute suspected of having formed offshore company aimed at tax evasion[53]. The request was approved and the proceedings initiated, despite the generic object and the lack of specification of the identity of the taxpayers in respect of which the information were requested. Against the orders of implementation request for cooperation issued by the FTA, some UBS clients appealed to the Federal Administrative Court, which in 2009 ruled in favor of the acceptance of the request for administrative assistance, although the request was indeed generic – almost as to set up a fishing expeditions, which would fall outside either the model of collaboration at Art. 26 of the OECD Model and in CDI

(Protocol of 21 March 2006 amending the Convention signed January 30, 1974 in Vienna between the Swiss Confederation and the Republic of Austria for the avoidance of double taxation with respect to taxes on income and wealth),Spain (Protocol of 29 June 2006 amending the Convention of 26 April 1966 between Switzerland Convention and Spain for the avoidance of double taxation with respect to taxes on income he and wealth), United Kingdom (Protocol of 26 June 2007 amending Convention of 8 December 1977 between the Swiss Confederation and the United Kingdom of Great Britain and Northern Ireland for the avoidance of double taxation with respect to taxes on income), in an additional agreement to the agreement signed with France (additional agreement of 12 January 2009 amending the Convention between Switzerland and France for the avoidance of double taxation with respect to taxes on income and wealth, whose approval process was, however, suspended after the announcement of the Swiss Federal Council of 13 March 2009, on which v. *infra* in the text).

52 Decisions of the Federal Administrative Court A-7342/2008 and A-7426/2008 of 5 March 2009.

53 For a commentary on such case, cf. A. Crazzolara, F. Lurà, *Lo scambio internazionale di informazioni e la giurisprudenza svizzera*, in *Dir. prat. trib. int.*, 2010, p. 551 ss.; Id., *Lo scambio internazionale di informazioni e la giurisprudenza svizzera – parte II*, in *Dir. prat. trib. int.*, 2010, p. 1019 ss.; Id., *Lo scambio internazionale di informazioni e la giurisprudenza svizzera – parte III*, in *Dir. prat. trib. int.*, 2010, p. 1507 ss. See. anche P. Mastellone, *La cooperazione fiscale internazionale nello scambio di informazioni*, in R. Cordeiro Guerra, *Diritto tributario internazionale*, Cedam, Padova, 2012, p. 257 ss.

bilaterally signed between the signatory countries of the same model[54] – since regarding American taxpayers, bank customers, not previously precisely identified because of the absence of information on them[55].

According to the reasoning of the the Federal Administrative Court, first, according to Swiss law the interposition of a foreign company in which undeclared titles were confer, together with the lack of declaration of participation in this society and on the incomes that the holder has earned, would qualify as tax fraud and not as tax evasion, since the taxpayers, in this case, did not use false documents. Second, the Court has given an interpretation of the prohibition on *fishing expeditions* very favorable for the authority requesting for assistance. Although appeals have been simply removed from the role since become devoid of purpose following to the decision of the FINMA with which has ordered to UBS the immediate transmission of the data relating to a number of clients to the American authorities, the Federal Administrative Court has proposed a quite elaborate disclosure in this second aspect. The Court admitted, in fact, that the identification of taxpayers involved in the procedure of administrative assistance could well take place not only through the precise indication of the name, but also by testing a behavioral model applicable to them. Thus, as it often happens with the interpretation of legislation carried out in courts of law, in fact, the Courts of Switzerland have anticipated the evolution of the international and conventional rules on exchange of information for tax purposes[56].

---

54 According to the applicants, such a formulation of the request constituted an impermissible fishing expeditions, as Switzerland could be obliged to lend its assistance only if it has been opened in the US a concrete proceedings against certain persons. The IRS relied on the fact that the DTC concluded with Switzerland did not provide as a condition of admissibility of requests for assistance to the preliminary identification of the taxpayers of the same object.

55 The evidence of tax evasion and fraud, on which was based the request for assistance, can be summarized in the discrepancy, on the identification of beneficial owners, resulting from the UBS statement submitted under the law of Switzerland and by the due statement according to US law for persons subject to the tax on investment income of US source.

56 In this sense, A. Buccisano, *Assistenza amministrativa internazionale dall'accertamento alla riscossione dei tributi*, Cacucci editore, Bari, 2013, p. 229. More precisely, the Federal Administrative Court did not deem that there was in this case a violation of the ban on fishing expeditions, relying first on the Federal Court concerning the administrative assistance provided by the Swiss domestic law in relations with the administrative and judicial authorities on the one hand, and fiscal, on the other (art. 112 DBG and 39, § 3 LAID). The Court has therefore repeatedly acknowledged that the bank documents seized in criminal proceedings may be made available to the tax authorities, which could also use it for the taxation of persons other than investigated. Finally, recalled that in the Swiss domestic

The described "jurisprudential opening" in the federal administrative cooperation in the field of tax fraud and similar behavior was not considered sufficient by the OECD, who was not long in denouncing the limits this interpretation. While, in fact, the principle of dual criminality – that the Helvetic legislator believed operates both on the level of judicial cooperation at the level of administrative cooperation – could have not been an obstacle to the exchange of information, once that the definition of tax infringements in requesting State and in the requested one was similar, if not entirely coincidental, otherwise the assistance would be seriously hampered in the different hypothesis, of definitions of divergent regulations.

Therefore, in two *Progress Report*[57], the OECD taxation Committee notes that, because of the restrictive definition of tax fraud and similar behaviour, contained in the latest CDI, the principle of dual criminality, to which Switzerland subordinated the exchange of information, represented an insuperable obstacle to administrative assistance.

It is not possible, then, to consider with surprise the growing pressure of the international community, accelerated by the financial and economic crisis, which led to the breakthrough announced in 2009. More precisely, with the famous press release of March 13 of the Federal Department of Finance (FDF), the Federal Government undertook to revoke the reserve made in 2004 to art. 26 of the OECD Model, pledging to negotiate revisions to the CDI in accordance with this latter[58].

---

law, to start the preliminary investigation is necessary an initial suspicion, which can, however, also be as simple as the existence of a crime suspect, without the request of any suspicion of a particular person as the author . Pending the dispute in question, it has come to the conclusion of an *Agreement between the Swiss Confederation and the United States on the request for information from the Internal Revenue Service of the United States of America regarding UBS AG, a corporation established under the laws of the Swiss Confederation*, concluded on August 19, 2009 and approved on June 17, 2010, aimed at expanding the possibility of granting the tax authorities of the requesting State the same information that the requested State may acquire in accordance with its domestic law. On this point Cf. A. Buccisano, *op. cit.*, p. 232.

57 Respectively in 2003 and 2007. Already in the Progress Report of 2003 records the agreement of all Member States of the OECD, with the exception of Switzerland and Luxembourg (with an Austrian reserve), around a common definition of fraud taxation, to include substantially all intentional infringements tax.

58 Cf. P. Bernasconi, *Scambio italo svizzero di informazioni fiscali. Rogatorie e convenzioni contro la doppia imposizione*, in *Dir. prat. trib. int.*, 2011, p. 15 ss., noting that the historic declaration of the Swiss Federal Council of 13 March 2009 constituted «*The turning point in the history of Swiss banking secrecy, consisting in the intention to comply with the OECD standards Swiss standards on the international exchange of information in tax matters, and it has been led by the threat*

Needless to say which effects followed the predicted statement. Basically, however, two are the main aspects on which Switzerland has been called to confront, in concluding the new CDI, since then: on the one hand, the extension of administrative assistance' application and, on the another, renunciation *de facto* to bank secrecy.

With regard to the first aspect, it is recalled that art. 26, par. 1 of the OECD Model included, and still provides today, for a very extensive collaboration, incorporating all the "foreseeably relevant" information for the application of the Convention or to the administration and enforcement of domestic legislation relating to all taxes. What has been requested to Switzerland, «*from this point of view, [was] especially of overcoming the concept that tax conventions exclusively serve to prevent double taxation, by accepting the idea that their purpose is also to prevent tax evasion*»[59].

However, a real impact on bank secrecy has been generated by par. 5 which explicitly addresses it[60].

To grasp the extent of compliance with the provisions in § 5, even by Helvetic national law, it should be remembered that art. 26, § 3 of the OECD Model admitted that the requested State may refuse to take, for assistance purposes, the administrative measures which derogate its legislation and its administrative practice, as well as to supply information which is not obtainable under the laws or in the framework of its normal administrative practice. A country whose legislation is opposed to bank surveys could therefore legitimately have refused to grant administrative assistance. This is precisely the result that the OECD has sought to avoid by introducing § 5 of art. 26, which provides that in no case the provisions of par. 3 shall be interpreted in

of the OECD, on the eve of the G20 of 2 April 2009 in London – at which will be proclaimed global war against fiscal evasion – to set up a black list, to post the States that had not yet comply with the expected standards art. 26 of the OECD Model». See also, from the same Author, P. Bernasconi, *Impatto delle iniziative fiscali internazionali rispetto al diritto ed alla prassi bancaria svizzera*, in *Atti del convegno Voluntary Disclosure*, organizzato a Milano il 1 ottobre 2014 from the A. Uckmar Foundation, p. 33 ss. e in particolare p. 34, where the Author states that: «*The Big Bang is located at a precise date: March 13, 2009, when the Swiss Government, together with that of Singapore, Liechtenstein and several others, raised the white flag, declaring publicly that Swiss legislation would be adequate to the OECD minimum standard. Nothing voluntary but a headlong rush, however, at the last minute, in view of the upcoming G20 summit on 2 April 2009 in London*».

59 Cf. A. Pedroli, *op. cit.*, p. 70.

60 Par. 5 of the rule in question was included in the OECD Model of 2005, in order to adapt the provisions in the Model TIEA 2002. On this point, see the Report Fiscal Affairs Committee of the OECD in 2000 *Improving Access to Bank Information for Tax Purposes*.

the sense of permitting to a Contracting State to refuse to transmit the information because they are held, among others, by a bank or another financial institution.

Thus, despite the above statement has led to an irreversible depletion of meaning to the words "bank secrecy", the same FDF hasten to point out that, the administrative assistance in the light of CDI, which may be concluded thereafter, i) would be limited to individual cases, with particular exclusion of fishing expeditions; ii) would be limited to the taxes contemplated by the CDI, or substantially taxes on income and on capital[61].

Another relevant date, is definitely that of 15 October 2013, day on which Switzerland has experienced new changes, coming to sign the OECD Convention, which represents the final confirmation of its commitment to the international and European fight against tax evasion and tax avoidance, as well as the shared goal of maintaining the integrity of its financial centre. The Convention of 2013, however, introduced the obligation on signatory States of spontaneous and, it should be noted, not the automatic, exchange of information, or of the transmission of information, regardless of any application for collaboration, implemented whenever the State in possession of certain information may deem it interesting for another signatory State. For the covering of this latter "flaw", the participating States at the G20 mandated the OECD to develop an international standard concerning the automatic exchange of information in tax matters. Standard that – as anticipated in the previous paragraph, § 2 – was approved by the OECD Council on 15 July 2014, and was confirmed by the G20 states on 20 and 21 September 2014.

---

61 The date of the press release, the Swiss Confederation has reviewed many existing CDI and concluded new DTAs and TIEAs that provide administrative assistance in accordance with the OECD standard; on 22 October 2014 launched a consultation on the design of the federal law concerning the unilateral application of OECD standards on information exchange (LASSI) laying down the conditions under which it is possible to grant administrative assistance in accordance with the standards of Art. 26 of OECD model to the States or territories that have concluded a double taxation agreement with Switzerland that does not meet this standard. On the basis of these premises, according to the designs of the Swiss legislature, the LASSI will no longer be applied to a State or territory once Switzerland and that State or territory concerned will exchange information on request according to international standard based on a CDI or another international agreement (e.g. multilateral Convention, if it is approved by the Federal Assembly and came into force in Switzerland). The LASSI is, therefore, transitional and will be repealed by the Federal Council as soon as all the States and territories concerned will exist a legal instrument which contains the internationally recognized standard of Art. 26 of the OECD Model.

As a result of these changes, even the Swiss Federal Council signed the MCAA on November 21, 2014.

Since not all the provisions of the Agreement are exhaustively detailed and, consequently, inferable and directly applicable in courts, it appeared necessary to the Federal Council to adopt a federal law of accompaniment and implementation, namely the law on the international automatic exchange of information on tax matters (hereinafter also "LSAI"), specifically designed to regulate the application of the standard for the automatic exchange of information and contains provisions on the organization, the procedure, the legal remedies and the criminal provisions[62]. The relevant draft law, resulting from the consultation carried out by the Council and completed last spring, is currently being considered by the Federal Assembly. Even if there were to be a referendum, then, the prospect of making the MCAA operative starting from 2017, and of implementing the first automatic exchange of information from 2018 will be respected.

With regards, however, to the specific level of relations between the European Union and the Swiss Confederation, these are regulated by numerous agreements, principally of bilateral nature[63]. This because, although, as noted, Switzerland is not among the EU Member States, who «*represents the main partner of the Swiss Confederation on both economic and political basis, also for its cultural and geographical proximity. So, and especially under the Directive, Switzerland is actively pursuing its "European policy" since the beginning of the 70s, based on bilateral sectoral agreements*»[64].

Limited to what is of interest here, for a first major package of bilateral agreements of 1999, followed by a second package of agreements, commonly known as Bilateral Agreements II[65], two of them having a very important value in terms of taxation, since the main effect of their entry into force was

---

62 The full text of the federal law in question is available on the following website http://www.admin.ch/bundesrecht/00568/index.html?lang=it.

63 For an historical recall over the relationships Switzerland/EU, Cf. C. Paolini, *op. cit.*, p. 395 ss.

64 In this sense C. Amalfitano, *op. cit*, p. 226.

65 Before the bilateral negotiations between Swiss and the EU in 1999 bilateral agreements I were signed, entered into force in 2002. These were seven agreements to the free movements of persons, technical barriers to trade, government procurement, air and land transport as well as Swiss participation in EU research programs. In 2004, Bilateral Agreements II negotiations expanded the cooperation to the Schengen/Dublin, the taxation of savings, the education, combating fraud and pensions. See A. Lang, I rapporti tra Svizzera e l'Unione europea: problemi generali, in A. Lang, C. Sanna (Eds.), *Federalismo e regionalismo. Esperienza Italiana, Svizzera e dell'Unione europea a confronto*, Giuffré, Milano, 2005, p.

clearly to extend the scope of application of administrative assistance from the Confederation towards the European Union States, with particular reference to tax offenses. Issue, in particular, of the Cooperation Agreement against fraud concerning both forms of administrative and judicial assistance[66] and of the Agreement on taxation of savings income, in the form of interest payments, concerning the sole administrative assistance[67].

Far from sacrificing its interests to the requests made by Brussels, the outcome of what can be considered to have been a real tug of war between the contracting parties, Swiss still managed to limit requests for cooperation to the hypothesis of requests for evasion of direct taxes. As far as indirect taxes are concerned, however, the federal government, while denying the administrative cooperation, decided to make available to Member States the same legal instruments that apply internally[68].

As mentioned above, remaining at the level of sunlight forms of administrative assistance, note the signing in October 2004 of the Cooperation Agreement against fraud concluded between the European Union and the Swiss Confederation[69], by virtue of which the parties are required to render to each

---

118 ss.; B. Nascimbene, *I rapporti tra la Svizzera e l'Unione europea. Gli accordi bilaterali e la politica europea della Svizzera*, in M. Condinanzi, *op. cit.*, p. 3 ss.

66 Commonly known as the Agreement on the form of interest payments, it came into force on 1.7.2005 and providing for measures equivalent to those laid down in Council Directive 2003/48/EC on taxation of savings income in the form of interest payments.

67 Commonly known as the European Union withholding tax Agreement entered into force on July 1, 2005, and providing for measures equivalent to those laid down in Council Directive 2003/48/EC on taxation of savings income in the form of interest payments.

68 Cf. A. Pedroli, *op. cit.*, p. 74, where the author notes that «*the authorities of the EU Member States can therefore have the same investigative tools that are already recognised in Switzerland to the Swiss authorities in the case of domestic proceedings. It is known that the enforceability of banking secrecy to the authorities pursuing the investigation of tax evasion is expected only in the context of the regulations on direct taxes and not even when it comes to indirect taxation, where the application is instead DPA. This is why the results of the agreements with the EU can be summarized with the notion of Inlandrbehandlung (national treatment)*».

69 Strongly backed by the EU, which insisted on the adoption of an international instrument that would allow the adoption of effective measures of the assistance, either judicial or administrative and even in cases where the merchandise do not touch Swiss. In fact, in order to increase the effectiveness in the fight against smuggling and costumes fraud at an international level, Swiss and the EU in 1997 had signed an additional protocol to the Free Trade of 1972 aiming to strengthen cooperation between their costumes authorities. In many cases, however, this goal was not achieved, despite the significant progress made, it was not possible to

other full judicial cooperation and administrative assistance on fraud and all other illegal activities, including crimes according to the field of customs and indirect taxes, related to trade in goods and services.

The scope of the Agreement is very broad: it is not limited to customs offences, but it also applies to every illegal activity falling in the field of indirect taxation (VAT and special consumption taxes, particularly on alcohol, tobacco, petroleum and motor vehicles). Direct taxes (including, for example, taxes on income, wealth or gains) are not however covered by this Agreement.

Very briefly and without pretending to be exhaustive, the Agreement, in order to speed up, facilitate and strengthen the cooperation between Switzerland, the European Union and its Member States, provides, among other, the following provisions: first, a commitment to provide legal assistance and administrative to the GPA and, secondly, the application – even in this case – of the so called principle of "National treatment", according to which, in the context of judicial and administrative assistance, Switzerland, the EU authorities and Member States have access to the same tools already applied in their national procedures.

The principle of "National treatment", however, must coordinate with the further principle/condition of "dual criminality", according to which any coercive measures can be applied only if the offense, in respect of which the assistance is requested, is considered punishable both in the requesting State than in the one required to provide such assistance.

In this context, however, it should be noted that the requesting administrative authority also has to submit an evidence, on the base of which the measure might be requested in its country, or the coercive measure would be granted by the Court (e.g. search warrant issued by a judge). And yet, according to the Agreement in comment, it is possible to dismiss the application for judicial and administrative assistance if the amount of the offense

eliminate some of the obstacles, in particular cumbersome procedures. For these reasons, at the request of the EU institutions themselves, they have been started new negotiations aimed at increasing cooperation between customs authorities, tax and legal in Switzerland and Europe, making it easier and faster. Moreover, it is stressed that the agreement in question has not yet entered into force: it is a mixed agreement, it must indeed be approved and ratified not only by the EU but also by individual Member States. Currently missing Ireland's ratification of Croatia (whose accession is recent). Some EU Member States, the EU itself and Switzerland, however, already apply the Agreement. In particular, Switzerland has ratified the Agreement 23 October 2008 and applies from January 2009 against the EU Member States which have ratified it in their turn, and adopted a declaration on its early application.

(or subtracted from the amount) is less than 25,000 Euros, or if the value of imported products or illegally exported does not exceed 100,000 Euros[70].

The second, but perhaps more important, agreement to be analyzed, it is the bilateral agreement on the taxation of savings income between Switzerland and the European Union[71], in the light of very recent amendments thereto.

Following a chronological order, the aforesaid agreement is the result of our efforts by the European institutions in order to standardize the detection of fiscal interest income within its territory[72]. In this context, the European Union has expressed interest in a partnership with certain third states, including Switzerland, which – while not participating "until yesterday" to the automatic exchange of information –, have always shared the request of the European Union, according to which the interest income of residents of a member State should be duly taxed. Therefore, it expressed its willingness

---

70 Always with reference to the purposes of this paper, is to be pointed out the provisions of art. 32 of the fraud, designed to regulate – to the detriment of the estate and the inviolability of banking secrecy – the following aspects: obtaining information on bank accounts (§ 1, lett. A); obtaining information on transactions carried out in a given period on a specified bank account (§ 1, lett. b); supervision of the operations that can be performed in the future on a specified bank account (§ 2); the guarantee that either the account holder or third parties to care knowledge provided (§ 3).

71 Which is also part of the Bilateral Agreements II signed on 26 October 2004 in Luxembourg by Switzerland and the European Union, entered into force on 1 January 2005. The existence of this agreement has raised many concerns about the compatibility between it and the Rubik model. On this point, among various contributions, Cf. B. Nascimbene, *op. cit.*, p. 21 and the doctrine recalled therein, and Cf. also C. Paolini, *op. cit.*, p. 410 where it is pointed out «*the states involved have had to renegotiate with the Swiss partners some clauses of these instruments in order to ensure their compatibility with European Union law. The changes have mainly affected the sphere of strict implementation of the agreements: the operating C.D. "Carve out, however, advocated by the Commission [...] have been excluded from the scope of the agreements in question the types of interests covered by the directive on taxation of savings income. Conversely, it is at least implicitly consecrated the freedom of Member States agreeing with third countries on the taxation of capital gains or any other stock of deposits. Furthermore, in order to avoid risk of overlapping with European Union law, the Protocols amending the agreements also include some of regularization mechanisms applicable to past tax defaults may not affect the Union's own resources and, therefore, apply to VAT*».

72 Always instrumentally, for this purpose it was enacted so-called Directive on the taxation of savings, analyzed above, aimed at ensuring taxation of cross-border interest payments aimed at individuals. In its current form, the directive on the taxation of savings is based on the so-called model of coexistence, namely the coexistence of the automatic exchange of information and the withholding tax.

to negotiate a solution equivalent to the internal EU rules, while calling for guarantees of safeguard for the protection of the privacy of bank customers.

The core of the agreement, which seems similar to the model of Rubik agreements, is the introduction of a withholding tax – initially by 15 percent with a gradual increase to 20 percent – as of July 2008 –, up to 35 percent in July 2011[73]. In this way it has been guaranteed, and it guarantees, the inability to evade the European fiscal rules through the transit of stakeholders on the Swiss financial centre. Simultaneously the protection of the privacy of bank customers, as governed by Helvetic law, was guaranteed[74] by the anonymity of the withholding tax.

The withholding tax applies to all interest payments that are not subject to withholding tax and are made by a paying agent in Switzerland – which is a credit institution – to a natural person having its tax residence in a Member State of the EU. It is also expected that foreign recipients of interest, can opt between the withholding tax or a voluntary declaration to the tax authorities of his State of residence. The voluntary declaration may, therefore, serve as an alternative to the withholding tax: upon presentation of an express provision of the beneficial owner, the paying agent submits a notification concerning the payment of interest; the information is forwarded to the tax authorities of the State of residence of the beneficial owner by the Swiss Federal Tax Administration.

According to art. 10 of the Agreement, the competent authorities of Switzerland and any of the MS shall exchange information on conduct constituting tax fraud in the state it requested or the "similar behavior", in relation to the only income covered by the Agreement itself. Likewise, paragraph 2 of the Memorandum of Understanding supplementing the Agreement also provides for an exchange of information concerning the income not subject to the provisions of the Agreement but covered by DTA between Switzerland and individual EU.

As far as the matter could still be considered as current, after the change as of March 13, 2009, the wording of the provision in question offers the familiar and *vexata quaestio* of the scope of the dual criminality principle in

73 Cf. art. 1.

74 This system has proved workable. The product of the withholding tax is up to the extent of 75 per cent to EU Member States, while the rest remain in Switzerland for its expenses (so-called revenue-sharing). The cantons are entitled to 10 percent of the Swiss share. In 2008, the gross revenue generated from the withholding tax on interest income of EU taxpayers in Switzerland amounted to 738.4 million francs. They were therefore poured 553.8 million francs to EU Member States. Switzerland has grossed 184.6 million francs, distributed at a rate of 166.2 to the Confederation and 18.4 to the cantons. For 2008 it was received about 43,000 voluntary communications, which include a sum in respect of 820,370,039 francs interests.

administrative assistance in the field of direct taxes. The question that arises facing the words "tax fraud" and "similar behavior", in fact, is if there is the intention to limit the exchange of information to those cases where under Swiss law there is fiscal evasion of direct taxes (*i.e.* the use of false or falsified documents) or if the collaboration shall be more extensive, such as it takes place in the bilateral relations with the US.

In this regard, the directions are contrasting: on the one hand, art. 10 refers to the notion of "tax fraud" to "rule of law of the requested State" (circumstances under which it would seem correct to assume that the criteria defined by Swiss law are crucial, and in particular art. 186 LIFD[75]); on the other side, are nevertheless mentioned the "similar behaviors" in relation to which it is first to be noted that they should have "*the same level of wrongfulness of tax fraud under the laws of the requested State*", and then, that Switzerland will enter into bilateral negotiations with each MS to define the individual cases that fall within its scope «*in accordance with the procedure of taxation in force in each of those States*». The latter reference is not justified by the important differences between the national taxation procedures: in the event that this provision was missing, it is not disputed the view that the strict application of the principle of dual criminality may ultimately prevent the administrative assistance.

In implementation of this Agreement, the federal government, 17 December 2004 adopted the "Federal Law on the agreement with the European Community on the taxation of savings income" (also "LFR")[76] which, at art. 10, par. 4 explicitly provided for the necessity to «preserve banking secrecy and other business secrets protected by law».

As anticipated, however, the agreement in question was just recently undergone modifications, agreed between the EU and the federal government in the month of May[77] last month, upon presentation of a Protocol amending the Agreement (the "SAI"), which will be applicable in the relations with all

75 Art. 186 LIFD, just for the first two paragraphs, provided: "*1. Anyone aiming to commit tax evasion within the meaning of articles 175-177 makes use, in order to cheat, of false, altered or inaccurate in content documents, such as books, balance sheets, income statements or wage certificates and other evidence of third, shall be punished by imprisonment or a fine of up to 30,000 francs. 2. It is saved the penalty for tax evasion*".

76 The latest version, updated to 2013, of the LFR can be consulted at the following Internet address: https://www.admin.ch/opc/it/classified-compilation/20042085/index.html.

77 The text of the Protocol of Amendment is available at the following address: http://data.consilium.europa.eu/doc/document/ST-8297-2015-INIT/it/pdf.
Under Art. 115 TFEU, the text has been subjected to prior consultation by the European Parliament, as per information available on the corporate website, at the

twenty-eight Member States. In concrete terms, the changes introduced during May consists substantially, even in the latter Code, in the introduction of the automatic exchange of information, as well as further ways of sharing already provided by artt. 16/24 of LFR[78]. In particular, as it regards the regulation of

following address: http://www.europarl.europa.eu/sides/getDoc.do?type=TA&reference=P8-TA-2015-0361&format=XML&language=IT.
As for the context that led to the amendments in question, already on May 14 2013 the Council of Ministers of Finance and Economy EU (Ecofin) gave a mandate to the European Commission to open negotiations for the adaptation of the Agreement on taxation of savings with Switzerland and other third countries (Andorra, Liechtenstein, Monaco, San Marino). After consulting the relevant parliamentary committees and the cantons, the Federal Council approved, December 18, 2013, a mandate for the revision of the concerned Agreement. The review was supposed to eliminate tax loopholes, so that it was not possible to circumvent the taxation of savings through intermediate or certain securities companies. The negotiations for this Agreement technical adjustment on the taxation of savings have been opened in mid-January 2014. Taking into account the developments at international level, in particular the introduction of global standards developed by the OECD, on 8 October 2014, the Federal Council approved a negotiating mandate to conclude an Agreement concerning the automatic exchange of data between the partner states – including the EU. In this way the negotiations on the revision of the Agreement on the taxation of savings have taken a different direction than was originally assumed.

78 In accordance with the provisions of art. 26 of the OECD Model, the federal law in question, it is above all provided a preliminary examination by the Federal Tax. Depending on the outcome of that review, there may be two cases: if it appears that the question can not be accepted since the act performed abroad does not constitute tax fraud pursuant to art. 10, § 1 of the Agreement or is a mere tax evasion if it had been made in Switzerland, the AFC informs the competent foreign authority, which may complete the application (art. 16); 2) if it appears that the requirements for granting assistance are fulfilled, the AFC shall inform the person who has such information in Switzerland (holder of information) regarding the submission of the application and the information it requests and invites him to provide that information, as well as to urge the interested party domiciled abroad in Switzerland to designate a person authorized to receive notifications. Again, the continuation of the procedure depends on the outcome of the request: if the owner of the information shall provide the requested information to the Federal Tax Administration, the latter shall consider it and take a final decision; if the holder of the information does not agree to provide the requested information within the deadline of thirty days from when he became aware of the steps initiated by the Federal Tax, the latter takes to the holder of the information a decision which requires the delivery of the information mentioned in foreign demand (art. 17). The law provides that it is also involved in the procedure the person concerned unless in the application it is not explicitly requested privacy (art. 18). Also, if the Federal Tax Administration has not obtained the information voluntarily by the holder thereof, may, *inter alia* by means of coercive measures (search of premises

the banking secrecy, Art. 2, par. 2 of the SAI provides that the information annually and automatically switches between the Swiss competent authority and the competent authorities of the Member States for the "*account subject to communication*", are: «*a) the name, address, NIF and, in the case of Natural Persons, the date and place of birth for each person of the Communication Object that is Account Holder and, in the case of an Entity that is Account Holder and that [...] has identified as having one or more persons who exercise control persons who are subject of Communication, the name, address and NIF Entity and the name, address, NIF and the date and the place of birth of each person of the Communication Object; b) the account number (or functional equivalent in the absence of an account number); c) the name and number, if any Financial Institution identification seal the Communication; d) the balance or the value of the account (including, in the case of a contract for which insurance is a Measurable Value Matured or an annuity contract, the Accrued Value or surrender value) at the end of the relevant calendar year, or other suitable reporting period or, if the account was closed during that year or period, the closure of the account*», as well as additional information in the specific cases of Custody Accounts or Deposit Accounts[79]. The remaining provisions of the 2004 Agreement are also incorporated in the new text, which is supplemented by a joint declaration in which the Contracting Parties shall determine the entry into force on 1 January 2017, provided that you have completed the approval process, in Switzerland and in the EU. The Swiss Executive plans to introduce the Accord in 2017 and proceed to a first exchange of data in 2018.

5 Final considerations

Recent developments concerning the bilateral relations between Switzerland and, on the one hand, the EU Member States[80], and, secondly, the States

---

and seizure of objects, documents and paper documents and other data carriers). Such measures are ordered by the Director of the Federal contributions, but they must be previously authorized by the competent court to decide on foreign requests for assistance in the canton in which they must be executed (Art. 19). The Federal Tax Administration's final decision concerning the provision of information may be subject to proceedings under the provisions of Federal proceedings (Art. 24) (jurisdiction the federal administrative court, which has the last word). is also provided for a simplified procedure, a final decision is not required if the person concerned agrees to provide the information to the competent foreign authority and shall inform in writing the Federal Tax Administration (Art. 22).

79 Cf. Art. 2, § 2, lett. e), f), g).

80 We recall the recent changes introduced to the CDI Italy-Switzerland, for the exchange of information concerning the Italian account holders, signed February 23,

Parties to the various international fora illustrated, are paradigmatic of the difficult situation in which both the EU and international bodies are called to work in pursuit of tax policy coordination among the different national tax systems, often very different between them.

Of course, the changes to the CDS and the Swiss-EU Bilateral Agreement herein just explained, that Switzerland is taking steps to implement into national law in order to avoid repercussions on the political and economic level within the international community, are a symptom of a inevitable change, that, as stated by the EU institutions themselves, is instrumental in order to conduct an effective fight against fraud and tax avoidance and, in particular, against tax evasion and tax avoidance by individuals and legal entities located in Union territory with the involvement of financial institutions in third countries.

All this, of course, will lead to the adoption of equally inevitable modifications to the Rubik agreements now in force for the Swiss Confederation, and to the LFR, in order also to elide the literal level of the provisions contained therein, any form of protection against the secret banking.

Symptomatic of these important changes, however, appears as of now the latest practice followed by Swiss banks, according to which, the so-called "International tax evaders" are forced to come to terms today, not only with the above mentioned and analyzed developments and evolutions of the law on international assistance in tax matters, but also with the more cautious attitude on the part of Swiss banks, which now seem to want to authorize the opening of new banking relationships, in particular the current accounts, exclusively by foreign taxpayers who are able to prove the lawfulness of the

---

2015. An acceleration at the end of Milan-Berne negotiations was impressed by the entry into force, with effect from 2 January 2015 of the law 186 of 15 December 2014 laying down provisions for the emergence and return of funds held abroad as well as for the strengthening the fight against tax evasion (better known as the "law on voluntary disclosure").

In essence, the Agreement between Italy and Switzerland marks the end of banking secrecy, and the effective exchange of information on request in relations between the two countries, set out the rules for administrative cooperation in tax matters between the tax authorities of the two States.

In particular, the Agreement: governs the exchange of information relating to Italian account holders, resulting in the end of bank secrecy (Art. 27) and possibility for Italian taxpayers to transfer (legitimately) capital abroad; contemplates a regularization procedure of banking activities undertaken and investments made in Switzerland by individuals resident in Italy; provides for a system of penalties rewarding for taxpayers who decide to "regularize" activities and capital held abroad; It provides for the possibility of cross-border workers, to be subject to taxation in both countries, according to, however, the splitting of the tax mechanism.

full tax assets conferred on deposit and current accounts compared to the rules of the country of residence.

The matter, as seen, is evolving rapidly and, of course, the conclusions of this long journey that began in the first decade of the twenty-first century and whose stages were marked by "attacks on banking secrecy from various fronts", have not yet been written. Nevertheless, if on one hand the practical consequences arising from all the aforementioned regulatory changes may not yet being known, on the other still seems logical to assume from the outset that one of the main pillars of the collective imagination against Switzerland, as synonym for tax haven and banking secrecy is inevitably doomed to collapse.

Gaetano Ragucci*

Tax Treatment of Cross-border Commuters and Effects of the ALC

Abstract: The chapter addresses the Italian tax regime applicable to incomes of employees who work abroad. Particular attention is devoted to taxation of salary as well as of pension rights of cross-frontier workers resident in Italy also with regard to the exemption.

1 Introduction

With the entry into force of the Agreement on the free movement of persons (ALC), Switzerland had to confront with the effects of a progressive opening of the job market and measures that facilitate immigration of foreign workers.

Quantitive investigations revealed how Swiss economy took remarkable advantage from the free movement of persons. Enterprises improved their capability in recruiting qualified workers among EU and European Free Trade Association (EFTA) countries. And this improved their competitiveness with regards to European competitors.

The economic development favored by immigration was however linked to financial imbalances due to the overloading of the infrastructures and the additional weight on the welfare state institutes. Studies commissioned by the State Secretariat for Economic Affairs (SECO)[1] also showed the effects of the increase of Italian cross-border workers on the budget of cantons where they are employed, resulting from the consequent increase in burden of financial compensation owed to the Italian municipalities of residence.

The phenomenon was particularly significant in the Ticino Canton, where it almost questioned the withheld of the agreements in force with Italy[2]. In fact, a comparative analysis of income tax regimes in both countries shows that the Swiss accession to the ALC reduced economic and legal asymmetries that in the

* Professore associato di Diritto Tributario, Università degli Studi di Milano.

1 http://www.personenfreizuegigkeit.admin.ch/fza/it/home/auswirkungen.html.

2 The crisis in relations between the two countries has gone up to the arrangement of the freezing of compensation due to Italy, disposed in June 2011 by the Council of State of Ticino.

past had led to grant favorable tributary treatment to Italian frontier workers[3]. Also, among the causes of the increase of immigrants from Italy there is the competitive advantage provided by Switzerland with respect to ordinary tax on personal income determined by national law.

From the Italian point of view, the problem is not only the elimination of double taxation on cross-border commuters income but, also, the correction of the imbalance that allocates the revenue from the levy on incomes of these persons on the Swiss canton in which the work was pursued against infrastructure and welfare costs that are paid also by Italian municipalities of residence.

The situation highlighted that a revision of the agreement on the taxation on income of frontier workers was necessary. The opportunity to start this revision was the signing of the Protocol between Italy and Switzerland for the amendment of the clause on exchange of information in the Convention against double taxation, which took place in Milan on 23 February 2015.

An overview of the current structure of the subject can be helpful to identify the lines of future reform, also in light of the relevant principles of the Italian and European taxation system.

2 Taxation in Italy of the income from employment pursued abroad

As a rule, any income in cash and in kind received by an Italian resident related to an employment paid abroad is taxable in Italy (Art. 3 c. 1 of the Consolidated Act on Income Tax – CAIT) except for the deduction of a tax credit, related to the taxes paid abroad, from gross calculated on the total income of the taxpayer.

In fact, when foreign incomes contribute in determining the taxable, the tax paid outright in that country should be written off the levy up to the amount corresponding to the ratio between the amount of income earned abroad, and the total gross income (Art. 165 CAIT). The taxpayer is not entitled to the deduction if he fails to file the tax return or, having submitted it, fails to indicate them.

The tax credit is a measure of national law aimed, if not at preventing, at least at mitigating the double taxation of foreign-source income, even in the absence of a special agreement. However, it is not very suitable for income arising from employment, because it only applies to taxes paid abroad out-

3 M. Bernasconi, D. Ferrari, *L'Accordo sui frontalieri tra Italia e Svizzera. Violazione del diritto di reciprocità*, in http://www.ti.ch/can/seggc/comunicazioni/gc/proposterisoluzione/allegato-propo-ris-13-12-2010.pdf.

right and is referred to gross tax due for the entire period, as wound up in the tax return.

Conversely, at the time of disbursement, incomes from employment suffer of a withholding tax, forcing the taxpayer to suffer a double withdrawal, with sensitive decrease in net assets available for theirs and their family's needs during the entire tax year. Moreover, in the absence of other taxable income in Italy, the taxpayer has no interest in referring it to any subsequent tax year in order to compensate with future tax liabilities, and this forces him to systematically opt for a refund. Therefore, the elimination of the duplication of the tax is deferred until further fulfillment of this obligation by the burdened administration. Hence widespread exceptions to the common system occur, aimed at eliminating double taxation of foreign-source income form employment. In fact, special rules can be found in domestic international tax law and in conventional sources.

To the first category of exceptions belongs the treatment of employees who work abroad as a continuous and sole object of the employment and who are resident in the foreign country for a period exceeding 183 days on twelve months.

These employees' incomes are set on the basis of conventional wages that the Ministry of Labour and Social Security defines each year (Art. 51 c. 8-bis CAIT). This is a form of lump-sum determination of the taxable fixed for income groups and sectors of activity, the result of which flows into the calculation of the taxable income of the period instead of the income actually received.

Once the deductions provided by the law are made, the credit set forth at Art. 165 of the CAIT can be subtracted from the taxable. However, its computation undergoes a correction since, according to the tenth paragraph of this provision, when the income produced abroad contributes only partly to the entire income (as it happens in this case) the foreign tax should be correspondingly reduced[4].

Those who can avail themselves of this discipline are not frontier workers. This regime requires that the work is carried out abroad on an ongoing basis, with extended stays that in the twelve months exceed 183 days. Different rules apply for persons traveling daily in the foreign state, to return to his own home at the end of the working day[5].

---

4 On the modalities of calculation: circ. min. n. 48 / E of 2013.

5 For the Art. 7 first paragraph of Annex I to the Agreement on the free movement of persons signed by the European Community and its Member States and the Swiss Confederation of 21 June 1999, «an employed frontier worker is a national of a Contracting Party who has his residence in the territory of a Contracting Party and who pursues an activity as an employed person in the territory of the other

This regime does not affect the application of special measures prescribed by conventions for the avoidance of double taxation signed by Italy, but this is not the appropriate place to discuss this issue.

3 Income taxation on frontier workers residing in Italy

Art. 175, § 1 of Law n. 147/2013 fixed a regulation that was originally disposed at art. 3 of the CAIT and hence expunged to be recovered in subsequent legislation, under which today the employment income practiced by Italian residents abroad in border areas, or in countries neighboring the national territory, on a continuous and sole object of the relationship, benefits an exemption of €. 6,700, raised to €. 7,500 with effect from 1 January 2015[6].

This measure is also intended to limit the double taxation of foreign-source employment income, and is the cause of a partial combination of foreign source income to the taxable gross in Italy. This event also affects the calculation of the tax credit, reducing the amount than ordinary (Art.165 c. 10 CAIT).

The discipline described above can be applied to Italian residents who render services in any neighboring country. Special rules may be contained in the agreements to prevent double taxation, concluded by Italy with one of these States. These agreements are not meant to prevail in any case, since they can be derogated by the more favorable relevant internal regulation (Art. 169 of the CAIT).

According to art. 15 of the Italy-Switzerland double taxation Convention dated 23 December 1978, n. 943, the employment income earned by an Italian resident for the work pursued in Switzerland shall be taxable only in this State. In addition, the applicable regime for frontier workers is governed by a separate agreement signed on October 3, 1974 (later amended in 1985), which is an integral part of the Convention (Art.15 c. 4 Agreement)[7].

The Agreement is intended to avoid double taxation on income of frontier workers, but it was originally also influenced by the consideration of the high number of Italian residents engaged in paid employment in Switzerland, the costs incurred by the Italian municipalities of residence, and the contribu-

---

Contracting Party, returning to his place of residence as a rule every day, or at least once a week».

6 Circ. min. n. 1/E del 2001, § 1.2.; circ. min. n. 2/E del 2003, § 9.

7 Agreement between the Italian Republic and the Swiss Confederation for the avoidance of double taxation and the regulation of certain other matters with respect to taxes on income and on capital (Published in the O.J. n. 42 of 12.02.1979). For the treatment of frontier workers resident in Switzerland: Guggiari Salari, *Spouses: unequal treatment based on residence of the border*, in *Novità fiscali*, 2014, n. 5, p. 8 ss.

tion that Italian workers bring at several levels to the economy of the Swiss cantons in which their services are rendered.

Relying on this, the Agreement restates a rule formerly expressed in the Convention for which the income tax of these persons belongs to Switzerland, but it also adds that the cantons concerned (Ticino, Grisons and Valais) are required to pay to the Italian municipality of residence a part of the gained annual revenue in compensation for expenses incurred for foreign workers[8].

The Agreement does not foresee similar charges for the Italian State upon occurrence of comparable situations, thus derogating to the reciprocity principle that rules the relations between States[9].

The coordination of the Conventional rule of tax exemption in Italy with the regime of partial exclusion from the taxable income set forth in Art.1 c. 175 Law n. 147/2013 is based on factual circumstances. To enjoy the full tax relief provided by the conventional rule, the employee must reside in one of the Italian border towns that enjoy the financial compensation provided for by the Agreement of 3 October 1974 and in subsequent reports that complement it. If he resides in a city other than those, he can take advantage of the less favorable regime of partial exclusion set forth under Art. 1 c. 175 Law n. 147/2013, like any other frontier workers.

4 (follow): imposition of pensions received by former frontier workers, and exemption from the statement of financial assets held in Switzerland

As a rule, under Italian law also all kinds of retirement benefits and allowances to them are treated as employment income (Art. 49 c. 2 lett. A, CAIT). However, this kind of disbursements, provided by Swiss law, are subject to another discipline.

Needless to reconstruct the whole regulatory framework. It will be simply said that Art. 18 of the Italian-Swiss double taxation of pensions and other payments of the same nature paid to a resident of a Contracting State in consideration of past employment shall be taxable only in that State[10]. Therefore,

---

8 This point of the agreement does not appear consistent with the current structure of Italian public finances, given that the levy on incomes is intended to the financing of general public expenditure, and that Italians municipalities count on independent sources of financing composed of their own tax revenues, integrated only by transfers of resources borne from state budget.

9 M. Bernasconi, D. Ferrari, *L'Accordo sui frontalieri tra Italia e Svizzera. Violazione del diritto di reciprocità*, in http://www.ti.ch/can/seggc/comunicazioni/gc/proposterisoluzione/allegato-propo-ris-13-12-2010.pdf.

10 On the subject, even if with reference to the different situation than the one considered in the text, and a different agreement: R. D'Alessio, *Il trattamento fiscale*

if paid directly in Italy, the AHV retirement pension acquired on the basis of social security contributions also taxed at source in Switzerland is subject to a withholding tax of 5%, and is therefore excluded from the total income to be reported in Italy (Art. 76 Law n. 413/1991).

The legal framework for supplementary pensions is more problematic. Supplementary pensions are already known by Swiss law as an income of the II Pillar paid by private employers[11]. Constructions proposed by the Italian practice are two.

According to one interpretation, it would regard activities carried out by third parties having relation with the terminated contract of employment, and it should therefore be treated as income from employment according to the regular discipline (Art. 49 c. 2 lett. A, CAIT). Therefore, such income would not be taxed in Italy, by virtue of concordant provisions of Art. 15 c. 4 of the Convention Italy-Switzerland against double taxation and of the Agreement of 3 October 1974[12].

A different interpretation leads the revenues of the II Pillar to the regime laid down by Art. 44 c. 1 lett. g) CAIT, relating to income from management of assets consisting of cash and properties entrusted to third parties, in the collective interest of a number of parties. They would therefore be subject to the withholding tax under Art. 6 Law n. 482/1985[13]. And they would not compete to the formation of the taxable in Italy by virtue of the exclusion of Art. 3 c. 3 lett. a) T.U.I.R.

The two solutions are both plausible, but they differ from the point of view of relations between the two States, because the first implies that the pension disbursements of the so called II Pillar increases the flow of financial compensation imposed on Swiss cantons where employee pursued the activity (and this is disputed by Swiss interpreters). Under an evolutionary perspective, the second one is preferable, since it anticipates the ineffectiveness on the financial compensation owed to Italy, assuring at the same time the resources to be transferred to border towns of residence, which would replace them.

It remains to be said that any frontier worker having another income to be taxed in Italy is required to submit a declaration even if the employment income related to the activity in Switzerland does not compete to the taxable. It remains to be said that any frontier worker having another income to be taxed in Italy is required to submit a declaration even if the employment in-

---

della pensione nel quadro di un sistema di sicurezza sociale: la corretta interpretazione della norma convenzionale, in *Dir. prat. trib.*, 2015, II, p. 418 ss.

11 If paid by public employers, Art. 19 of the Convention Italy-Switzerland double taxation applies, on which basis the levy is up to Switzerland.

12 Agenzia delle Entrate del Piemonte, response to question n. 954-56/2007.

13 Agenzia delle Entrate della Lombardia, response to question n. 904-359/2004.

come related to the activity in Switzerland does not contribute to the taxable income. In these cases they are not required to exhibit in the RW box of the declaration their investments and foreign activities of financial nature held in the country where they work, thus derogating the legal framework set forth by Art. 4 D. L. n. 167/1990 (art. 38 c. 13 Law n. 122/2010).

The exemption from the obligation to indicate stocks amount on the Swiss current accounts holds for those who have only credited their own wages. In case of availability from other sources, the ordinary discipline applies again.

5 The line of the reform

During negotiations which would have led to the signing of the Protocol amending the Convention of 1976 to avoid double taxation, representatives of the tax authorities of the two countries signed a political document which set the course of further negotiations on other relevant issues. Among these, we can also find the taxation of employment income for cross-border workers residing in both countries[14].

From this point of view, the goal that Italy and Switzerland aim to achieve through the planned revision of the 1974 Agreement is the reallocation of the taxation on frontier workers on reciprocal basis. Therefore it lies ahead the overcoming of the regime of total exemption from taxation of income in the country of residence, in force today. The point was however agreed that the taxes owed to the country where the frontier worker will carry out his activities may not exceed 70% of the ordinary taxes applied to residents. And the State of residence of the worker can apply their own taxes, with the obligation, however, to eliminate double taxation.

In addition, with the help of Italian and Swiss tax authorities, the burden of financing public services using the revenue of applicable taxes will be up to both countries, who will face them through the revenues collected according to their national laws. As for Italy, it will burden the budget of the State, of Regions located at the Swiss border and of the border towns where workers reside in accordance with the allocation prescribed by Art. 117 Cost. and with the primary legislation that gave effect starting from the Law n. 42/2009.

The line of future negotiations is completed by the mutual commitment to create a system of electronic exchange of periodic information, aimed at enabling the State of residence to receive and process on time all data relat-

14 http://www.mef.gov.it/inevidenza/documenti/Roadmap_initialled_on_19.12.2014.pdf.

ing to the income earned from cross-border workers in the State where the income is produced[15].

6. Problems and constraints

The future structure of the taxation of employment income of border commuters departs significantly from the Model of Convention OECD against double taxation, Art. 15 of which reserve the imposition to the source State. In addition, implementary rules will be subject to the limitations resulting from the EU Court of Justice settled case law on the guarantees securing the freedom of movement of persons.

In judgment of 19 November 2015, related to Case C-241/2014, Bukovanský, the European Court of Justice (section II) states that settled case law regarding the relationship between primary European Union law and conventions against double taxation treaties between Member States can be applied through analogical interpretation to the relationship between the Agreement on the free movement of persons and the conventions aimed at preventing double taxation concluded between Member States and the Swiss Confederation[16].

In the Court's vision, Member States are free to determine the connecting factors for the allocation of fiscal jurisdiction by inserting specific clauses in bilateral agreements for the avoidance of double taxation, but in the exercise of the power of taxation so allocated they are also required to respect the principle of equal treatment enshrined in Art. 9, Annex I of the Agreement on free movement – according to which the employee and his family members should enjoy the same tax and social advantages as national employed persons and members of their families – as well as the freedom of movement grounded in Art. 45 TFEU[17].

The resulting framework is open to different evaluations for the reciprocity of commitments made by the signing of the document attached to the Protocol of 23 February 2015. Two are the situations on which Italy will have to take action for the implementation and they relate to the processing of the employment income of Swiss residents working in Italy, and the treatment of Italian residents working in Switzerland.

---

15 There are also provisions for the case of the output from the ALC Switzerland, which does not dwell because not directly relevant to the subject.

16 Abovementioned judgment, § 39.

17 Court of Justice judgment of 12 May 1998, C-336/96, *Gilly*, § 30; judgment of 16 October 2008, C-527/06, *Renneberg*, §§ 48 to 51; judgment of 12 December 2013, C-303/12, *Garcet Imfeld*, §§ 41 and 42.

As for the first, the internal international tax regulation provides that non-resident workers suffer the levy on income from employment paid in Italy, even if it is composed of fees paid by worker cooperatives, allowances and compensation against third parties (Art. 23 c. 1 lett. c, CAIT). Tax applies on total income, from which only some of the many and various charges recognized to residents are deductible (Art. 24 c. 2 CAIT). An analogous restriction is provided for tax deductions (Art. 24 c. 2 CAIT).

Abstractly, Italian commitment to limit the tax at 70% of the ordinary taxes due from an Italian resident can be realized through a reduction of the taxable, net of deductions or through a reduction of the tax, net of permitted deductions. It is likely that the final result is more favorable than the one achievable by the employee in Italy using all deductions allowed on 100% of the taxable.

However, in order to assess the compatibility of the rule with the principle of equal treatment, it should be taken into account the treatment in Switzerland of the remaining 30% of incomes that, in addition to the tax levied in Italy, could lead to a result altogether more onerous than the common regime applied to employment income in Italy. Compatibility issues with the European legal order are hence foreseeable, issues that are not immediately solvable simply on the recognition of equivalent treatment to that given to national resident[18].

Considerations over the case of an Italian resident who lends its work abroad must be different. In fact, Italy will apply ordinary taxes to the employee, but will also have to respect the burden of eliminating double taxation. Given the structural failure of the tax credit system to ensure the elimination of double taxation on abroad employee income, it will be necessary to find out an alternative solution. A partial exemption could be ensured by Art. 1, § 175, of Law n. 147/2013 to any frontier worker, exemption that Italy could extend to employees in Switzerland simply by failing to introduce a derogating scheme reserved for them.

It should otherwise be borne in mind that that provision would also mark a limit on the legislative intervention on the matter since, as mentioned above, it prevails over conventional exceptional arrangements if more favorable.

18 As of the leading houses of the Court of Justice judgment 14 February 1995, C-279/93, *Schumacker*, especially relevant to the principles established in terms of comparability of the situations at the end of the application of the principle of non-discrimination, on which P. Boria, *European tax Law*, Giuffré, Milano, 2015, p. 177 ss., which concludes on the point: «*you can argue that discrimination does not simply constitute a different tax treatment between resident and non-resident entities, but rather a difference in tax treatment does not reasonably based on an assessment the overall situation of resident and non-resident individuals*».

Therefore, at level playing field, for the taxpayer the treatment of taxable employment income in Swiss cantons could not be more onerous than the one recognized through the deduction of e 7,500 from the calculation of the taxable, completed by the credit deduction for taxes paid in Switzerland, reduced on the basis of the rules set forth at § 10 of Art. 165 T.U.I.R..

Similar considerations apply also to the tax treatment of pension payments and of supplementary welfare benefits of the s.c. Pillar II, under appropriate adjustments.

7. Displacement abroad of the Italian residence

The foregoing evaluations assume that the frontier worker retains his residence in Italy. For completeness it is appropriate to indicate those conditions that according to the Italian legal system integrate the status of a resident and cases in which this status is lost, with the caveat that the periodic nature of taxation on income requires that verification of their occurrence is accomplished year per year[19].

The tax law concept of residence does not coincide with the one provided by the Civil Code. To income tax purposes, resident in Italy are considered all individuals who for most of the tax period are recorded in the General Register at the resident position (Art. 2 CAIT)[20].

However, a person may be a resident even if not recorded in any Register. This happens when he has in Italy his domicile, intended as the place where his personal and financial interests are centered (Art. 43 c. 1 cod. Civ.), or his residence as defined in the Civil Code. Taken the concept of residence in the latter sense, may be considered a resident also the person that keeps his habitual dwelling there in Italy (Art. 43 c. 2 cod. Civ.).

The necessary coordination between the tax law and civil law imposes to conclude that those conditions must last for most of the year, hence for more than six months, so that the tax residence notion may be considered consolidated for income tax purposes.

In addition, with a view of contrasting the phenomenon of false residences, the Italian tax law considered as residents in Italy those individuals who deleted from the Registers and moved to the States or territories which enjoy preferential tax regimes (Art. 2 bis CAIT). In this case, the taxpayer has the

---

19 R. Baggio, *Loss and purchase of tax residence: overview and controversial aspects*, in *Riv. dir. trib.*, 2006, I, p. 357 ss.

20 This condition makes the status of indisputable residence: Cass. n. 677/2015, in *GT Riv. swore. trib.* 2015, 288 ss., with F. Roccatagliata note, *The Internal Rules and international standards on the subject of "tax residence": a coexistence by seemingly conflicting aspects.*

responsibility to prove that he did not conserve in Italy neither the center of his own affairs and interests, nor his ordinary residence after deletion from the Register[21].

Switzerland is among those states enjoying more favorable tax regimes (the list is contained in the Decree of 4 May 1999) and remained in the list even after the signing in Milan, on 23 February 2015, of the Protocol for the modification of the clause on exchange of information. In fact, the direct effect of the signature has been the commitment of Italy to delete Switzerland from the blacklists solely based on the presence of limits to the exchange of information to incorporate it in the collaborative countries list. These lists are linked to particular disciplines applicable to the taxation of business income, and are affected by a reorganization intervention foreshadowed by the new provisions contained in the 2015 Stability Law, not yet accomplished[22].

The list concerned by the rule of presumption of residence in Italy dictated by Art. 2 bis CAIT indicates those countries whose tax system is characterized by preferential regimes attributable to tax competition techniques considered harmful among the States. Switzerland is included in the list because of the presence of companies that are not subject to cantonal and municipal taxes, such as holding, auxiliary and domicile companies. Its deletion from the list provided by Art. 2 bis will follow the elimination of these measures. Switzerland committed to perform this removal with the signing of the joint declaration with the EU Member States concerning the taxation of businesses, which took place in Bern on 14 October 2014[23].

Moreover, the presumption of residence provided by Art. 2 bis of the CAIT works at interior international tax law level, and is not by itself sufficient to attract all the incomes of the taxpayers who moved to Switzerland under the sole Italian fiscal jurisdiction. The effect of the presumption is in

---

21 The ability to prove the contrary implies that the burden imposed by Art. 2 bis of the CAIT serious on the subject that intends to rebut the presumption that there is regulated, even when this is the financial administration: Cass Court. n. 21438/2014, in *GT Riv. swore. trib.* 2015, 127 ss., With note Antonini Septa, *The presumption of residence between the burden of proof allocation rule and enforceability to the financial administration.*

22 A. Albano, Penned, *The new criteria for the identification of tax havens*, in *Corr. Trib.*, 2014, p. 3047 ss.; R. Rizzardi, *The exchange of tax information internationally*, ibid, 2015, p. 2085 ss.

23 Moreover, issues of common interest on which Italy and Switzerland have committed to continue negotiations also includes the tax competition between the two systems. The two countries will work together to identify new tax regimes to attract new investments in Switzerland. Italy will inform Switzerland of the countermeasures that could be taken, as well as the rules which, if necessary, itself intends to take, in order to achieve the same result.

fact to increase the recurrence cases of dual Italian and Swiss residency, that have to be eliminated by applying the relevant provisions of the Convention.

According to the provisions of Art. 4 of the Convention, elimination of this condition occurs with the application of auxiliary criteria (prevalence of taxing rights of the state in which there is the permanent home; if not, in the following order: the center of vital interests, the usual residence; nationality and, ultimately, through the mutual agreement of the competent authorities of the two States).

It is therefore clear that, without coming into direct conflict with the conventional rules, the presumption expressed by Art. 2 bis of the CAIT imposes anyway a burden of the material conditions for transferring the residence, functional to contrast the competition between tax systems, and the application of direct anti-abuse measures of domestic law to contain tax evasion .

The just mentioned constraints respond to interests that do not concern the conduct of frontier workers, whose condition was indirectly affected by the fiscal policy options carried out at the level of financial taxation and enterprise.

Maria Pierro*

Administrative Cooperation between Switzerland and the EU: the Exchange of Information

Abstract: The author outlines the current legal framework governing exchange of information between tax authorities and transparency in the light of the art. 26 of the OECD Convention Model. She then identifies and comments on the relevant rules applicable to the exchange of information and to the rights granted to the taxpayers in the context of fiscal surveillance procedures.

1 Automatic exchange of information and fiscal transparency

The increase in cross-border transactions, their transnational dimension and the increase in the movement of capital and persons produced numerous positive effects (investments in developing countries, international mobility of workers), but have also favoured financial instability and the worsening of economic and financial crimes, among which we highlight the infidel and the omitted tax return, tax evasion, money laundering, insider trading.

The globalization of economic phenomena, in fact, led small and large taxpayers, on the one hand, to take advantage of tax incentives in the domestic law to attract investments in the territory and encourage the localization of activity and/or production initiatives and, on the other hand, to exploit the complexity and asymmetries of domestic, European and non-EU countries regulations to mitigate the tax burden.

The use of so called "aggressive mechanisms" for tax planning allowed to move the wealth (tax base) from countries with high taxation to "spaces" or jurisdictions where it is (was) possible to submit relevant income shares to a minimum taxation or to complete exclusion from taxation (via exemption in the place of residence of the taxpayer, and in the production place)[1]. With

---

* Professore Associato di Diritto Tributario (Università degli Studi dell'Insubria, Varese).

1 The Communication from the Commission to the European Parliament and the Council on fiscal transparency to combat tax evasion and tax avoidance of March 18, 2015 n. 136, indicated that «using aggressive tax planning techniques, some companies exploit loopholes in tax systems and mismatches between national

the effect of: a) eroding tax bases (and simultaneously maximize profits); b) altering the distribution of the tax burden among taxpayers; c) affecting the tax collection with a significant drop in tax revenue; d) altering, in general, the proper functioning of the single market and fair competition between Member.

The main cause of these phenomena has been detected in the absence of transparency[2], so in the impossibility for the tax authorities to access information of financial and patrimonial nature, needed for a correct determination of the taxpayer's wealth to be taxed. This inability was determined by the lack of cooperation and collaboration between countries that enables both to ensure a fair taxation, and to allocate the "stolen evasion" resources to the promotion of new economic activities and to the strengthening of the existing ones.

The need to encourage the exchange of information, useful for the assessment of taxes, has always been unanimously felt[3].

The Organisation for Economic Co-operation and Development (OECD) and the European Union have long been engaged on this front and, at the

---

rules to avoid paying their fair share of taxes. In addition the tax systems of many countries allow companies to artificially shift profits in their jurisdictions, with the effect of encouraging the aggressive tax planning».

http://www.parlamento.it/web/docuorc2004.nsf/8fc228fe50daa42bc12576900058cada/7f5700cb678b3647c1257e0d003d73a4/$FILE/COM2015_0136_IT.pdf.

In the literature, on the subject, it should be noted the essay by S. CIPOLLINA, *I redditi 'nomadi' delle società multinazionali nell'economia globalizzata*, in *Riv. dir. fin. sc.*, 2014, I, p. 23 ss.

2 The 2001 OECD report, § 37 shows that «the absence of non-transparent features in the tax jurisdiction of a certain» system can only be countered with the attribution to the Governments of the ability to access bank data (which might be relevant for tax purposes, criminal and civil) and those that enable the identification of the beneficial owner of assets entities, financial or income of any kind. The acquired data must then be made available to the administrative authorities of the requesting States in order to enable an effective fight against tax evasion and international tax evasion.

3 On the subject, for a general overview see M.C. FREGNI, *Problemi e prospettive dell'Unione fiscale europea*, in *Raff. trib.*, 2013, p. 1061 ss.; on this subject, in particular P. BORIA, *Diritto tributario europeo*, Giuffré, Milano, 2015, p. 421 ss.; M. BARASSI, *Lo scambio d'informazioni nella UE*, in *RDT Internazionale*, 2001, p. 327 ss.; ID., *Cooperazione tra amministrazioni fiscali*, in *Diz. Cassese*, Milano, 2006, p. 1525 ss.; ID., *Exchange of tax information. The legislative framework – Lo scambio di informazioni in materia fiscale. La normativa vigente*, in *RDT Internazionale*, n. 1-2/2009, p. 99 ss.; F. FERNANDEZ MARIN, *Il principio di cooperazione* tra le amministrazioni finanziarie, in AA.VV., A. DI PIETRO (Eds.), *I principi europei del diritto tributario,* Cedam, Padova, 2013, p. 380 ss.; ID., *La tutela de la Unión Europea al contribuyente en el intercambio de información tributaria*, Atelier, Barcellona, 2007, p. 29 ss.

request of the Finance Ministers and central bank Governors of the G20 (19 April 2013), they have identified the *automatic exchange of information* between tax authorities as the most effective and appropriate tool to prevent and combat system distortions and to fight elusive, illegal, and fraudulent phenomena.

The haven to this "advanced" mode of information exchange is a relatively recent acquisition, resulting from a progressive path that has seen converging, more or less of course, the will of EU and of the G20 governments and also of third countries; all sharing the desire to counter the elusive phenomenon[4] behind which sometimes offenses are hidden which contribute, along with other factors, to fuel also the phenomena of international terrorism.

The classical scheme of sharing tax information between governments has always been the exchange of information *on request*[5] governed, first of all, by the convention model against double taxation elaborated by the OECD.

However, the free movement of financial assets and the need to streamline the verification activity and tax collection have weakened the effectiveness of this tool, leading the governments up to invoke – always in order to foster the emergence of hidden wealth – for the identification of a more efficient mode of exchange of information (tax-sensitive), in addition to the strengthening of the existing ones.

Mode, as mentioned, that has found its concrete expression first in the identification and proposition, and then in the adoption at international, European and domestic level of the automatic exchange of information, or so-called *Standard for automatic Exchange of financial account information in tax matters*, technique borrowed from the FATCA legislation (bilateral agreement on the exchange of information signed between the United States and Third Countries)[6] that constitutes the model by which the G20 countries

---

4 Please refer to R. Cordeiro Guerra, *Criminalità economica e paradisi fiscali*, Lecture given at the National Meeting of the Italian Association of Tax Law Professors in Naples on 14-15 October 2015 on «New items taxpaying capacity and hidden wealth», p. 12 ss. typescript, http://www.aipdt.it/atti-provvisori-convegno-annuale-aipdt-2015/, in which the impact of international fiscal cooperation on anti-money laundering regulations is analysed.

5 Art. 26 of the OECD Convention Model is the reference standard on transparency and exchange of information. § 9 of the Commentary regulates three types of information exchange: on request, spontaneous and automatic as it will be explained in the text.

6 The FATCA legislation has been adopted by the United States in 2012 and entered into force in 2013. It requires the foreign financial intermediaries (Foreign Financial Institutions – FFI) the obligation to automatically communicate and yearly the US tax authority (Internal Reveue Service- IRS) the names of the US tax persons (US citizens) who have foreign accounts (financial information: interest, dividends,

and the European Union have then been inspired for the implementation of the new methodology.

The new *Standard* takes into account a scheme of intergovernmental agreement (*Multilateral Competent Authority Agreement* – MCAA[7]), which defines the rules governing the automatic exchange of information – only usable for tax purposes and for a specific period – and it is the text of reference on the basis of which bilateral agreements can be concluded.

The *Standard*, in addition to MCAA, provides for common rules that regulates procedures for the implementation of the obligation for correct verification and communication (*Common Reporting Standard – CRS*[8]). In particular, it identifies the type of financial information subject of automatic exchange (*i.e.* the data identifying the account holder [*reportable account*], the number and the account balance, interest, dividends, revenues from the sale of transited assets from accounts held by individuals and legal entities, as well as the intermediary identification data, only for the financial accounts subject to disclosure, identified through *due diligence*), and the procedures that financial institutions must adhere to, for their acquisition and transmission.

The adoption of the *Common Reporting Standard* might allow to take a census on information related to investors holding bank accounts and deposits at financial Institutions (banks, financial intermediaries, brokers, insurance companies, collective investment schemes [UCITS], mutual funds) banks, financial intermediaries, brokers, insurance companies, collective investment schemes [UCITS], mutual funds of a State, and to share them periodically (yearly) – without prior request, on a spontaneous initiative of the governments – with the administrative authorities of the States of the investor's

---

balance of current accounts, the income received from the sale of financial instruments). On topic, cf. M. BARBIERI, *International exchange of information in tax matters: recent developments in the lights of the conclusion of. FACTA – related intergovernamental agreements – Scambio internazionale di informazioni in materia fiscale: i recenti sviluppi alla luce della conclusione degli accordi intergovernativi FACTA*, In *Diritto del commercio internazionale*, 2015, p. 137 ss.

7 The MCAA, international agreement on the principles relating to the execution of the exchange of information, was signed 29 October 2014 by 51 States and territories.

8 The *Model of Common Reporting Standard*, published on 13 February 2014 (http://www.oecd.org/ctp/exchange-of-tax-information/automatic-exchange-of-financial-account-information.htm), disclosed in July 2014, including commentaries on the model agreement on common standards for providing information, and approved by the Ministers of Finance and Governors of central banks of the G20 in September 2014, was drawn up by the OECD in collaboration with some countries (Italy, France, Spain, Germany and England) on the basis of a similar agreement signed with the US (FATCA Agreement – *Foreign Account Tax Compliance Act*).

residence who joined the Standard and/or that have entered into bilateral agreements providing for their implementation.

The Standard, which will contribute decisively to verify incomes and financial resources, even when shielded (companies, trusts or opaque entities, so-called "look-through approach"), was adopted by some states through bilateral agreements (first of all the FATCA agreement) and/or with the accession to multilateral agreements (Strasbourg Convention on mutual administrative assistance in tax, signed in 1988, an essential foundation for the subsequent conclusion of bilateral agreements that implemented it), as well as, like the EU did, through the adoption of Directive 2014/107/EU[9], which guarantees «*the uniformity of the frame of reference regulations, leaving vice versa to the states to adapt thereto their own internal system*»[10].

---

9 The Directive 9 December 2014/107/EU – entered into force in Italy since 5 January 2015 – December 8, 2015 and Directive n. 2015/2376 (OJEU n. 332, 18 December 2015, L) – entered into force in Italy from 18 December 2015 – have amended Directive 2011/16/EU on administrative cooperation in the tax area (the latter transposed in Italy with Legislative Decree 4 March 2014, n. 29). With these two measures has been gradually extended of the automatic exchange of information the objective scope. Originally planned in relation to income from work, to the remuneration of directors and/or managers, to life insurance not covered in other EU legal instruments on the exchange of information and other similar measures, pensions, and the properties and real estate income, the automatic exchange of information has been automatically extended (2014) also to income from capital such as interest, dividends and similar types of income, account balances and income from financial assets annuities, and (2015) estimates the ruling and the Advance Pricing agreements transfer prices. The Directive imposes the obligation on financial intermediaries both to gather information relating to current accounts and financial investments, and to forward them to the competent administrative authority that should made them automatically available for the States that may be interested therein .European states have committed to adopt the Standard as of 1 January 2016, with the exception of Austria, for which the application is planned from 1 January 2017 (art. 2).
Directive 2014/107/EU and Law 18 June 2015, n. 95 were implemented by Decree 28 December 2015 published in OJ n. 303 of December 31, 2015 – General Series. We note that the with law n. 95/2015 Italy has not only ratified the Agreement with the United States Government aimed at improving international tax compliance and to implement FATCA legislation, but also introduced provisions relating to the obligations to which they are kept the Italian financial institutions for the implementation of the automatic exchange of information resulting from other agreements and technical agreements concluded by Italy with the governments of foreign countries according to the OECD standard.

10 S. Dorigo, *Scambio di informazioni nel diritto tributario internazionale*, in *Digesto delle discipline privatistiche, sez. Commerciale*, Giappichelli, Torino, 2015, p. 480 ss. and spec. p. 486.

The automatic exchange of information could then be adjusted simultaneously from multiple sources (nothing excludes, in fact, that the same country may have entered into a bilateral agreement, signed the Strasbourg Convention and be EU country), and their overlap can potentially result in the purpose of applying, in system distortions, despite the Standard is common to all disciplines. In these cases, if should there be any conflicts or uncertainties in the implementation of the exchange of information, the administrative authorities should opt, as suggested by the legislative indication (art. 1, § 3 Directive 2011/16/UE[11] and art. 27, § 2 Multilateral Convention of Strasbourg on Mutual Administrative Assistance[12]) for the application of the solution which promotes administrative cooperation between States, which solely is able to guarantee not only the interest of revenue but also the rights of the subject for which the information is claimed[13].

Switzerland – always and universally recognized as a stronghold where to allocate assets of which either the origin or the destination, or the existence or holding was not to be known – in order to avoid being excluded from the most important financial centres and suffering commercial and financial "penalties", had to give its consent to the action plan for combating tax evasion and tax fraud. And for that reason, it had to put tax transparency among its main objectives and had to commit to renounce the banking secrecy, until recently guaranteed to all those who had invested in the territory, residents and non-residents.

In the following paragraphs, after presenting the rules on administrative assistance between States provided for by Art. 26 OECD Model, we will illustrate the basic steps taken by the Swiss Confederation towards the, first on request and then automatic, realization of the information exchange with the European Union.

---

11 The provision states that the directive «shall not affect any obligations of the Member States in relation *to wider administrative cooperation ensuing from other legal instruments, including bilateral or multilateral agreements.*» (Italics added by the author).

12 Art. 27 of the Multilateral Convention of Strasbourg on Mutual Administrative Assistance provides that «1. The possibilities of assistance provided by this Convention do not limit, nor are they limited by, those contained in existing or future international agreements or others arrangements between the Parties concerned or other instruments which relate to co-operation in tax matters. 2. Notwithstanding § 1, those Parties which are member States of the European Union can apply, in their mutual relations, the possibilities of assistance provided for by the Convention in so far as they allow a wider co-operation than the possibilities offered by the applicable European Union rules».

13 On this point cf. S. Dorigo, *op. cit.*, p. 486.

2 The Normative Sources of Information Exchange: the Art. 26 of the OECD Model Convention

The exchange of information between tax authorities is governed by different legal sources, and their coordination is not easy, because the texts, though united by the same goals – transparency and fight against tax evasion – were adopted at different times and in totally different contexts. Interventions occurred at international, European and domestic level.

The exchange of information finds its legal basis in Art. 26 of the OECD Model[14], a provision which is reproduced in the bilateral agreements signed between States. The arrangement, compared to its first version (1963)[15], has undergone a number of modifications – the last in July 2012[16] – which extended its scope of application[17] both in subjective and objective terms.

It has been going from the *exchange of "necessary" information* for the application of conventional and national rules, concerning "taxes considered" by the Convention with reference to the taxpayers resident in a Contracting State, to the exchange, between authorities, of *information "foreseeably relevant"*[18], concerning taxes of every kind and classification (although not expressly provided for by the Convention), applied within their respective

14 On the OECD Model cf. for all R. Coedeiro Guerra, *Il Modello OCSE contro la doppia imposizione internazionale, in Diritto tributario internazionale. Istituzioni*, Cedam, Padova, 2012, p. 341 ss.

15 Art. 26 OECD Model 1963.

16 On topic S. Garufi, C. Garbarino, *Le modifiche all'art. 26 del modello OCSE sullo scambio di informazioni*, in *Fiscalità & Commercio Internazionale*, 2013, p. 19 ss.

17 The exchange of information (bilateral, between states) was introduced and institutionalized at the international level originally to avoid the phenomenon of double taxation (or non-taxation through a distorted use of conventional systems), and only later to fight tax evasion and implement the national tax regulations concerning taxes, as well as to fulfil "*a broader function, allowing States to share information ... for further purposes, and different from those typical of the sole treaty instrument*". It was qualified "in all respects, as an independent form made available for the international community as a whole and within the specific organizations, also regional, which compose it, aimed at pursuing their goals, not necessarily related to tax matters." As by S. Dorigo, *Scambio di informazioni nel diritto tributario internazionale*, in *Digesto delle discipline privatistiche, sez. Commerciale*, Giappichelli, Torino, 2015, p. 480 ss. and spec. p. 482.

18 This change was introduced in 2005. The qualification of "foreseeably relevant" was unspecified in the version of Art. 26 published by the OECD on July 18, 2012 (OCSE, *Update to Article 26 of the OECD Model Tax Convention and its Commentary*, Paris, 2012). The requirement is integrated when the request for information relates to a single or a plurality of taxpayers, provided that they are specifically identified (Art. 5.2 new commentary).

legal systems (including those of local authorities), with regard to resident taxpayers even in countries other than those of contractors.

The exchange of information can be on request, spontaneous or automatic (Art. 26, § 9 OECD Commentary).

A. Exchange of information on request

The requesting State, in the exercise of fiscal control function, "having exhausted all" its domestic remedies for the acquisition of data and information, relevant to the investigation activity aimed at rectification or levying the tax, can (has the right to) claim for *information*, which are required to be, according to an *ex ante* evaluation, *relevant (foreseeably relevant) "to the widest possible extent"* for the purposes of the tax position of a taxpayer who owns availability or economic interests in the State to which the request is addressed. The application must be detailed: in addition to explicitly state the purpose for which it is submitted and the resulting facts and circumstances on the basis of which the administrative authority decided to submit the request, it shall include the information required for the identification of the subject in relation to which information are sought or, in the case in which it relates to more contributors, the detailed description of the features that qualify the class or group of people, and the reasons for which it is assumed that the behaviours, adopted by the subject in relation to which the request for assistance was advanced, may be fiscally illegal or illicit.

Requests related to a group (*group requests*) should not amount to so-called "*fishing expedition*", "*speculative requests that have no apparent nexus to an open inquiry or investigation*"[19], in other words "*speculative requests that have no apparent nexus to an open inquiry or investigation*"[20].

---

19 The OECD Commentary, as amended on 17/07/2012, section 5.1 states that this hypothesis does not configure the event that the name or address (or both) of the taxpayer, subject to investigation or verification, is shown in a non corrected way, or in a different format from the Standard. In such cases, the requesting state must provide adequate and sufficient information to enable the identification of the taxpayer.
In fact, the group (or collective) request is allowed if the requesting State demonstrate the ability of the financial operator of the foreign State to attract – offer shelter – to tax evaders" Cf. http://www.oecd.org/ctp/exchange-of-tax-information/120718_Article%2026-ENG_no%20cover%20(2).pdf.

20 The need to rule out the possibility to ask indeterminate and general questions meets the need, on the one hand to protect the sovereignty of the State to which the request is made, and on the other to limit the use of this form of cooperation only to cases in which it proves essential.

If there are doubts about the "relevance" of the required information or even just a part of these, States must consult and submit their comments. In any case the State to which the request was made, in the case it has no information, should take steps to find them by following the procedure provided for under its legislation, and can not oppose its refusal when the application is supported by such evidences that the application submitted by the requesting State might do to feel justified.

To ensure the timely acquisition of information, the Member may then agree on a *deadline* to provide for the exchange; the term can be extended in the presence of legal impediments to the useful acquisition of data. In the absence of agreement on the point, the term (to be considered non peremptory[21]) for the exchange is two months from the request, if the authority already holds the information, or, otherwise six[22].

The acquired information (Art. 26, § 2) must be kept secret (*duty of confidentiality*) and must be communicated to those (including courts and administrative bodies) who might use them for fiscal purposes, in administrative procedures (control, detection, collection, refunds) and/or before the courts (tax litigation). A different use (think of criminal cases) is now only permitted in cases where it is expressly provided for by the law of both Contracting States, and the authorities of the States to which the request has been forwarded have given their consent.

The acquisition of the data and information required and disclosed in communication, shall take place in accordance with uniform rules, applicable in all the Contracting States, so as not to create inequality or system asymmetries (principle of reciprocity). The obligation for administrative assistance and the obligation to exchange information are no longer met then, if the State Party is obliged to carry out administrative measures at variance with its laws or administrative practice, or to deliver data that would not be acquired on the basis of laws or the application of the administrative authority indication, or which would disclose a commercial, industrial, professional or trade process secret, or the disclosure of which would be contrary to public policy.

The requested State shall not, however, refuse to cooperate when the particulars of the application for transmission are not considered relevant for the administrative authority to which an application is made (so-called *domestic tax interest* – Art. 26, § 4) or when – and this is the most relevant fact – they are held by a bank or other financial institution or otherwise covered by bank secrecy (Art. 26, § 5). Many bilateral agreements have long provided for a reserve to Art. 26, and opposed the prohibition to the exchange for informa-

21 Failure to meet the deadline should not be considered as cause of unusable or inadmissibility of the acquired information.

22 § 10.4 of OCSE Commentary.

tion covered by banking secrecy. This is the situation where, in more recent times, were Austria, Belgium, Luxembourg and Switzerland who have now removed the veto, and opened the possibility to exchange information on request and, as will be said, even on an automatic basis.

On 23 February 2015, the Swiss Confederation and Italy signed a protocol[23] amending the bilateral agreement on double taxation (signed on March 9, 1976 and amended on April 28, 1978), and that enables the exchange of information upon request for tax purposes (Art. 27) in a manner that is not governed by Art. 26 OECD[24]. The ratification process is not yet completed. However, once concluded the process that will allow the entry into force of the Protocol, the Italian tax authorities may require Switzerland for information even related to banking relationships existing since the moment of the signing of the agreement (overcoming of bank secrecy) relating to taxpayers (not necessarily resident in either country) who have transferred and/or hold assets, activities, and capital abroad and failed to declare them in Italy. The agreement, concluded on the occasion of the adoption, in Italy, of the so called *voluntary disclosure*[25], enabled Switzerland to be not considered as a *black list* Country, for the purpose of the implementation of regulation on the voluntary cooperation, resulting in the limitation of the tax years in dispute, to those of ordinary assessment (five years in case of non-declaration)[26] and reduction of administrative sanctions (3% instead of 6% of the assets that should have been listed annually in the return).

---

23 The Protocol in particular covers requests relating to current accounts closed after the agreement, but before its execution; in current accounts that have been emptied or have a zero balance as a result of the behaviour of the owner during the period going from the signing of the agreement and its entry into force. The introduction of a discipline of detail is aimed at simplifying the investigative obligations incumbent on the applicant State.

24 Besides Switzerland, even Liechtenstein (February 26, 2015) and the Principality of Monaco (March 2, 2015) signed agreements providing for the exchange of information upon request for tax purposes in accordance with the OECD standard.

25 On this point, Cf. P. Marongiu, *La Voluntary disclosure nei rapporti tributari fra principi generali e interventi legislativi*, in *RTDT*, 2015, p. 636 ss. *Voluntary disclosure*, introduced by the n. 186/2014, entered into force on 1 January 2015, has had a limited period of application, which ended December 30, 2015 (deadline for submission of reports concerning the requests applied for no later than November 30, 2015).

26 To take advantage of the short term (basic period of assessment) it was also necessary that the taxpayer would release to the financial intermediary from whom the activities are or were detained, the permission to transmit (waiver) to the Italian financial Administration all datas undergoing the procedure, and would attach to the instance for financial cooperation a copy of the authorization countersigned by the intermediary.

B. Spontaneous exchange of information

In the event that the tax authorities, became aware during the investigation of facts and figures relating to persons resident in other States, assume that these information might be potentially relevant or of interest for the foreign government, it may decide to pass them spontaneously to the competent foreign authority, which decides if and how to use them. As a rule, this form of cooperation is exercised in cases where infringements bearing on criminal (tax fraud) are configured, also if aimed or related to the commission of other crimes. As it happened with the so-called Falcianì list – which indicated the foreign taxpayers who held accounts at a Swiss branch of a British bank (Geneva offices of HSBC) – in possession (behind payment of consideration) of the French governmental authorities. France has considered appropriate to send a copy of the document to the countries whose nationals were included in the list, using the spontaneous exchange of information. The use of this mechanism has also enabled national tax authorities, in an entirely objectionable way, to clean/"recycle" the information contained in the list, and to consider them as usable for securing the assessment in Italy, regardless of the illegality of their original acquisition[27].

---

27 Refer to Cass., sez. VI, Ord. n. 8605-8606 as of April 28, 2015 that stated «*The tax authority, in its activities of assessment of tax evasion, can – in principle – use any means with circumstantial value, with the exception of those whose uselessness derives from a legal provision or by the fact that they have been acquired by administration in violation of a right of taxpayers. In consultation with the taxpayer, bank data acquired by the unfaithful employee of a banking institution may therefore be used, without any relevance for any offense committed by the employee and the violation of the right of confidentiality of banking data (which does not benefit of the protection before tax authorities). Then it will be up to the trial court, in the case of tax charges made to the taxpayer, to assess whether the data concerned are reliable, even in the light of the feedback arising from the defences of the taxpayer*». The Ordinance has been commented upon by A. Turchi, *Legittimi gli accertamenti fiscali basati sulla lista Falciani*, in *Giur. it.*, 2015, p. 1614 ss. who notes that the ordinance stirs reserves, both in the part where the right of taxpayers to the administrative consultation is devaluated, both where it accept the evaluation of any means of evidence, even if illegally obtained, that the judge might qualify as "possible point of support to demonstrate the existence of a relevant fact and not directly known". See also the comment by S. Armella, *Ammesso l'uso della lista Falcianì per gli accertamenti fiscali, ma è mero indizio*, in *Corr. Trib.*, 2015, p. 1995 ss. which shows that the Court considers as licit the use of evidence obtained in violation of law, because the wrongful conduct is attributable to a third party and occurred before any action of the French tax administration. The author also points out that it did not deal with the issue of conventional provisions on exchange of information between Contracting States, instead, which is possible only in relation to information lawfully acquired on the

C. Automatic exchange of information

The automatic exchange of information provides for the sharing by the States of banking, financial, equity and income data, systematically and periodically updated. The implementation of this mechanism requires the preparation of a common platform in which to bring together the information acquired by the Member from its financial institutions and from which the administrative authorities of such Countries that have opted for the application of this form of administrative assistance, may gain at any time useful information for the purpose of tax collection, or of any other fiscally relevant administrative activity.

As mentioned, the automatic exchange of information – by replacing the one on request – has become the Standard shared by the OECD (see § 1) and has been the subject of a multilateral agreement, the Multilateral Competent Authority Agreement, on the basis of which those States that adhered to it pledged to take the necessary steps to implement the centralized collection of data held by financial institutions, with regard to accounts and investments owned or held by individuals, corporations, trusts, foundations etc. automatically shared data.

3 Switzerland and the Exchange of Information

Switzerland has always been considered as a tax haven, not only for "modest" levels of income taxation (rates applied at the federal and cantonal level), but also and above all because it refused the exchange of information on matters other than those relating to the application of the provisions of the Conventions for the avoidance of double taxation, and opposed to requesting States the confidentiality of relations and banking secrecy.

This position has been tempered through the time, even though in between the limits of those "suspected of tax fraud" behaviours (or "similar cases")[28] for which, on request, the Swiss government is obliged to exchange information.

---

basis of its internal legislation and with the normal activity investigation. Furthermore, please refer to P. Mastellone, *Tutela del contribuente nei confronti delle prove illecitamente acquisite all'estero*, in *DPT*, 2013, p. 791 ss. Sul tema Cf. F. D'Ayala Valva, *Acquisizione di prove illecite. Un caso pratico: la lista Falciani*, in *Riv. Dir. Trib.*, 2011, II, p. 396. On the possibility to use the acquired information in criminal procedures, Cf. P. Bernasconi, *Effetti fiscali del trafugamento di informazioni dal Liechtentein a favore delle autorità fiscali dei paesi dell'Unione Europea*, *DCoI*, 2008, II, p. 259 ss.

28 The exchange of information between Switzerland and EU countries, face to tax fraud offenses, was set forth under art. 10 of the Agreement on the Savings and its

The Swiss Confederation, in any event, in response to the OECD solicitations, had formally committed to take action to create conditions that would allow the exchange of information and, as a natural consequence and despite bank secrecy, in year 2000 was not included in the blacklist of "uncooperative tax haven", elaborated by the OECD.

However, in 2009 after the decision of the G20 to tighten up the enforcement action against non-cooperative countries and ascertained the fact that, despite having take a commitment, instructions placed by the OECD on the exchange of information had not been followed, Switzerland was included in the *Grey list*. To get out of it, it was necessary to withdraw the reserve opposed to art. 26 OECD on the exchange of information and to conclude at least 12 agreements that would provide an extended administrative assistance

---

Memorandum EC – SWITZERLAND JOINT COMMITTEE of 26 October 2004 (OJCE L 385 as of 29 December 2004), and entered into force on 1 July 2005, subscribed by and between the European Community and the Swiss Confederation on measures equivalent to those laid down in Directive 2003/48/EC on taxation of savings income in the form of interest payments, in accordance with which «*the competent authorities of Switzerland and any Member State shall exchange information on conduct constituting tax fraud under the laws of the requested State, or the similar offenses, for income covered by this agreement*». For "similar offenses" is intended only offenses with "*the same level of wrongfulness of tax fraud under the laws of the requested State*". Italy has reached an agreement with Switzerland on the identification of similar cases of tax evasion in respect of which, on request, the exchange of information is granted (Press Release 25 October 2005). The State provides the requested information to the requesting Country in case of reasonable suspicion that the conduct would constitute tax fraud or a similar violation. The suspects, about tax fraud or a similar violation, may be based on documents, whether authenticated or not, including, but not limited to, business records, books or documents relating to bank accounts; statements by the taxpayer; information obtained from an informer or other third person, which are supported by sources and/or independent elements or otherwise appears credible or circumstantial evidence.

The requested Country provides information on the basis of a request duly justified, which will be examined on an administrative, civil or criminal level. The information must be exchanged in accordance with the procedures provided for by international conventions against double taxation in force between Switzerland and the Member States concerned. The confidential treatment of such information is ensured in the ways provided for in the Conventions. The preliminary examination of applications is entrusted to the Federal Tax Administration that also has the task to inform foreign authorities whether the application may or may not be accepted, if the reported case subject of the request for information does not constitute fraud tax. is now expected the entry into force of the new EU-Switzerland agreement, based on the provisions of the Protocol of 27 May 2015, of which will be described in the text.

clause regarding tax (*TIAE – Tax Information Exchange Agreement*). As it has been done in less than two years, even through the renegotiation of the Conventions against double taxation previously signed off[29].

Switzerland, at this stage removed from the *grey list*, had not taken steps towards the effective abolition of banking secrecy yet. For this reason, the pressure on the Federal Government, as on other Countries that still had not effectively adhered to the OECD's directives, has not been loosened.

In view of the numerous recommendations of the *Global Forum*[30] on Transparency and Information exchange set by the OECD, Switzerland has therefore entered into new agreements which provide for forms of enlarged assistance, and launched a consultation on a law that provides for the unilateral application of the exchange of information on request (LASSI)[31]. Not only this. To make its financial centre still "competitive, stable, and integrates with

---

29 On 13 March 2009, the Federal Council decided to adapt to the OECD indicator in terms of information exchange and withdraw its reservation to art. 26 OECD. On November 27, 2015, Switzerland has signed a total 53 CDI according to international standard, of which 46 are in force, and 10 TIEAs, 7 of which are in force. https://www.sif.admin.ch/sif/it/home/themen/internationale-steuerpolitik/doppelbesteuerung-und-amtshilfe.html.

30 The Global Forum, OECD organism (http://www.oecd.org/tax/transparency, «*The Global Forum is the continuation of a forum which was created in the early 2000s in the context of the OECD's work to address the risks to tax compliance posed by non-cooperative jurisdictions. The original members of the Global Forum consisted of OECD countries and jurisdictions that had agreed to implement transparency and exchange of information for tax purposes. The Global Forum was restructured in September 2009 in response to the G20 call to strengthen implementation of these standards. The Global Forum now has 130 members on equal footing and is the premier international body for ensuring the implementation of the internationally agreed standards of transparency and exchange of information in the tax area. Through an in-depth peer review process, the restructured Global Forum monitors that its members fully implement the standard of transparency and exchange of information they have committed to implement. It also works to establish a level playing field, even among countries that have not joined the Global Forum.*»), monitors compliance with the international standards of transparency and exchange of information through a comprehensive evaluation process, and between countries. The Peer Reviews take place in two phases. In the first phase it is examined the existence of the legal basis for the exchange of information on request. In the second phase it is evaluated the application of the exchange of information in practice. Switzerland was admitted to the second stage of the assessment on March 15, 2015. The Global Forum has recognized the efforts made to fulfil the international standards for exchange of information on request.

31 To speed up the process of adjustment of the Conventions against double taxation, the Federal Council on 19 February 2014 a consultation on the draft Federal Law that provides for the unilateral application of the exchange of information on

conditions internationally accepted" in March 2009[32] it has lent its consent to the implementation of the exchange of information on request.

However, while Switzerland was about to take the first steps on the path of cooperation and administrative assistance, the majority of the States – European and OECD's – had identified in the automatic exchange of information the most efficient instrument for ensuring fiscal transparency, and as said, it had been elevated to a common standard OECD, combining it in the Strasbourg Convention (2010) with the exchange on request, and the spontaneous exchange.

The Strasbourg Convention on Mutual Administrative Assistance in Tax Matters (Convention MAAT) subordinated (Art. 6), however, the introduction of the new Standard to a specific agreement (Multilateral Competent Authority Agreement – MCAA) – which was repeatedly mentioned – signed by the competent authority in 2014, and that helps to ensure uniform application of the Standard (CRS) for the automatic exchange of information OECD.

This agreement (MCAA) – as already anticipated – provides for the automatic exchange of information to be implemented bilaterally between the signatory States. So that to give effect to the automatic exchange of information is necessary that the Members concerned have ratified the Strasbourg Convention, signed the MCAA and adopted the legislative measures necessary to give effective implementation.

The Swiss Federal Council, to stay up to date, on October 15, 2013 decided to (could not do anything but) sign the Multilateral Convention of

---

request (LASSI), with all States with which Switzerland that signed agreements against double taxation and that still do not meet the international standard. https://www.news.admin.ch/message/index.html?%20%20lang=it&msgid=54902%20[13 April 2015.

The unilateral application of the exchange of information on request, (excluding the automatic and the spontaneous one) must be accomplished by reciprocity and in such a way to guarantee to safeguard the confidentiality of the information exchanged. This law is residual, as it can be applied only if the State or territory concerned is not equipped with the regulatory instruments which enable it to submit the request for administrative assistance. It could come into force in 2016, to be repealed as soon as signed, for all states and territories concerned, an agreement (bilateral or multilateral) which provides for an exchange of information on request complies with Standard OECD originally planned. It does not apply against Italy following the signing of the Protocol amending the DTA CH-ENG of 23 February 2015, and that, once ratified, will enter into force with effect from the date of signature.

32 On 13 March 2009 the Swiss Federal Council has joined the OECD Standard (in those years on request), namely the extension of the exchange of information even in the cases where the circumstances defined profiles simple "tax evasion". As did Austria, Luxembourg and Singapore.

Strasbourg – already signed by the Member of the Council of Europe and the OECD (25 January 1988 n. 127)[33] – which guarantees the assistance between States, in particular: a) in tax audits carried out simultaneously and in those conducted abroad that require the presence of officials of the requesting State; b) in the activity of collecting tax credits from abroad also through the adoption of executive measures; c) in the notification of relevant documents.

After the Global Forum 2014 report, in which it was considered that «*since 2009, Switzerland has made significant progress in the field of administrative assistance, but [...] in some parts it does not meet or only partially meets the conditions required for an effective exchange of information*», the Federal Assembly decided for the decree of approval and execution[34] of the Convention as amended, entered into force June 1, 2011 and, simultaneously, approved the MCAA and the Federal Law on international automatic exchange of information for tax purposes (LSAI). All legislation that, even in the absence of a referendum, provide Switzerland with the legal basis for introducing the automatic exchange of information with the countries concerned[35].

Meanwhile, as mentioned, some European countries (Italy, France, Spain, Germany and England) had promoted inter-governmental agreement with the United States, which was concluded with the adoption of the FACTA legislation, a real systematic disclosure of financial data relevant for tax purposes.

---

33 Italy has ratified the Strasbourg Convention on Mutual Administrative Assistance in Tax Matters with Law as of February 10, 2005, n. 19, entered into force on May 1, 2006. On May 27, 2010 was signed in Paris on Protocol amending the Convention, in order to align it with the OECD standard on the automatic exchange of information. It provides, *inter alia*, that the state in which information is requested can not refuse to provide assistance on grounds of bank secrecy or domestic tax interest. And the parts that are EU Member States ensure, in their mutual relations, effectiveness of the provisions of the Conventions whenever they allow for greater cooperation with respect to the possibilities offered by the applicable legislation of the European Union. The Protocol was ratified by Italy 17 January 2012 and entered into force on 1 May 2012. On this S. Dorigo, *La cooperazione fiscale internazionale dopo il protocollo di modifica alla Convenzione di Strasburgo: qualche luce e molte ombre*, in *Riv. dir. trib.*, 2011, p. 157 ss.

34 18 December 2015.

35 To introduce automatic exchange of information with a partner State it is necessary to sign a bilateral agreement which implies the recognition of the country with which Switzerland wishes to introduce automatic exchange of information in a list to be deposited with the Secretariat of the Organ of the MCAA coordination. The Federal Council has had the mandate to report that Switzerland signed in January 2016 joint statements for the introduction of automatic mutual exchange of information for tax purposes with the British Crown Dependencies, Jersey, Guernsey and the Isle of Man, with Iceland and Norway.

The FATCA legislation requires the signature of an agreement or between governmental authorities (agreement between states)[36] or between financial institutions and American governmental authorities. This second option was chosen by the states that do not wish to exchange information on an automatic basis, and who want to delegate the transmission of data directly to the financial Institute (thus not by the administrative authority) who have collected form the US customer a prior consent to the transmission .

Switzerland has chosen this path and on February 14, 2013 signed the FATCA Agreement, which entered into force on June 2, 2014, providing for "direct notification [of banking information] by Swiss financial institutions to the US tax authorities (Internal Revenue Service)". Direct notification, without any mediation, allows to 'exonerate' the Swiss tax authorities from the obligation to automatic exchange and authorizes Swiss intermediaries to release the data upon request (Art. 5 provides for a "favoured" application of the legislation).

With the signing of this Agreement, Switzerland has made a very important step on the road to fiscal transparency. Step that, however, has not been spontaneous, as a natural outcome of the process aimed at implementing international cooperation, but was rather determined by the need to avoid being excluded from the US financial market. Failure to adhere to the FACTA would in fact result in the application of a withholding tax of 30% (improper sanction) on all types of US origin payment – regardless of whether the beneficiary of the proceeds of American origin was or not tax resident in the US – causing a real loss for the financial intermediary.

Switzerland signed the FACTA legislation, approved the Strasbourg Convention, the MCAA and the law on the automatic exchange of information has finally made further progress, and Switzerland has also signed an understanding with the EU (19 March 2015) on the automatic exchange of information in tax matters[37]. Understanding that has resulted in a real agreement

---

36 Italy has chosen this solution and signed an intergovernmental agreement with the United States (IGA Intergovernmental Agreement ratified by Law n. 95/2015, which entered into force on 8 July 2015) according to which the Tax Agency undertakes to transfer the data acquired by the Italian Financial institutions directly to the IRS.

37 During 2015, the EU has signed similar agreements with Liechtenstein, the Republic of San Marino and Andorra. On 22 February 2016, the Principality of Monaco and the European Union initiated the agreement on fiscal transparency with which binds them to each other to automatically exchange financial information to their residents, from 2018. Information that may be collected by the competent authorities of the Contracting Parties as early as 1 January 2017. The Agreement is expected to be officially signed before the summer of 2016, once the EU Council has formally approved the proposal of the European Commission.

signed in Brussels on 27 May 2015 which provides for the adoption of the Common Reporting Standards and, therefore, for the definitive disappearance of banking secrecy for foreign residents who hold financial assets in the Confederacy.

Formally it is a protocol that processes and modifies the agreement on the taxation of savings income, in force since 2005[38], between Switzerland and the EU, which established for measures equivalent to those laid down in Directive 2003/48/EC on taxation of savings income, and it is converted into an agreement on the information exchange. It provides for and regulates the exchange of information automatically and on request, and the exemption to apply to tax on interest and dividends and cross-border payments between associated companies.

The agreement will be implemented with regards to the automatic exchange of information only by the appropriate law (LSAI – law on the automatic exchange of information) submitted to the Parliament, and in cases of exchange on request, according to the Law administrative assistance (LAAF).

The protocol was published in the European Official Journal of 19 December 2015, and will enter into force presumably from 1 January 2017, with automatic exchanges from 2018, provided that the approval procedures in Switzerland and the EU are concluded in time. For this purpose, it is necessary that the Agreement is ratified and/or subjected to administrative approval procedures designed to ensure its implementation and compliance with the rules envisaged in the field of communication and of diligent assessment in tax matters.

When the *iter* will be finalized Switzerland, like all EU countries, will be considered a collaborative State in all respects. The achievement of the automatic exchange of information, not imaginable until recent times, is the result of a long process that will enable the Swiss Confederation to be differently perceived and valued from the past, so to be considered as a solid and efficient financial centre for services provided by its banking system, not just as a refuge for capital and investments not declared, or for outcomes and profit that, it is assumed, derive from no legitimate or lawful activities.

The path followed by Switzerland in the recent years aiming at implementing the cooperation between States, while respecting the rights of the taxpayer, will lead to a turning point. The federal government, once the provisions that

38 This agreement provides for the application of the withholding of 35% tax on interest paid to the taxpayer who wanted to remain anonymous and did not allow the exchange of any information, and the distribution of revenue from an investment between Switzerland (25%) and the residence of the recipient. In the new agreement it does not move the withholding tax exemption for dividends, interest and royalties between associated companies.

provide for the exchange of information on request and/or automatic will come into force, will not only be deleted from the list of Countries considered Blacklisted in all respects, but will also be confirmed as a territory where the rights and fundamental freedoms of the individual are always guaranteed and respected as well as the interests, not only fiscal, of the Member.

4 The Participation of the Taxpayer in International Cooperation Procedures and the Swiss Discipline.

The analysis of taxpayers' rights during the acquisition of information deserves special attention[39].

International law, as well as that of Europe, do not provide the taxpayer – against whom it was forwarded a request for administrative assistance – with neither the right to be informed of the request made by the state that is doing the monitoring, nor the right to be consulted, nor the right to participate in the data collection phase to contest, if necessary, their authenticity as well as the assumed unlawfulness of the acquisition mode.

In particular, the OECD Model doesn't state anything on this point.

The Strasbourg Convention merely highlight that «*Nothing in this Convention may limit the rights and safeguards secured to persons by the laws or administrative practice of the requested State*».

European Directives (77/799/EEC, 2011/16/EU, 2014/107/EU) use generic formulas and claim that the legislation guarantees the «*fundamental rights and observes the principles recognized in particular by the European Union Charter of Fundamental Rights, including the right to the protection of personal data*».

There are thus no express provisions for the protection of the taxpayer[40], even though the Protocol of Amendment to the Strasbourg Convention pro-

---

39 On this, please see P. Adonnino, *Lo scambio di informazioni fra amministrazioni finanziarie*, in V. Uckmar (Ed.), *Corso di Diritto tributario internazionale*, Milano, 1999, p. 1126; G. Melis, *Coordinamento fiscale nell'Unione europea*, in *Enc. dir.*, Annali, I, Milano, 2007, p. 394 ss.; L. Del Federico, *Scambio di informazioni fra autorità fiscali e tutela del contribuente: profili internazionalistici, comunitari ed interni*, in *RDT internazionale*, 2010, p. 221 ss.; P. Selicato, *Scambio di informazioni, contraddittorio e Statuto del contribuente*, in *Rass. Trib.*, 2012, p. 321.

40 P. Boria, *Diritto tributario*, Giappichelli, Torino, p. 413 where it is stated that «*Community and international legislation does not contain references to forms of protection of the taxpayer in cases where it is determined an injury in the course of the investigation, since it merely defines the circumstances in which the information should not be transmitted (trade secret, business, professional, contrary to public order) and to impose a general obligation of confidentiality for all data received. Therefore, in cases where the information is transmitted in violation of the re-*

vides that cooperation between Member assures "*adequate protection to the rights of taxpayers*". In the best cases, the international and/or European legislations makes reference to the national legislations that usually, on this point, at this stage could only concern "*preliminary investigation*"[41], and does not provide for any rule to protect the taxpayer[42].

On the other hand the requirement of "relevance", or rather the "pertinence", which should qualify the information required in accordance with Art. 26 OECD, postulates that the elements and the facts that constitute the object may, but need not, be used in the investigation process by the tax authority who requested it.

Basically it is not necessary that the data offered in communication prove to be in practice actually needed for the purpose for which they were requested, or that they will be used in domestic environment for fiscal purposes. It requires, instead, that the information is configured as *potentially useful* for the purpose pursued by the Authority of the requesting State.

This solution, which addresses the need to first of all protect the State's interest for an effective exchange of information, might look questionable, when taking into account the fundamental need to ensure the protection of the individual/taxpayer's rights, and among these, in particular the right of defence.

However, it is understood that the right of the person to be informed of the request for assistance and his right to participate in the proceedings for his defence, should only be guaranteed when negative consequences may

---

quirements or do not respect the procedural rules laid down, it poses a problem of protection of the taxpayer. The issue in this case does not concern relations between states, but moves in the security of a legal position guaranteed to the taxpayer by the regulatory system». In this sense before A. Fedele, *op. cit.*, p. 49 ss.

41 On this point, cf. P. Mastellone, *op. cit.*, p. 791 ss. which shows that the protection of the taxpayer, in the silence of European and international regulations concerning international tax cooperation, is left to the "*incoherent regulatory recover in domestic legislation*" which frequently attributes a key role to the tax Courts. The lack of protection – continues the author – become alarming in persistence of "*pathological*" situations such as what might occur in the cases of "sale" by the tax authorities of bank data stolen abroad by employees of banks, and used to the detriment of taxpayers.

42 Again P. Boria, *op. cit.*, who noted that, in relation to the Italian domestic situation, «*regarding the effectiveness, the national protection against the unlawful investigation may not be sufficient to ensure protection in line with European standards, especially in light of strong resistance (national) on the immediate protection or that attemptable plan on a different plane than the merits of the claim for additional taxes*». The author hopes, therefore, that under the principle of effectiveness of protection, are identified "*in the future more effective forms of protection*" for the protection of the taxpayer and third parties involved.

derive for him from the use of the acquired information, as it emerges both from the European legislation, both from the national ones (Art. 41 CED and art. 6, § 2, of the Statute of the taxpayer rights)[43]. Possibility that is realized only when the requesting authority[44], at national headquarters, once assessed as relevant the data made available, decides to assume them as evidence or circumstantial evidence grounding a "proposal" (not claim) for rectification (minutes of finding, subpoena, a wrongful act of protest, request for clarification, etc.), which is transmitted to the taxpayer and which precedes the adoption of a final court decision.

Out of these cases, when the tax authorities consider the information transmitted "irrelevant" for such assessment, it is believed that the information and participation of the taxpayer are not only undue, but rather not recommended, as they may compromise the effectiveness of investigation activities. Even the Court of Justice ruled in this sense, stating, moreover, that «*it is necessary to distinguish, in the context of fiscal surveillance procedures, the investigative stage during which the information is collected and that includes the request for information by a tax administration to another, from the* inter partes *stage, between the tax authorities and the taxpayer to whom is directed, which starts with the notification to the latter of a proposal for correction*»[45].

---

43 On topic, please accept to refer to M. Pierro, *Il dovere di informazione dell'Amministrazione finanziaria*, Giappichelli, Torino, 2013, p. 52 and p. 91 ss. where it is noted that the right to defense in proceedings – inalienable right – is guaranteed by Art. 41 of the European Charter of Fundamental Rights (right to good administration), implemented by the Lisbon Treaty, which entered into force in 2009, and as such, applicable in the national legal framework of all the EU countries, and implemented also, as reinforcement, by national laws of many countries, and in Italian Art. 6, § 2, of the Statute of the taxpayer rights and other specific provisions.

44 It could not be excluded the possibility that certain elements related to the taxpayer and the data can be acquired in an unlawful manner, in violation of the constitutionally guaranteed rights. In this case, the rule of law, the protection of the taxpayer can be guaranteed being deferred, through the provision of appeal that the financial authorities adopted, or if you are activating the administrative or judicial remedies of the State in which its the offense has been committed.

45 It comes to Court of Justice of the EU, October 22, 2013 (judgment Sabou – Case C-276/12) in comment F. Fernandez Marin, *La tutela nazionale del contribuente nello scambio comunitario d'informazioni*, in *Rass. Trib.*, 2014, p. 1421 ss. See also, in particolar; P. Mastellone, *L' Unione Europea non riconosce 'participation rights' al contribuente sottoposto a procedure di mutua assistenza amministrativa tra autorità fiscali*, in *Riv. Dir. Trib.*, 2013, p. 349 ss. who notes how the Court excludes that from Directive n. 77/799/EEC may be derived by means of interpretation the s.c. *participation right* of the taxpayer subject to procedures

The situation is different for Switzerland, which has instead opted for a more protective solution.

Unlike the international and European legislation, Law on International Administrative Assistance in Tax Matters (LAAF) of 28 September 2012, entered into force on 1 February 2013 and subsequently amended, puts in charge the Contribution Tax Administration of the obligation to inform in advance either the person with respect to which information was requested, the persons who may be involved in the proceedings[46], and persons who are part of a group in those cases where a collective request is submitted[47].

The recognition of the right to information of the subjects, in relation to which the request for assistance is transmitted, allows the taxpayer not only to know in advance which the alleged violations are and to assume the behaviours deemed most appropriate to its protection, but also to prepare the defence on time, in case is decided to challenge the decisions which may be adopted as a result of this administrative stage (Art. 19 LAAF). However, in exceptional cases, *i.e.* in those cases where the preliminary information could defeat the purpose of administrative assistance, affecting the success of the procedure, or rendering investigative activities ineffective by endangering Switzerland's relations with the foreign State, the Federal Tax Administration is required to maintain the confidentiality and to inform the interested persons only after the termination of the exchange of information (Art. 21 to LAAF). This provision, result of a reforming action determined by solicitations of

for mutual administrative assistance in tax matters; the Court considers that the activity of collection of tax-relevant information is not – by itself – capable of affecting negatively the sphere of the individual, since the right of defence will still be guaranteed in the possible subsequent phases of investigation, as well as adjusted by the domestic laws of the Member States.

46 Art. 14 provides that the person concerned should be informed about the key elements of the application, while it excludes that he should know of the investigative measures taken until then by the requesting State, who may have an interest in keeping it secret. If the person resides abroad, the Administration provides to inform him directly – if there is a bilateral agreement with the foreign state – or through the holder of the information (credit institution, bank, etc.). On topic, and in particular with reference to the advanced group letters rogatory to Switzerland, see P. Bernasconi, S. Schusch, *Fishing expedition e rogatorie di gruppo nella cooperazione internazionale con la Svizzera in materia fiscale. Norme e prassi recenti ed imminenti*, in *RDT*, IV, 2015, p. 109 ss.

47 In these cases, the obligation is put on credit institutions or on the banks, which have to invite their client or former client to designate an attorney in Switzerland. It is considered unnecessary to identify the s.c. holder of information, being sufficient that the model of behaviour adopted by the different parties belonging to the same group are clearly identifiable, and then linked to a certain type of entities that hold the information requested.

the Global Forum on transparency[48] has forced the Swiss Confederation to a reinterpretation, in a pejorative sense, of the guarantees granted to individuals, with the introduction of limits on the right of taxpayers to be informed.

It is hoped that the limitation of the rights and guarantees will end.

The problem is to determine whether the legislation of the State that will use the data acquired through international cooperation provides for forms of protection with respect to the taxpayer, before the acquired information become the basis of a definitive measure. Otherwise the position of the subject undergoing verifications would be greatly affected.

The primary need of the OECD and the G20 is to contrast evasion offenses and fiscal erosion, for the recovery of tax bases and tax revenues. This need however, should always be evenly balanced with the recognition of the rights of the taxpayer in domestic environment, among which, first of all, there is the right of defence that has to be guaranteed, even at procedural stage.

48 *Terms of Reference*, B.2.1 (n. 4); OCSE Commentary "*Agreement on Exchange of Information on Tax Matters*", p. 14, art. 1, n. 6.

Bibliography

ABASS A., *International Law*, Oxford University Press, Oxford-New York, 2012.

ACEVEDO A., *The EEC Dyestuffs Case: Territorial Jurisdiction*, in *Modern Law Review*, 1973, p. 317.

ADAM R., *Limiti esterni delle norme comunitarie sulla concorrenza*, in *Riv. dir. int.*, 1975, p. 254.

ADINOLFI G., *Il sostegno congiunto UE-FMI: è necessario un ripensamento della politica di condizionalità?*, in G. ADINOLFI, M. VELLANO (Eds.), *La crisi del debito sovrano degli stati dell'aerea euro. Profili giuridici*, Giappichelli, Torino, 2013, pp. 3-27.

ALBANO A., PENNED, *The new criteria for the identification of tax havens*, in *Corr. Trib.*, 2014, 3047.

ALFORD R.P., *The Extraterritorial Application of Antitrust Laws: The United States and the European Approaches*, in *Virginia Journal of International Law*, 1992, p. 1.

ALMUNIA M., BÉNÉTRIX A.S., EICHENGREEN B., O'ROURKE K.H., RUA G., *From Great Depression to Great Credit Crisis: Similarities, Differences and Lessons,* National Bureau of Economic Research, Inc, Cambridge MA, 2009.

AKEHURST M., *Jurisdiction in International Law*, in *British Yearbook of International Law*, 1973.

AMALFITANO C., *Conflitti di giurisdizione e riconoscimento delle decisioni penali nell'Unione europea*, Giuffré, Milano, 2006.

AMATO G., GUALTIERI R. (Eds.), *Prove di Europa unita. Le istituzioni europee di fronte alla crisi,* Passigli Editore, Firenze, 2013.

ANDENAS M., *Jurisdiction, Procedure and the Transformation of International Law: From Nottebohm to Diallo in the ICJ*, in *European Business Law Review*, 2012, p. 127.

ARMELLA S., *Ammesso l'uso della lista Falciani per gli accertamenti fiscali, ma è mero indizio*, in *Corr. Trib.*, 2015, p. 1995.

ATHANASSIOU P., *Withdrawal and Expulsion from The EU and EMU: Some Reflections, ECB Legal Working paper Series n. 10*, December, 2009, pp. 1- 43.

Atwood J.R., *Blocking Statutes and Sovereign Compulsion in American Antitrust Legislation*, in *Swiss Review of International Competition Law*, 1986, p. 5.

Bader G.K., *The Keiretsu Distribution System of Japan: Its Steadfast Existence Despite Heightened Foreign and Domestic Pressure for Dissolution*, in *Cornell International Law Journal*, 1994, p. 365.

Baggio R., *Loss and purchase of tax residence: overview and controversial aspects*, in *Riv. dir. trib.*, 2006, I, 357.

Bagus P., *The Eurosystem: Costs and Tragedies*, in D. Howden (Ed.), *Institutions in Crisis: European Perspectives on the Recession*, Routdlege, London, 2011, pp.117-141.

Baker D.I., *Antitrust Conflicts between Friends: Canada and the United States in the Mid-1970's*, in *Cornell International Law Journal*, 1978, p. 168.

Baker D.I., Ayer D.B., *Anti-trust Imperialism*, in *European Competition law Review*, 1993, p. 3.

Ballarino T., *Manuale di diritto dell'Unione europea*, Cedam, Padova, 2011.

Balzaretti R., *L'importanza della cooperazione Schengen – Dublino per la Svizzera: situazione attuale e prospettive*, in AA.VV., *Accordi bilaterali Svizzera-Unione europea. Atti della giornata di studio del 4 giugno 2007*, Lugano, 2008.

Barassi M., *Lo scambio d'informazioni nella UE*, in *RDT Internazionale*, 2001, 327.

Barassi M., *Cooperazione tra amministrazioni fiscali*, in *Diz. Cassese*, Milano, 2006, p. 1525.

Barassi M., *Exchange of tax information. The legislative framework – Lo scambio di informazioni in materia fiscale. La normativa vigente*, in *RDT Internazionale*, n. 1-2/2009, p. 99.

Barbieri M., *International exchange of information in tax matters: recent developments in the lights of the conclusion of. FACTA – related intergovernamental agreements – Scambio internazionale di informazioni in materia fiscale: i recenti sviluppi alla luce della conclusione degli accordi intergovernativi FACTA*, in *Dir. comm. intern.*, 2015, p. 137.

Bariatti S., *La cooperazione giudiziaria in materia civile del terzo pilastro dell'Unione europea al titolo V del Trattato CE*, in *Diritto dell'Unione europea*, 2001.

Bariatti S., *Cases and materials on EU Private International Law*, Hart Publishing, Oxford-Portland, 2011.

Baroncini E., *Il* treaty making power *della Commissione europea,* Libreria Bonomo, Bologna, 2008, p. 261 .

Barucci P., Rabitti Bedogni C. (Eds.), *Vent'anni di antitrust. L'evoluzione dell'autorità garante della concorrenza e del mercato*, Giappichelli, Torino, 2010, p. 137.

Basedow J., *Souveraineté territoriale et globalisation des marchés: le domaine d'applications des lois contre les restrictions de la concurrence*, in *Recueil des cours – Académie de Droit International de La Haye*, M. Nijhoff, The Hague-Boston-London, 1997, p. 123.

Bassan F., *Una regolazione per i fondi sovrani*, in *Mercato concorrenza e regole*, 2009, pp. 95-132.

Bassan F., *The Law of Sovereign Wealth Funds*, Edward Elgar Publishing, Cheltenham-Northampton, 2011.

Bastianon S., *Il carattere speciale (pro-integrazionista) del diritto antitrust alla luce del Protocollo n. 27*, in M. Frigessi di Rattalma-P. De Cesari, *Nuove sfide in tema di concorrenza e aiuti di Stato nell'Unione europea*, Editoriale Scientifica, Napoli, 2013, p. 23.

Batista P.A., *Confronting. Foreign "Blocking". Legislation: A Guide to Securing. Disclosure from Non-resident. Parties to American Litigation*, in Journal of International Law, 1983, p. 61.

Bavasso A., *Boeing/McDonnel Douglas: Did the Commission Fly Too High?*, in *European Competition Law Review*, 1998, p. 243.

Bennett S., *The European Commission v. Gazprom*, in *Wisconsin International Law Journal*, 2014, p. 886.

Berge G.W., *Case of the S. S. Lotus*, in *Michigan Law Review*, 1928, p. 361.

Bernasconi P., *Effetti fiscali del trafugamento di informazioni dal Liechtentein a favore delle autorità fiscali dei paesi dell'Unione Europea, DCoI*, 2008, II, p. 259 .

Bernasconi P., *Scambio italo svizzero di informazioni fiscali. Rogatorie e convenzioni contro la doppia imposizione*, in *Dir. prat. trib. int.*, 2011, p. 15.

Bernasconi P., Schusch S., *Fishing expedition e rogatorie di gruppo nella cooperazione internazionale con la Svizzera in materia fiscale. Norme e prassi recenti ed imminenti*, in *RDT*, IV, 2015 p. 109.

Bertoli P., *Corte di giustizia, integrazione comunitaria e diritto internazionale privato e processuale*, Giuffré, Milano, 2005.

Biagioni G., *L'art. 6 della Convenzione europea dei diritti dell'uomo e l'ordine pubblico processuale nel sistema della Convenzione di Bruxelles*, in *Riv. Dir. Intern.*, 2001, p. 723.

Biagioni G., *L'abolizione dei motivi ostativi al riconoscimento e all'esecuzione nella Proposta di revisione del Regolamento di Brussels I*, in *Riv. dir. int. priv. e proc.*, 2011, p. 971.

Bieber R., *On lacunae of legitimacy and the contradictions of financial crisis management in the European Union*, in *EUI Law Working Papers*, n. 16, 2011.

Biscottini G., *La natura giuridica delle Comunità Europee*, in *Tavole rotonde di diritto comunitario*, Giuffré, Milano, 1980.

Bishop B., *The Boeing/McDonnel Douglas Merger*, in *European Competition Law Review*, 1997, p. 417.

Bonomi A. (Ed.), *Diritto internazionale privato e cooperazione giudiziaria in materia civile*, Giappichelli, Torino, 2009.

Bonomi A., Cashin Ritaine E., Romano G. (Eds.), *La Convention de Lugano. Passé, présent et dèvenir*, Schulthess, Génevre-Zurich-Basel, 2007.

Boria P., *Diritto tributario europeo*, Giuffré, Milano, 2015.

Boria P., *European tax Law*, Milano, Giuffré, Milano, 2015.

Breibart E., *The Wood Pulp Case: The Application of European Economic Community Competition Law to Foreign Based Undertakings*, in *Georgia Journal of International and Comparative Law*, 1989, p. 149.

Breitenmoser S., *Sectoral Agreements between the EC and Switzerland: contents and context*, in *CMLR*, 2003, pp. 1137-1186.

Brierly J.L., *The Law of Nations: An Introduction to the International Law of Peace*, Clarendon Press, Oxford 1963, p. 162.

Broberg M.P., *The European Commission's Extraterritorial Powers in Merger Control. The Court of First Instance's Judgment in Gencor v. Commission*, in *International and Comparative Law Quarterly*, 2000, p. 172.

Bronckers M., Vallery A., *No longer presumed guilty? The impact of fundamental rights on certain dogmas of EU competition law*, in *World Competition*, 2011, p. 535.

Buccisano A., *Assistenza amministrativa internazionale dall'accertamento alla riscossione dei tributi*, Cacucci editore, Bari, 2013.

Bucher A. (Ed.), *Loi sur le droit international privé*, Convention de Lugano, Helbing, Basel, 2011.

Burdeau G., *L'Exercice des Competences Monetaires par les Etats*, in *Recueil des cours de l'Académie de droit international de La Haye*, 1988, pp. 236-237.

Burnside A., *Ge, Honey I sank the Merger*, in *European Competition Law Review*, 2002.

BUTTIGIEG E., *Competition Law: Safeguarding the Consumer Interest. A comparative Analysis of US Antitrust Law and EC Competition Law*, Kluwer Law International, Alphen aan den Rijn, 2009.

CANALE R., NAPOLITANO O., *The Recessive Attitude of EMU policies: Reflections on the Italian Experience*, 1999-2008, in *MPRA Paper* n. 20207, 2009.

CANNIZZARO E., *Le relazioni esterne della Comunità: verso un nuovo paradigma unitario?*, in *Diritto dell'Unione Europea*, 2007.

CANOVA V.T., *The Transformation of U.S. Banking and Finance: from Regulated Competition to Free Market Receivership*, in *Brooklyn Law Review*, 1995, pp. 1295-1354.

CAPOTORTI F. (Ed.), *Il fenomeno delle concentrazioni di imprese nel diritto interno e internazionale*, Cedam, Padova, 1989, p. 81.

CAPOTORTI F., *Cours général de droit international public*, in *RCADI*, tome 248, IV, 1994.

CARBONE S.M., *Lo spazio giudiziario in materia civile e commerciale*, Giappichelli, Torino, 2009.

CARBONE S.M., FRIGO M., FUMAGALLI L., *Diritto processuale civile e commerciale comunitario*, Giuffré, Milano, 2004.

CARBONE S.M., LUZZATTO R., SANTA MARIA A., *Istituzioni di diritto internazionale*, Giappichelli, Torino, 2011.

CARREAU D., *Souveraineté et Coopération Monétaire Internationale*, Editions Cujas, Paris, 1971.

CARRERA S., GUILD E., EISELE K., *No Move without Free Movement: The EU-Swiss controversy over quotas for the free movement of persons*, in CEPS Policy Briefs, Brussels, April 2015, n. 331.

CAVARÉ L., *L'arrêt du "Lotus" et le positivisme juridique*, in *Travaux Juridiques et Economiques de l'Université de Rennes*, 1930, p. 144.

CEJNAR L., BURGESS R., *Challenging the need for a "Global" Competition Law*, in *European Competition Law Review*, 2014, p. 461.

CHAN S.S.H., *InnoLux Corp v. European Commission: Establishment of the effects doctrine in extra-territoriality of EU competition law?*, in *European Competition Law Review*, 2015, p. 463.

CHEVALIER P., *L'execution des decisiones jurisdictionelles etrangres hors espace judiciare europeen: etat de lieu de la jurisprudence*, in *Rev. gén. dr. int. public*, 2013, p. 503.

CHRISTIN T., TRESCHEL A.H., *Joining the EU? Explaining Public Opinion in Switzerland*, in *European Union Politics*, December 2002, vol. 3, n. 4, pp. 415-443.

CHURCH C. (Ed.), *Switzerland and the European Union*, Routledge, London, 2007.

CINTIOLI F., *The interpretation of competition law between the legal method and the economic approach*, in *Dir. Un. Eur.*, 2007, p. 873.

CIPOLLINA S., *I redditi 'nomadi' delle società multinazionali nell'economia globalizzata*, in *Riv. dir. fin. sc.*, 2014, I, p. 23.

COEDEIRO GUERRA R., *Il Modello OCSE contro la doppia imposizione internazionale, in Diritto tributario internazionale. Istituzioni*, Cedam, Padova, 2012.

COLANGELO G., *T-Mobile Netherlands e GlaxoSmithKline. La giurisprudenza comunitaria torna indietro*, in *Mercato Concorrenza Regole*, 2010, p. 527.

COLESANTI V., CONSOLO C., GAJA G. (Eds.), *Il diritto processuale civile nell'avvicinamento giuridico internazionale. Omaggio ad Aldo Attardi*, Cedam, Padova, 2009.

COLLINS L., *Blocking and Clawback Statutes: The United Kingdom Approach*, in *Journal of Business Law*, 1986, p. 372.

CONDINANZI M. (Ed.), *Unione europea e Svizzera tra cooperazione e integrazione*, Giuffré, Milano, 2012.

CONFORTI B., *La dottrina di diritto comunitario: questa sconosciuta*, in *Dir. Un. Eur.*, 1-2004.

CONFORTI B., *Diritto internazionale*, Editoriale Scientifica, Napoli, 2014.

CONTALDI G., voce *Politica economica e monetaria (Diritto dell'Unione europea)*, in *Enc. dir.*, Annali VII, Giuffrè, Milano, 2014, p. 826.

COPPEL J., *A question of Keiretsu: Extending the Long Arm of US Anti-trust*, in *European Competition Law Review*, 1992, p. 192.

CORBET H., ROBERTSON D. (Eds.), *Europe's Free Trade Area Experiment. E.F.T.A. and Economic Integration*, Pergamon, Oxford, 1970.

CRAZZOLARA A., LURÀ F., *Lo scambio internazionale di informazioni e la giurisprudenza svizzera*, in *Dir. prat. trib. int.*, 2010, p. 551.

CSERES K.J., *The Controversies of the Consumer Welfare Standard*, in *Competition Law Review*, 2007, p. 121.

CUNIBERTI G., *The recognition of foreign judgments lacking reasons in Europe: access to justice, foreign court avoidance and efficiency*, in *International and Comparative Law Quaterly*, 2008.

DABBAH M.M., *International and Comparative Competition Law*, Cambridge University Press, Cambridge, 2010.

D'ALESSANDRO E., *Il riconoscimento delle sentenze straniere*, Giappichelli, Torino, 2007.

D'Alessio, *Il trattamento fiscale della pensione nel quadro di un sistema di sicurezza sociale: la corretta interpretazione della norma convenzionale*, in *Dir. prat. trib.* 2015, II, 418.

Dammann J.C., *The Right To Leave the Eurozone*, in *Texas International Law Journal*, 2013, pp. 125-155.

Davidow J., *Application of U.S. Antitrust Laws to Keiretsu Practices*, in *World Competition*, 1994, p. 5.

D'Ayala Valva F., *Acquisizione di prove illecite. Un caso pratico: la lista Falciani*, in *Riv. Dir. Trib.*, 2011, II, p. 396.

De Cesari P., Frigessi di Rattalma M. (Eds.), *La tutela transazionale del credito*, Giappichelli, Torino, 2007.

Degan V.D., *Sources of international law*, Nijoff (ed.), The Hague-Boston, 1997.

De Grauwe P., *Crisis in the Eurozone and How to Deal with it*, in *CEPS Policy Brief, n. 204*, February, 2010.

De Guttry A., Ronzitti N., *I rapporti di vicinato tra Italia e Svizzera*, Giuffrè, Milano, 1989.

De Lange R., *The European Public Order, Constitutional Principles and Fundamental Rights*, in *Erasmus Law Review*, 2007, 12.

Del Federico L., *Scambio di informazioni fra autorità fiscali e tutela del contribuente: profili internazionalistici, comunitari ed interni*, in *RDT internazionale*, 2010, p. 221.

Delors J., *Mémoires*, Plon, Paris, 2004.

Demedts V., *International Competition Law Enforcement: Different Means, One Goal?*, in *Competition Law Review*, 2012, p. 223, spec. p. 233.

De Mestral A., *The extraterritorial extension of laws: how much has changed*, in *Arizona Journal of International & Comparative Law*, 2014, p. 43.

Denozza F., Toffoletto A., *Contro l'utilizzazione dell'«approccio economico» nell'interpretazione del diritto antitrust*, in *Mercato Concorrenza Regole*, 2006, p. 563.

De Pasquale P., *L'applicazione extraterritoriale delle regole antitrust*, in L.F. Pace (Ed.), *Dizionario sistematico del diritto della concorrenza*, Napoli, 2013, p. 144.

De Schoutheete P., *La coopération politique européenne*, Labor, Bruxelles, 1986.

De Schoutheete P., Wallace H., *Le Conseil européen*, Études et Recherches n. 19, Notre Europe, September, 2002.

De Smet D., *The diametrically opposed principles of US an EU antitrust policy*, in *European Competition Law Review*, 2008, p. 356.

Detter I., *Law Making by International Organizations*, P.A. Norstedt & Söners, Stockholm, 1965.

Dony M., Kaddous C. (Ed.), *D'Amsterdam à Lisbonne: dix ans d'espace de liberté, de sécurité et de justice*, Bruylant, Bale-Bruxelles-Paris, 2010.

Donzallaz Y., *La Convention de Lugano du 16 septembre 1998 concernant la competence judiciaire et l'exécution des décisions en matière civile et commerciale*, 1998 (Ed.), Switzerland and the European Union, Routledge, London, 2006.

Dorigo S., *La cooperazione fiscale internazionale dopo il protocollo di modifica alla Convenzione di Strasburgo: qualche luce e molte ombre*, in *Riv. dir. trib.*, 2011, p. 157.

Dorigo S., *Scambio di informazioni nel diritto tributario internazionale*, in *Digesto delle discipline privatistiche, sez. Commerciale*, Giappichelli, Torino, 2015.

Draetta U., *Si estende la collaborazione internazionale in materia antitrust*, in *Dir. comm. internaz.*, gennaio, 1997, p. 225.

Draetta U., *The international jurisdiction of the E.U. Commission in the merger control area*, in *Revue de droit des affaires internationals*, 2000, p. 201.

Ducrey P., *The agreement between Switzerland and the Eu concerning cooperation in the application of their competition laws*, in *Journal of European Competition law & practice*, 2013, p. 438.

Dupont C., Sciarini P., Eggli C., *Entre coherence et efficacité: la Suisse dans les négotiations bilatérales avec l'Union Européenne*, in *Rev. Suisse de Science Politique*, 7, n. 4/2001, p. 5-37.

Dupont C., Sciarini P., *Back to Future: the First Round of Bilateral Negotiations with Europe*, in C. Church (Ed.), *Switzerland and the European Union*, Routledge, London, 2006.

Eeckhout P., *External Relations of the European Union. Legal and Constitutional Foundations*, Oxford University Press, Oxford, 2004.

Egeberg M., Trondal J., *Differentiated Integration in Europe: The Case of EEA Country*, in *Journal of Common Market Studies*, 37, n. 1/1999, p. 133-142.

Ehlermann C.D., *The modernization of EC Antitrust Policy: a Legal and Cultural Revolution*, in *Common Market Law Review*, 2000, p. 537.

Eisele K., *The External Dimension of the EU's Migration Policy. Different Legal Position of Third-Country Nationals in the EU: A Comparative Perspective*, Leiden, Brill Nijhoff, pp. 218-224.

EMMERT F., *Switzerland and the EU: Partners, for Better or for Worse*, in *European Foreign Affairs Review*, 10/1998, p. 367.

EVANS M. (Ed.), *International Law,* Oxford University Press, Oxford, 2006.

FABBRINI F., *Il pareggio di bilancio nelle Costituzioni europee*, in *Quaderni costituzionali*, 2011 pp. 933-935.

FACHIRI A.P., *The Case of the S.S. Lotus*, in *British Year Book of International Law*, 1928, p. 131.FARINA M., *Titoli esecutivi europei ed esecuzione forzata in Italia*, Aracne, Roma, 2012.

FELDER D., KADDOUS C. (Ed.), *Accords bilatéraux Suisse – UE (Commentaires)*, Basel-Geneva-Munich-Bruxelles- Paris, 2006.

FENGER N., SANCHEZ RYDELSKI M., VAN STIPHOUT (Eds.), *European Free Trade Association (EFTA) and the European Economic Area (EEA)*, Alphen aan den Rijn, Kluwer, 2012.

FERACI O., *L'abolizione dell'*exequatur *nella proposta di revisione del regolamento n. 44/2001: quale destino per i motivi di rifiuto del riconoscimento e dell'esecuzione delle decisioni?*, in *Riv. dir. int.*, 2011, p. 833.

FERACI O., *L'ordine pubblico nel diritto dell'Unione europea*, Giuffré, Milano, 2012.

FERNANDEZ MARIN F., *Il principio di cooperazione tra le amministrazioni finanziarie*, in AA.VV., A. DI PIETRO (Eds.), *I principi europei del diritto tributario,* Cedam, Padova, 2013.

FISHER F.M., *Transnational competition law and the WTO*, in *Journal of International Trade Law & Policy*, 2006, p. 42.

FOX E.M., *U.S. and European merger policy-fault lines and bridges*, in *Concorrenza e mercato*, 2002.

FRANZINA P., *Le condizioni di applicabilità del regolamento (CE) 44/2001 alla luce del parere 1/03 della Corte di giustizia*, in *Riv. dir. intern.*, 2006, p. 948.

FREGNI M. C., *Problemi e prospettive dell'Unione fiscale europea*, in *Rass. Trib.*, 2013, p. 1061.

FREI D., *Switzerland and the EEC: Facts and Trends*, in *Journal of Common Market Studies*, 1973, vol. 12, n. 3, pp. 248-264.

FRIEDBERG J.J., *The Convergence of Law in an Era of Political Integration: The Wood Pulp Case and the Alcoa Effects Doctrine*, in *University of Pittsburgh Law Review*, 1991, p. 289.

FRIEND M., *The Long Arm of Community Law*, in *European Law Review*, 1989, p. 169.

Frowein J., *The European Convention on Human Rights as the Public Order of Europe*, in *Collected Courses of the Academy of European Law*, Vol. I, Book 2.

Gambaro Edoardo E., Mazzocchi F., *Le regole dell'Unione europea alla prova della crisi dei debiti sovrani: il caso Pringle*, in *Dir. comm. Inter.*, 2013, pp. 545 – 569.

Garufi S., Garbarino C., *Le modifiche all'art. 26 del modello OCSE sullo scambio di informazioni*, in *Fiscalità & Commercio Internazionale*, 2013.

Garvey E.G., *The Foreign Trade Antitrust Improvements Act of 1981*, in *Law and Policy in International Business*, 1982, p. 1.

Gerotto S., *Svizzera*, Bologna, il Mulino, 2011.

Ghidini G., Arezzo E., *L'assalto fallito? Riflessioni sulla proposta rivisitazione in chiave «più economica» dell'abuso di dominanza?*, in *Mercato Concorrenza Regole*, 2010, p. 115.

Giannini C., *L'età delle banche centrali. Forme e governo della moneta fiduciaria in un prospettiva istituzionalista*, il Mulino, Bologna, 2004.

Gigante A., Ligustro A., *Il diritto internazionale degli investimenti alla sfida dei fondi sovrani*, in *Diritto pubblico comparato ed europeo*, 2010, pp. 1179-1221.

Ginsberg R., *Conceptualizing the European Union as an International Actor: Narrowing the Theoretical Capability-Expectations Gap*, in *Journal of Common Market Studies*, Vol. 37(3)/1999, pp. 429-454.

Giscard d'Estaing V., *Le Pouvoir et la Vie*, Compagnie 12, Paris, 1988.

Grewlich A.S., *Globalisation and Conflict in Competition Law*, in *Journal of World Competition*, 2001, p. 367.

Grolimund N., Vahl M., *Integration without Membership: Switzerland's Bilateral Agreements with the European Union*, Centre for European Policy Studies, Brussels, 2006.

Gualco E., *L'opposizione al decreto di* exequatur *nel regolamento 44/2001: la natura atecnica della nozione di "ricorso" secondo la giurisprudenza della Corte di Cassazione italiana,* in *Dir. mar.*, 2012, p. 1072 .

Gubner S.T., *Wood Pulp – The European Economic Community and Effects Doctrine Jurisdiction: The Community's New Weapon*, in *Transnational Lawyer*, 1990, p. 759.

Guzman A. (Ed.), *Cooperation, Comity, and Competition Policy*, Oxford University Press, Oxford, 2010.

Hall B., Peel Q., *Paris and Berlin at Odds over Default System*, Financial Times 2010, October, 26.

HAUSCHILD W.M., *L'importance des conventions communautaires pour la création d'un droit communautaire*, in *Rev. trim. droit eur.*, 1975, p. 6.

HAYMANN M., *Extraterritorial Application of Antitrust Law. The Swiss Approach*, in *Revue Suisse du droit international de la concurrence*, 1981, p. 17.

HELOU A., *The Nature and Competitiveness of Japan's Keiretsu*, in *Journal of World Trade*, 1991, p. 99.

HÉRITIER A., *Common goods: reinventing European and international governance*, Rowman&Littlefield, Boulder, CO, 2002.

HÉRITIER A., LEHMKUHL D. (Eds.), *The Shadow of Hierarchy and New Models of Governance*. Special issue *Journal of Public Policy* 28(1)/2008.

HESS B., *The Brussels I Regulation: recent Case Law of the Court of Justice and the Commission's proposed recast*, in *Comm. Mar. Law Rev.*, 2012, p. 1101.

HILDEBRAND D., *The European School in EC Competition Law*, in *World Competition*, 2002.

HILLION C., KOUTRAKOS P. (Eds.), *Mixed Agreements Revisited: The EU and its Member States in the World*, Hart Publishing, Oxford, 2010.

HOFMEISTER H., *Goodbye Euro: Legal Aspects of Withdrawal from the Eurozone*, in *Columbia Journal of European Law*, 2011, pp. 111-134.

HOFSTETTER K., LUDESCHER M., *Fines against Parent Companies in EU Antitrust Law: Setting Incentives for "Best Practice Compliance"*, in *World Competition*, 2010, p. 55.

HUGHES P., *Competition Law Enforcement and Corporate Group Liability – Adjusting the Veil*, in *European Competition Law Review*, 2014, p. 68.

IBÁÑEZ COLOMO P., *Intel and Article 102 TFEU Case Law: Making Sense of a Perpetual Controversy*, London School of Economics Law, Society and Economy Working Papers n. 29/2014.

JACHTENFUCHS M., *The Governance Approach to European Integration*, in *Journal of Common Market Studies*, Vol. 39(2)/2001, pp. 245-264.

JACQUÉ J.-P., *Eléments pour une théorie de l'acte juridique en droit international public*, Librairie générale de droit et de jurisprudence, Paris, 1972.

JACQUÉ J.-P., *Droit institutionel de l'Union Européenne*, Cours, 2015.

JONES A., SUFRIN B., *EU Competition Law: Text, Cases and Materials*, Oxford University Press, Oxford-New York, 2014, p. 1294.

JOHNSON J.E., *Keiretsu: Their Effect on Business and How American Government and Business Can Confront Them*, in *Brigham Young University Law Review*, 1992, p. 1155.

Joshua J., Botteman J., Atlee L., *"You Can't Beat the Percentage" – The Parental Liability Presumption in EU Cartel Enforcement*, in *Global Competition Review*, 2012, p. 3.

Kaczorowska A., *International Competition Law in the Context of Global Capitalism*, in *European Competition Law Review*, 2000, p. 117.

Kaddous C., *L'arrêt France c. Commission de 1994 (accord concurrence) et le contrôle de la "légalité" des accords externes en vertu de l'art. 173 CE: la difficile réconciliation de l'orthodoxie communautaire avec l'orthodoxie internationale*, in *Cahiers de droit européen*, 1996, p. 613.

Kaddous C., Jametti Greiner M., *Accords bilatéraux II Suisse-UE et autres accords récents/BilteralAbkommen II Schweiz-UE und andereneueAbkommen*, Bâle-Genève-Munich-Bruxelles-Paris, 2006.

Kahn T.J., *The Protection of Trading Interests Act of 1980: Britain's Response to U.S. Extraterritorial Antitrust. Enforcement*, in *Northwestern Journal of International Law and Business*, 1980, p. 476.

Kaniel M., *The Exclusive Treaty-Making Power of the European Community up to the period of the Single European Act*, Kluwer, The Hague, 1996.

Kohler Ch., *Interrogations sur les sources du droit international privé européen après le traité d'Amsterdam*, in *Revue critique de droit international privé*, 1999, p. 1.

Korah V., *The EEC Dyestuffs Case*, in *Journal of Business Law*, 1972, p. 319.

Kramer E. X., *Cross Border Enforcement and the Brussels I-*bis *Regulation: Towards a New Balance between Mutual Trust and National Control over Fundamental Rights*, in *Netherlands Int. Law Rev.*, 2013, p. 343.

Krugman P., *The Return of Depression Economics and the Crisis of 2008*, Norton Publications, London-New York, 2009.

Kux S., Sverdrup Ul., *Fuzzy borders and adaptive outsiders, Norway, Switzerland and the EU*, in *Journal of European Integration*, Vol. 22/2001, pp. 237-270.

Kulms R., *Capitale privato ed investimenti: Governance d'impresa attraverso il diritto societario?*, in *Rivista di Diritto Societario*, 2009, pp. 433-455.

La Malfa G., *L'Europa legata. I rischi dell'Euro*, Rizzoli, Milano, 2000.

Lang A., Sanna C. (Ed.), *Federalismo e regionalismo. Esperienza Italiana, Svizzera e dell'Unione europea a confronto*, Giuffré, Milano, 2005.

Lange D.F.G., Sandage J.B., *The Wood Pulp Decision*, in *Common Market Law Review*, 1989, p. 137.

La Pergola A., *Unione europea tra il mercato comune e un moderno tipo di confederazione. Osservazioni di un costituzionalista*, in *Riv. trim. dir. e proc. civ.*, 1993.

La Rocca L., *The controversial issue of the parent-company liability for the violation of EC competition rules by the subsidiary*, in *European Competition Law Review*, 2011, p. 68.

Lastra R.M., *Legal Foundations of International Monetary Stability*, Oxford University Press, Oxford, 2006.

Lavenex S., *Switzerland's Flexible Integration in the EU: A Conceptual Framework*, in *Swiss Political Science Review*, 15(4), p. 547-575.

Lavranos N., *Opinion 1/03, Lugano Convention*, in *Common Market Law Review*, 2006, p. 1087.

Lazzeri V., *Economia e finanza degli hedge funds*, in *Banca, Impresa e Società*, 2000, pp. 383-414.

Lein E. (Ed.), *The Brussels I Review Proposal Uncovered*, 2012, London, British Institute of International and Comparative Law.

Leupold B., *Effective enforcement of EU competition law gone too far? Recent case law on the presumption of parental liability*, in *European Competition Law Review*, 2013, p. 570.

Levrat N., *Switzerland's Relation with the EU after the adoption of Seven Bilateral Agreements*, in *EFA Rev.*, 2001, p. 335.

Lopes Pegna O., *I procedimenti relativi all'efficacia delle decisioni straniere in materia civile*, Cedam, Padova, 2009.

Lorca Susino M., *The Euro in The 21 Century: Economic Crisis and Financial Uproar*, Routdlege, London, 2013.

Lotti P., *L'ordine pubblico internazionale*, Giuffré, Milano, 2005.

Lowe V., *International Law and the Effects Doctrine in the European Court of Justice*, in *The Cambridge Law Journal*, 1989, p. 9.

Malatesta A., *La Banca centrale europea, Gli aspetti istituzionali della banca centrale della Comunità europea*, Milano, Giuffrè, 2003.

Malatesta A., Bariatti S., Pocar F. (Eds.), *The external dimension of EC private International law in family and succession matters*, Cedam, Padova, 2008.

Mangiameli S. (Ed.), *Italian Regionalism: Between Unitary Traditions and Federal Processes.* Essays on Federalism and Regionalism I, Springer, Heidelberg, 2014, pp. 281-306.

Mann F.A., *The Dyestuffs Case in the Court of Justice of the European Communities*, in *International and Comparative Law Quarterly*, 1973, p. 35.

MANN F.A., *The Public International Law of Restrictive Practices in the European Court of Justice*, in *International and Comparative Law Quarterly*, 1989, p. 375.

MARESCEAU M., *Bilateral Agreements concluded by the European Community*, in *Collected Courses of the Hague Academy of International Law*, 2004, vol. 309, p. 412 .

MARI L., *Il diritto processuale civile della Convenzione di Bruxelles, I. Il sistema della competenza*, Cedam, Padova, 1999.

MARKERT K.E., *The Dyestuff Case: A Contribution to the Relationship between the Antitrust Laws of the European Economic Community and Its Member States*, in *Antitrust Bulletin*, 1969, p. 869.

MARONGIU P., *La Voluntary disclosure nei rapporti tributari fra principi generali e interventi legislativi*, in *RTDT*, 2015, p. 636.

MASTELLONE P., *Tutela del contribuente nei confronti delle prove illecitamente acquisite all'estero*, in *DPT*, 2013, p. 791.

MELIS G., *Coordinamento fiscale nell'Unione europea*, in *Enc. dir.*, Annali, I, Milano, 2007, p. 394.

MENDEZ M., *The Legal Effects of EU Agreements. Maximalist Treaty Enforcement and Judicial Avoidance Techniques*, Oxford University Press, Oxford, 2013.

MONTESA A., GIVAJA A., *When Parents Pay for Their Children's Wrongs: Attribution of Liability for EC Antitrust Infringements in Parent-Subsidiary Scenarios*, in *World Competition*, 2006, p. 555.

MOREILLON L. (Ed.), *Aspects pénaux des Accords bilateraux Suisse/Union européenne. Accords de Schengen, Dublin et autres engagements bilatéraux*, Helbing Lichtenhahn, Basel, 2008.

MORRIS P.S., *Iron Curtain at the border: Gazprom and the Russian blocking order to prevent the extraterritoriality of EU competition law*, in *European Competition Law Review*, 2014, p. 601.

MORVIDUCCI C., *I diritti dei cittadini europei*, Giappichelli, Torino, 2014.

MOSCONI F., *Un confronto tra la disciplina del riconoscimento e dell'esecuzione delle decisioni straniere nei recenti regolamenti comunitari*, in *Riv. dir. int. priv. proc.*, 2001, p. 545.

MOSTACCI E., *Dal 'dialogo' al decalogo: le OMT nel primo rinvio pregiudiziale del 'Bundesverfassungsgericht'*, in *Diritto pubblico comparato ed europeo*, 2014, pp. 36-43.

MUNARI F., *Il diritto comunitario antitrust nel commercio internazionale: il caso dei trasporti marittimi*, Cedam, Padova, 1993.

MURPHY D.T., *Moderating Antitrust Subject Matter Jurisdiction: The Foreign Trade Antitrust Improvements Act and the Restatement of Foreign*

Relations Law (Revised), in *University of Cincinnati Law Review*, 1986, p. 779.

NAPOLITANO G. (Eds.), *Uscire dalla crisi. Politiche pubbliche e trasformazioni istituzionali*, il Mulino, Bologna, 2012.

NASCIMBENE B., *Aspetti internazionali della politica di concorrenza comunitaria,* in *Dir. comm. internaz.*, 2/2001, p. 309.

NASCIMBENE B., *Riconoscimento di sentenze straniere e ordine pubblico comunitario*, in *Riv. dir. intern. priv. e proc.*, 2002, p. 658.

NEUWAHL N.A., *Joint participation in international treaties and the exercise of power by the EEC and its member States: mixed agreements*, in *Common Market Law Review*, 1991, pp. 717-740.

NIELSEN P.A., *The new Brussels I Regulation*, in *Comm. Mar. Law Rev.*, 2013, p. 524.

NIHOUL P., *The Ruling of the General Court in Intel: Towards the End of an Effect-based Approach in European Competition Law?*, in *Journal of European Competition Law & Practice*, 2014, 521.

NUYTS A., *La reforme du règlement Bruxelles I* bis, in *Rev. crit. DIP*, 2013, p. 22.

O'KEEFE D., SCHERMERS H.G. (Eds.), *Mixed Agreements*, Deventer, Kluwer, 1983.

ORTINO S., *La Banca centrale nella costituzione europea*, in *Quaderni costituzionali*, 1993, pp. 33-69.

OSTI C., PARDOLESI R., *Falsi amici: le concentrazioni in Europa e negli Stati Uniti*, in *Giur. comm.*, 2002.

OTHENIN-GIRARD S., *La réserve d'ordre public en droit International privé suisse*, Schulthess, Zurich, 1999.

ÖZKAN A.F., *The Intel judgment: the Commission threw the first stone but the EU courts will throw the last*, in *European Competition Journal*, 2015, p. 69.

PALERMO F., *La forma di Stato dell'Unione europea. Per una teoria costituzionale dell'integrazione sovranazionale*, Cedam, Padova, 2005.

PAPADOPOULOS A.S., *The international dimension of EU competition law and policy*, in *The Cambridge Antitrust and Competition Law Series*, Cambridge, 2010.

PANEBIANCO M., *Quale* leadership *democratica nel nuovo Trattato di Roma?*, in *Dir. com. e degli scambi int.*, Vol. 3/2005, pp. 421-435.

PATRONO M., *Il governo della prima Europa*, Cedam, Padova, 2003.

Paredes T.A., *On the Decision to Regulate Hedge Funds: the Sec's Regulatory Philosophy Style and Mission*, in *University of Illinois Law Review*, 2006 pp. 975-1027.

Parret L., *Do we (still) know what we are protecting?*, TILEC Discussion Paper 2009-2010.

Pauer N.I., *The Single Economic Entity Doctrine and Corporate Group Responsibility in European Antitrust Law*, Alphen aan den Rijn, 2014.

Pedroli A., *Lo scambio di informazioni fiscali*, in *Accordi bilaterali Svizzera-Unione europea, Atti della giornata di studio del 4 giugno 2007*, State Chancellery of the Canton of Ticino and Helbing Lichtenhahn, Basel, 2009.

Peers S., *Mission accomplished: EU Justice and Home Affairs Law after the Treaty of Lisbon*, in *Common Market Law Rev.*, 2001, p. 661.

Pera A., *Changing Views of Competition, Economic Analysis and EC Antitrust Law*, in *European Competition Journal*, 2008, p. 127.

Pera A., Auricchio V., *Consumer Welfare, Standard of Proof and the Objectives of Competition Policy*, in *European Competition Journal*, 2005, 153.

Perez R., *La nuova disciplina del bilancio in Germania*, in *Giornale di dir. amm.*, 2011, pp. 95-99.

Peroni G., *Il commercio internazionale dei prodotti agricoli nell'accordo WTO e nella giurisprudenza del Dispute settlement Body*, Giuffrè, Milano, 2005, pp. 87-115.

Peroni G., *La crisi dell'euro: limiti e rimedi dell'unione economia e monetaria*, Giuffrè, Milano, 2012.

Peroni G., *L'azione dell'Unione europea in campo sociale e la crisi economica*, in G.P. Milano, L. Daniele, C. Malinconico, M.C. Ciciriello (Eds.), *Il Trattato di Lisbona due anni di applicazione. Atti della Giornata di studio in ricordo di Francesco Caruso (Roma, 7 ottobre 2011)*, Editoriale Scientifica, Napoli, 2013, pp. 409-424.

Peroni G., *Il difficile equilibrio tra austerità e solidarietà nell'Unione economica e Monetaria,* contributo *in corso di pubblicazione* in Raccolta degli Atti del Convegno AUSE, *The European Economic Union: Economic, Social and Institutional Aspects,* Venezia, 17-19 Luglio, 2015.

Peroni G., *Il recesso dall'euro: una via percorribile, ma non auspicabile*, in *Studi sull'integrazione europea*, 2015, vol. 1, pp. 85-108.

Peroni G., *The failure of the Latin Monetary Union: a Forerunner of Euro Crisis?*, in R. Leboutte, S. Aprile (Eds.), *Un Europe de papier: projets et programmes européennes au milieu du XIX siècle,* Editions du Septentrion – Universitè de Lille, Lille, 2015, pp. 235-247.

Peterson J., Shackleton M. (Eds.), *The Institutions of the European Union*, Oxford University Press, Oxford, 2012.

PETIT N., *Intel, leveraging rebates and the goals of Article 102 TFEU*, in *European Competition Journal*, 2015, p. 26.

PICONE F. (Ed.), *Diritto internazionale privato e diritto comunitario*, Cedam, Padova, 2004.

PIERRO M., *Il dovere di informazione dell'Amministrazione finanziaria*, Giappichelli, Torino, 2013.

PINELLI C., *Ipotesi sulla forma di governo dell'Unione europea*, in *Riv. trim. dir. pubbl.*, 1989, p. 315.

POCAR F., *La comunitarizzazzione del diritto internazionale private: una "European Conflict of Law Revolution"?*, in *Riv. Dir. Inter. Priv.*, 2000, p. 873.

POCAR F. (Ed.), *Commentario breve ai Trattati della Comunità e dell'Unione europea*, Cedam, Padova, 2001.

POCAR F., *Con la nuova proposta di abolizione dell'*exequatur *lo spazio giuridico europeo cerca il rafforzamento*, in *Guida al diritto*, 2011, p. 9.

POHL B., *EU Foreign Policy and Crisis Management Operations. Power, purpose and domestic politics*, New York, Routledge, 2014.

PONZANO P., *Un nuovo metodo dell'Unione*, in G. AMATO, R. GUALTIERI (Ed.), *Prove di Europa unita. Le istituzioni europee di fronte alla crisi*, Astrid, Firenze, 2013.

PROCTOR C., *Mann on the Legal Aspects of Money*, Clarendon press, Oxford, 2005.

PROCTOR C., *The Future of Euro. What Happens if a Member State Leaves?* in *European Business Law Review*, 2006, pp. 909-937.

RAFFAELLI A. (Ed.), *Antitrust tra diritto nazionale e diritto dei consumatori*, Giuffrè, Milano, 2009.

RIGAMONTI S., *I principi della* «comitas gentium» *negli Accordi tra Comunità europee e Stati Uniti in materia di concorrenza*, in *DUE*, 1997, p. 835.

RISHIKESH D., *Extraterritoriality versus Sovereignty in International Antitrust Jurisdiction*, in *World Competition*, 1991, p. 33.

ROSENTHAL D.E., KNIGHTON W.M., *National Laws and International Commerce. The Problem of Extraterritoriality*, Royal Institute of International Affairs, London, 1982.

ROSSI L.S., *L'incidenza dei principi comunitari sul diritto internazionale privato: dalla «comunitarizzazione»* alla «costituzionalizzazione», in *Riv. dir. int. priv. proc.*, 2004, p. 63.

ROSSI L.S., *Conclusione di accordi internazionali e coerenza del sistema: l'esclusività della competenza comunitaria*, in *Riv. Dir. Intern.*, 2007, p. 1008.

ROSSI L.S., *From EU Pillar to Area: The Impact of the Lisbon Treaty on the External Dimension of Freedom Security and Justice*, in *Dir. Un. Eur.*, 2011, p. 999.

ROTH R., AMIRDIVIANI B., *L'entraide judiciaire Suisse en matière pénale à un tournant? Etat de la question à la veille d'une adhésion à Schengen*, in G. DE KERCHOVE, A. WEYEMBERGH (Ed.), *Sécurité et justice: enjeu de la politique extérieure de l'Union européenne*, Ed. Université de Bruxelles, Bruxelles, 2003, p. 247.

ROUBINI N., UZAN M., *International Financial Crisis and the New International Financial Architecture*, Edward Elgar Publishing, Cheltenham-Northampton, 2005.

RUFFERT M., *The European Debt Crisis and European Union Law*, in *Common Market Law Review*, 2011, p. 1787.

SABALOT D.A., *Shortening the Long Arm of American Antitrust Jurisdiction: Extraterritoriality and the Foreign Blocking Statutes*, in *Loyola Law Review*, 1982, p. 213.

SAGGIO A., IANNONE C., *Le informazioni riservate e i segreti commerciali nel diritto comunitario della concorrenza*, in *Riv. Dir. eur.*, 1997, p. 547.

SALOP S.C., *Question: What is the Real and Proper Antitrust Welfare Standard? Answer: the True Consumer Welfare Standard*, in *Loyola Consumer Law Review*, 2010, p. 336.

SALVIOLI G., *Il caso del Lotus*, in *Rivista di Diritto Internazionale*, 1927, p. 521.

SAMADEN G. H., *Les septs accords bilatéraux entre la Suisse et l'Union européenne*, in *Revue du Marché commun de l'Union européenne*, n. 433/1999, p. 696-699.

SANNA C., *Gli accordi bilaterali tra la Svizzera e l'Unione europea*, in *Dir. comm. int.*, 2000, p. 547.

SAPELLI G., *La crisi economica mondiale: dieci considerazioni*, Bollati Boringhieri, Torino, 2008.

SARTORI N., *The European Commission vs. Gazprom: An issue of Fair Competition or a Foreign Policy Quarrel?*, Istituto Affari Internazionali Working Papers n. 13/2013.

SCHEPISI C., *Le relazioni esterne in materia di concorrenza: gli accordi CE/USA e CE/Canada tra dimensione internazionale e dimensione comunitaria*, in *Dir. Un. Eur.*, 2001, p. 149.

SCHEPISI C., *Le relazioni esterne in materia di concorrenza: gli accordi CE/USA e CE/Canada tra dimensione internazionale e dimensione comunita-*

ria, in L. DANIELE (ed.), *Le relazioni esterne dell'Unione europea nel nuovo millennio*, Giuffré, Milano, 2001, p. 311.

SCHWOK R., *Les accords sectoriels Union europèenne-Suisse: une nouvelle forme de flexibilité dans la dimension extérieure de l'UE*, in *RMCUE*, 1999, p. 613.

SCHWOK R., *Switzerland's Approximation of its Legislation to the EU Acquis. Specificities, Lessons and Paradoxes*, in *European Journal of Law Reform*, 2007, vol. 9/3, pp. 449-465.

SCHWOK R., *Switzerland-European Union: An Impossible Membership?*, Brussels, Peter Lang, 2009.

SCIPIONE L., *Prime riflessioni sulla legittimità delle OMT e sul ruolo della BCE alla luce di una recente sentenza della Corte costituzionale tedesca*, in *Dir. banca e mercato fin.*, 2014 pp. 183-235.

SCORDAMAGLIA V., *Merger Control Rules in the EU and their Extraterritorial Application*, in *Medjunarodni Problemi*, 2008, p. 47.

SEATZU F., *Diritto alla difesa, ordine pubblico dello Stato richiesto dell'exequatur e Convenzione di Bruxelles del 1968*, Litotipografia operai Cagliari, 2001.

SELICATO P., *Scambio di informazioni, contraddittorio e Statuto del contribuente*, in *Rass. Trib.*, 2012, p. 321.

SHER B., *Keep Calm – Yes; Carry on – No! A Response to Whish on Intel*, in *Journal of European Competition Law & Practice*, 2015, 219.

SHUSTER M. R., *The Public International Law of Money*, Clarendon press, Oxford, 1973.

SMITS R., *The European Central Bank Institutional Aspects*, *Law International*, The Hague-London-Boston, 1997.

STIGLITZ J.E., *I ruggenti anni Novanta. Lo scandalo della finanza e il futuro dell'economia*, Einaudi, Torino, 2004.

SORRENTINO F., *Profili costituzionali dell'integrazione comunitaria*, Giappichelli, Torino, 1996.

SVETLICINII A., *Parental liability for the antitrust infringements of subsidiaries: a rebuttable presumption or probatio diabolica? ("Arkema SA v European Commission", ECJ (Second Chamber), judgment of 29 September 2011, C-520/09 P; and "Elf Aquitaine SA v European Commission", ECJ (Second Chamber), judgment of 29 September 2011, C-521/09 P)*, in *European Law Reporter*, 2011, p. 288.

TAVERNIER B. (Ed.), *Quelle Europe pour les droits de l'homme?*, Bruylant, Bruxelles, 1999.

TENAGLIA AMBROSINI M.G., *La moneta e l'Europa: da Bretton Wodds a Maastricht e oltre,* Giappichelli, Torino, 1996.

TESAURO G., *Diritto dell'Unione Europea*, 7 ed., Cedam, Padova, 2012.

THEMELIS A., *The Internet, Jurisdiction and EU competition Law: The Concept of 'Over-territoriality' in Addressing Jurisdictional Implications in the Online World*, World Competition, 2012, p. 325.

THOMAS S., *Guilty of A Fault One has not Committed. The Limits of the Group-Based Sanction Policy Carried out by the Commission and the European Courts in EU-Antitrust Law*, in *Journal of European Competition Law & Practice*, 2012, p. 11.

TIZZANO A., *La convenzione europea di estradizione*, in *Annuario di diritto internazionale*, 1965, p. 204.

TIZZANO A., *Relazione sui protocolli relativi all'interpretazione da parte della Corte di giustizia della Convenzione di Roma del 19 giugno 1980 sulla legge applicabile alle obbligazioni contrattuali*, in GUEU C 219, 3 September 1990.

TIZZANO A., *L'applicazione «decentrata» degli art. 85 e 86 Ce in Italia*, in *Il Foro Italiano*, 1997, vol. 120, n. 1, p. 33.

TIZZANO A., *Appunti sulla cooperazione internazionale in tema di concorrenza*, in *Dir. Un. Eur.*, 1999, p. 695.

TREVES T., *Il controllo dei cambi nel diritto internazionale privato*, Cedam, Padova, 1967.

TREVES T. (Ed.), *Verso una disciplina comunitaria della legge applicabile ai contratti*, Cedam, Padova, 1983.

TORREMANS P., *Extraterritorial Application of E.C. and U.S. Competition Law*, in *European Law Review*, 1996, p. 280.

TOSATO G.L., *L'integrazione europea ai tempi della crisi dell'euro*, in *Riv. Dir. Inter.*, 2012, p. 689.

TOVIAS A., *Exploring the "Pros" and "Cons" of Swiss and Norwegian Models of Relations with the European Union: What Can Israel Learn from the Experiences of These Two Countries?*, in *Cooperation and Conflict*, Vol. 41(2)/2006, pp. 203-222.

TUO C. E., *La rivalutazione della sentenza straniera nel regolamento di bruxelles I: tra divieti e reciproca fiducia*, Giuffré, Milano, 2012.

TURCHI A., *Legittimi gli accertamenti fiscali basati sulla lista Falciani*, in *Giur. it.*, 2015, p. 1614.

UCKMAR V. (Ed.), *Corso di Diritto tributario internazionale*, Milano, 1999.

Vahl M., Grolimund N., *Integration without membership. Switzerland's bilateral agreement with the European Union*, CEPS, Brussels, 2006.

Valvo A., *Futuri assetti decisionali ed istituzionali dell'Unione europea*, in *Riv. cooperaz. giur. int.*, 2003, 13, p. 111.

Van Den Bergh R., Giannaccari A., *L'approccio più economico nel diritto comunitario della concorrenza. Il più è troppo o non (ancora) abbastanza?*, in *Mercato concorrenza regole*, 2014, p. 393.

Van Gerven Y., Hoet L., *Gencor: Some Notes on Transnational Competition Law Issues – European Court of First Instance 25 March 1999, T-102/96, Gencor Ltd. v. Commission*, in *Legal Issues of Economic Integration*, 2001, p. 195.

Venit J.S., *Case T-286/09 Intel v Commission – The Judgment of the General Court: All Steps Backward and No Steps Forward*, in *European Competition Journal*, 2014, 203.

Vidal D., *Rapport introductif*, in *Rev. Aff. Eur.*, n. 2/2005, p. 139.

Vincente R., *L'espace deliberate, de sécurité et de justice après le traité de Lisbonne*, in *Annuaire Suisse de droit européen*, 2010, p. 37.

Viterbo A. M., Costamagna F., *L'impatto sociale della politica di condizionalità nel contesto della crisi dell'euro,* in N. Napoletano, A. Saccucci (Eds.) *Gestione internazionale delle emergenze globali. Regole e valori*, Editoriale Scientifica, Napoli, 2013, p. 167.

Zanettin B., *Cooperation Between Antitrust Agencies at the International Level*, Hart Publishing, Oxford, 2002, p. 195.

Zanghì C., Istituzioni di diritto dell'Unione europea; verso una costituzione europea, 4 ed., Giappichelli, Torino, 2005.

Zerk J.A., *Extraterritorial Jurisdiction: Lessons for the Business and Human Rights Sphere from Six Regulatory Areas*, Harvard Corporate Social Responsibility Initiative Working Paper n. 59, 2010, p. 99.

Zoromè A., *Concept of Offshore Financial Centers: in Search of an Operational Definition*, in *IMF Working Paper* (WP/07/87), April, 2007.

Waldhoff C., *Art. 127*, in Siekmann (Ed.), *Kommentar zur Europaisschen Wahrungsunion*, Tubingen, 2013, p. 287.

Walther H., *L'affaire du 'Lotus' ou de l'abordage hauturier en droit pénal international*, Paris, 1928.

Whish R., *Intel v Commission: Keep Calm and Carry on!*, in *Journal of European Competition Law & Practice*, 2015, 1.

Whish R., Bailey D., *Competition Law*, Oxford University Press, Oxford, 2012.

WILS W.P.J., *The judgment of the EU General Court in Intel and the so-called 'more economic approach' to abuse of dominance*, in *World Competition*, 2014, 405.

WINCKLER A., *Parent's Liability: New case extending the presumption of liability of a parent company for the conduct of its wholly owned subsidiary*, in *Journal of European Competition Law & Practice*, 2011, p. 231.

WOOD D.P., *The Impossible Dream: Real International Antitrust*, in *University of Chicago Legal Forum*, 1992, p. 277.

WOOD D.P., *Soft Harmonization Among Competition Laws: Track Record and Prospects*, in *Antitrust Bulletin*, 2003, p. 305.

Finito di stampare
nel mese di ottobre 2016
nella Stampatre s.r.l. di Torino – Via Bologna 220